REVISED EDITION

CONVERTIBLE

Bonds

The
Low-Risk,
High-Profit
Alternative
to Buying
Stocks

Thomas C. Noddings

Foreword By Earl Zazove

PROBUS PUBLISHING COMPANY
Chicago, Illinois

Library of Congress Cataloging-in-Publication Data

Noddings, Thomas C.
    Convertible bonds : the low-risk, high-profit alternative to
buying stocks / Thomas C. Noddings.
        p.   cm.
    Rev. ed. of: Low-risk strategies for the high-performance
investor. 1985.
    Includes bibliographical references and index.
    ISBN 155738-148-8 : $29.50
    1. Convertible bonds.   I. Noddings, Thomas C.   Low-risk
strategies for the high-performance investor.   II. Title.
HG4651.N63   1991
332.63'23—dc20   90-21132
                                                  CIP

Printed in the United States of America
BB
1   2   3   4   5   6   7   8   9   0

CONTENTS

PREFACE

In revising *Low Risk Strategies for the High Performance Investor* and *SuperHedging*,[1] I have chosen to condense the material into one definitive book. Since it is aimed towards individual investors and tax-exempt trusts who may not wish to learn about all the intricacies of convertible bonds, technical material can be found in the appendixes.

This edition is more than an update on the convertible market and its strategies. It's also about building and maintaining one's wealth. Convertible bond strategies can indeed be the ultimate wealth builders for many investors in the 1990s.

Few market participants know that most "conservative" investments are destined to destroy wealth after taxes and inflation are taken into account. Chapter 1, for instance, documents how money market instruments and bonds have failed miserable as safe investment havens. The alarming truth is that common stocks are the only traditional area within the financial markets which has performed well over time. So, whether you are trying to accumulate assets in preparation for retirement, or try-

---

1. Thomas C. Noddings, *Low Risk Strategies for the High Performance Investor.* Chicago, Illinois, Probus Publishing Company (1985). Thomas C. Noddings, *SuperHedging.* Chicago, Illinois, Probus Publishing Company (1986).

ing to maintain your principal during retirement, you must usually turn to the riskier stock market. But how do you handle its volatility?

Fortunately, alternatives for savvy investors do exist. This book will show you ways to avoid the stock market's rollercoaster ride while earning stock-market rates of return. Chapter 4, for example, introduces the 80/40 performance advantage. By selecting convertible bonds offering 80 percent or more of their stock's upside potential—at no more than 40 percent of the downside risk—a diversified convertible bond portfolio should beat the stock market over the long run.

This concept is confirmed by two managed convertible bond indexes maintained by my firm. Our former *Low Risk* convertible index has been updated and renamed the Noddings *Large-Cap* convertible bond index. At a 19.3 percent annual compounded rate of return, it significantly outperformed the riskier stock market since its inception in 1976. Similarly, our former *Aggressive* convertible index, updated and renamed *Medium-Cap*, turned in a 20.8 percent compounded rate of return over the same fourteen-year time frame.

Chapter 6 introduces an exciting new investment strategy using convertible bonds issued by small companies. It was born about 1986 when more and more small companies turned to the convertible bond market to raise capital. My firm has tracked performance of issues purchased for our managed accounts through the Noddings *Small-Cap* convertible bond index. Carefully chosen small-company convertible bonds have also been outperforming small-company stocks.

The last three chapters update the strategies nearest to my heart, convertible hedging: from the short sale of common stock against undervalued convertibles to the use of index options for hedging total portfolios. The Noddings *Convertible Hedge* index, a track record of actual account performance using various hedging strategies since 1976, is introduced in Chapter 9. It dramatically highlights how truly conservative strategies beat the market.

Convertible preferreds were excluded intentionally since they are primarily purchased by corporations to gain tax advantages via partially tax-free dividends. As a result, they are typically overpriced relative to convertible bonds. In addition, neither a preferred's dividends nor its principal are guaranteed. Thus, individuals and tax-exempt trusts can find better opportunities in the convertible bond market.

Throughout the years, my books have offered investors not only the result of years of research and actual experience within the convertible market, they have also been presenting by investment philosophy as it evolved. I place strong emphasis on broad portfolio diversification and a long-term investment outlook as key factors for success. I warn you against being seduced by the latest fads and against succumbing to the allure of misrepresented, yet highly touted "investment products." And I explain how to take advantage of hidden inefficiencies within the nooks and crannies of the markets unavailable to large institutional money managers.

In preparing the book I have been aided by many friends and associates. Chief among them was Earl Zazove of Zazove Associates, Inc., a Chicago-based investment advisory firm. Dr. Zazove is a nationally recognized expert in the field of convertible securities. I sincerely appreciate his invaluable contributions.

Special thanks also to my firm's professional staff who encouraged and helped me throughout the project. I am especially indebted to Connie Castañuela Helbling. After gently prodding me into updating the books, she made essential contributions to the text and edited the manuscript as well.

Thomas C. Noddings

FOREWORD

I t's very easy for most Americans to lose money in the stock market.

Strange, isn't it; we live in the quintessential capitalistic country of all time, yet we're seldom taught how to invest money. We're taught how to *make* it (and how to spend it), but not how to *invest* it.

Why is competent instruction so hard to obtain?

There's certainly no shortage of volunteers. New litters of instant investment experts are born every week, but their teaching qualifications are dubious at best. With "facts" that are sometimes open to question (and sometimes completely wrong), they tend to be cocksure and arrogant in a field that calls for caution and humility. The risk of being taught by people who don't know what they're talking about is obvious, yet almost invariably it's the least qualified and most flamboyant investment mavens the public hears about.

That's an unfortunate result of modern journalism. News has become a commodity—like cars and cosmetics—where quality of product is subordinate to its promotion. In such an atmosphere, the interests of the instant experts and the media dovetail. The former make provocative statements and get their names publicized, while the latter get dramatic stories to help sell advertising space. Such statements are usually worthless for the very reason that got them into the media.

Worthless information of another kind is disseminated by many market advisory services. Publishers of these periodicals are likely to be more concerned with their subscription renewal rate than with accuracy (Can you blame them?). Thus most advisory services simply echo their readers' current hopes and fears.

Specious information and advice comes from the brokerage community too. Here the purpose is to increase portfolio activity, so we get an immense outpouring of opinion, bulletins, recommendations, figures, reports, and predictions from Wall Street. Their value, if any, is shortlived by design.

Further muddying the water are government statistics and forecasts, eagerly awaited and pounced on by traders. These figures are issued in increasing number and variety—but primarily for political purposes.

In addition to the difficulties already mentioned, investors must contend with latter-day changes in the securities markets themselves. Once upon a time, these markets were auctions that responded to millions of individual buyers and sellers. No longer, though; today they're dominated by a few hundred large institutions. There's also a continuous influx of newly-minted investment vehicles, which appear with bewildering frequency and bewildering acronyms—STRIPs, TRANs, PRIMEs, CMOs, TIGRs, SCOREs, and so forth, a proliferation of species unparalleled since the Paleozoic Era.

For all these reasons, it's not surprising that so many Americans—lacking a bona fide investment education, overloaded with information, seduced by questionable advice, and steamrollered by the institutions—lose money in the stock market.

But not everyone does.

A few individuals have set themselves apart from the crowd. Calmly and confidently, they ignore gratuitous advice and opinions, whether from self-styled experts, advisory services, the government, or the brokerage industry. The institutions can't be ignored, but these investors don't even try. Instead, they beat the giants on their own turf by exploiting their weaknesses: their enormous size, their legal constraints, and their need to dress up quarterly reports. The investors I'm referring to take impressive profits out of Wall Street, while keeping their risk prudently low at all times. Furthermore, they do so with only a reasonable expenditure of time. Their secret? The advanced investment strategies they use.

This book will teach you how to use those strategies.

It's one of the most important works since Graham and Dodd, and a lot easier to read. Extraordinary in the fullest sense of the word, it's the definitive book on a vital but seldom understood investment opportunity. Where others recommend tired, weatherworn strategies or resort to complex formulas, this one will teach you a way to invest that's both fresh and understandable.

If you're about to discover its author for the first time, get ready for some straight talk. Tom Noddings doesn't promise any short cuts to wealth; there isn't a hot tip in this entire volume. But *convertible securities* and *hedging* are exciting concepts, in a capitalistic way, and even if you're an experienced investor you'll find a revelation of stock market technique and philosophy, a piece of The Truth. Soundly based on original research, it won't let you shrug your shoulders and walk away. Noddings writes in a quiet voice—which makes his logic all the more devastating—but he cuts through half-baked investment nonsense as with a surgeon's scalpel. Between these covers, an entire herd of sacred cows is neatly disposed of.

Meanwhile, in richly-detailed chapters, the author explains advanced investment strategies step by step. He offers plain proofs as he goes along; no arcane arithmetic here, no economic forecasts, no earnings estimates. There aren't many writers who are prolific, yet maintain a consistently high standard. Noddings is one of the few who do, which is why his work always gets an especially warm welcome from sophisticated investors. A seasoned engineer, he's trained to look, question, and study. Here he applies this training, enhanced by a thinking mind, to the stock market. You'll be surprised and delighted by his investment insights.

The consummate test of a stock market professional is his ability to bring it all together where it counts: in the real world. Theories are fine, but without application, they're esthetic and sterile. On the other hand, proven investment strategies are fascinating, and Tom Noddings has tested his with millions of dollars of cold cash in the hot forge of the market.

For a generation now, he's been the professional investor's professional. Though you may not get the opportunity to work with him personally, you have a superb stand-in: the book you hold in your hands. Make it truly your own by studying it. Once you do, I guarantee you'll never look at stocks and bonds the same way again.

It may be difficult to acquire a solid investment education in America, but it's easier to become rich if you do. Why not open your mind and get started?

Earl Zazove

Chapter 1

BUILDING AND PRESERVING WEALTH

An investor usually has two objectives in mind when working to build wealth. The most important is to assure a comfortable standard of living during retirement and the other is to leave an estate. Assuming these are your goals, how much wealth will you need and how do you go about accumulating it?

This book encompasses pre- and post-retirement investment strategies available in the financial markets, both of which are equally important and hard to master. However, if we can acknowledge that maintaining our lifestyle in retirement, while preserving principal, is the more difficult challenge, then creating wealth in preparation for retirement becomes a less daunting task. Therefore, let's break with tradition by first delving into the retirement years.

For illustration purposes, assume you enter retirement with a million dollars, free of income tax obligations (e.g., an after-tax, lump-sum distribution from your company's profit sharing plan plus personal savings). Whether or not this hypothetical million represents an estate sufficient to meet your dual retirement objectives will depend not only on your lifestyle, but on how wisely you invest.

Investing in Retirement

The financial markets offer three basic investments: money market instruments, bonds and common stocks. Within each investment category lie alternative strategies. The money market, for example, includes T-bills, CDs and mutual funds employing a number of other short-term instruments. Bonds include governments, corporates and tax-exempt municipals, all ranging from short- to long-term maturities. Governments also include mortgage-backed securities such as Ginnie Mae certificates. Corporates and municipals range from high quality to junk. And strategies involving common stocks are even more numerous. How can we select from these countless possibilities?

Assume, for the moment, that you wish to avoid the high volatility inherent in the stock and bond markets. You thus opt for the safety of Treasury bills or fully-insured bank certificates of deposit, which may be viewed as comparable investments for all practical purposes. If you make T-bills or CDs your ongoing investment strategy, *as most retirees do,* will you be able to meet your dual objectives?

Before proceeding, it's important to understand that *real investment returns* are defined as returns net of taxes and inflation. For example, if an investor receives an annual 10 percent return, is in the 30 percent tax bracket (federal, state and local) and inflation is running at 5 percent, the real investment return is only 2 percent (7 percent after taxes minus 5 percent inflation). If inflation was 10 percent, the real return would be a negative 3 percent.

Contrary to popular belief, risk-free money market instruments have seldom provided *real* returns. During the sixty-two year period, 1926-87, Treasury bills averaged 3.5 percent while the rate of inflation averaged 3.0 percent—negative real returns for most tax payers. During the past few years, T-bill returns of 2 to 3 percent above inflation were realized, about break-even after taxes; yet, as recently as 1973-80, T-bills actually underperformed inflation before taxes (7.5 percent vs 9.3 percent annually). This was catastrophic for people trying to live on interest without dipping into their principal.

Potential problems for retirees can best be illustrated if we make a few fundamental assumptions: inflation remains at the 5 percent level we have experienced in recent years; T-bills (or CDs) earn 6 percent; and federal, state and local income taxes total 33.3 percent. Various investment strategies consistent with these assumptions are evaluated in the following illustrations.

Investing in Retirement—A Typical Strategy

The most often recommended strategy has retirees investing in Treasury bills and living on their after-tax earnings. At a 6 percent interest rate, this works out to $60,000 each year on a million dollar retirement account, leaving $40,000 in spendable income net of the one-third tax bite. Excluding Social Security payments for ease of illustration, Table 1-1 demonstrates what inflation can do to your principal *and* purchasing power as you try to maintain your lifestyle at this $40,000 per year level. After ten years, the principal's *value* will have dropped from $1,000,000 to $600,000 and the annual *purchasing power* will have decreased from $40,000 to $24,000. After twenty years, the numbers are $360,000 and $14,000. Does $360,000 represent the estate you originally planned to leave? Will you and your spouse be able to live on $14,000. What happens if your life span exceeds twenty years, or you experience a serious uninsured illness? What happens if inflation heats back up to the 10 percent level of the 70s—or higher? What if taxes are raised?

The disturbing truth is that inflation can destroy both your wealth and standard of living. How many retired people who fight for higher Social Security and other benefits are aware that inflation, fueled by government printing presses, is destroying their other dollar-denominated assets: namely their money market funds, their bonds, their pensions, their annuities?

These discouraging numbers leave you with two difficult, but necessary, decisions: cut back your intended lifestyle *and* increase the earning power of your investment capital.

Table 1-1. Investing $1,000,000 in Retirement—A Typical Strategy

Assumptions

- Investment strategy: buy T-bills at 6.0 percent interest
- Inflation is 5.0 percent
- Interest earned is taxed at 33.3 percent
- All earnings are spent each year

	Years into Retirement		
	0	*10*	*20*
Investment Capital			
Investment in T-bills	$1,000,000	$1,000,000	$1,000,000
Adjusted for inflation	1,000,000	600,000	360,000
Annual Earnings			
Pre-tax interest earned	60,000	60,000	60,000
Taxes	20,000	20,000	20,000
After-tax earnings	40,000	40,000	40,000
Earnings reinvested	0	0	0
Earnings spent	40,000	40,000	40,000
Purchasing power	40,000	24,000	14,000

Investing in Retirement—An Alternative Strategy

The first decision is analyzed in Table 1-2. It shows what will happen if you *spend only half* of your after-tax earnings—$20,000 in the first year instead of $40,000—while *reinvesting the remaining half* each year. This tactic will add 2 percent to the capital base every year and raise future spendable income above the $20,000 starting point. Although this approach improves the long-term outlook, it falls far short of your original goals. After twenty years, your capital, having a nominal value of

---

Table 1-2. Investing $1,000,000 in Retirement—An Alternative Strategy

Assumptions

- Investment strategy: buy T-bills at 6.0 percent interest
- Inflation is 5.0 percent
- Interest earned is taxed at 33.3 percent
- 50 percent of after-tax earnings are spent each year
- 50 percent of after-tax earnings are reinvested each year

	Years into Retirement		
	0	*10*	*20*
Investment Capital			
Investment in T-bills	$1,000,000	$1,220,000	$1,500,000
Adjusted for inflation	1,000,000	730,000	540,000
Annual Earnings			
Pre-tax interest earned	60,000	74,000	90,000
Taxes	20,000	24,000	30,000
After-tax earnings	40,000	50,000	60,000
Earnings reinvested	20,000	25,000	30,000
Earnings spent	20,000	25,000	30,000
Purchasing power	20,000	15,000	11,000

$1,500,000, is worth only $540,000, and your annual purchasing power has dropped from $20,000 to $11,000.

Bluntly stated, after-tax earnings from "risk-free" money market instruments are illusory. They cannot be expected to provide a comfortable standard of living or to protect an estate's value. Therefore, you must bolster your capital's earning power.

The investment area most individuals should logically turn to is the stock market.

Investing in Retirement—A High-Performance Strategy

Table 1-3 brings in the second decision by increasing your capital's earning power. It combines stock market investing with a starting spendable income, set midway between the first two strategies, of $30,000. This high-performance investment approach assumes a *total return* (dividends plus capital gains) at 6 percent *above* the T-bill rate, an assumption in line with the historically higher returns produced by the stock market during the past sixty years. Of the 12 percent total return for stocks, assume dividends of 3 percent and capital gains of 9 percent both taxed at the 33.3 percent rate. As a result, purchasing power remains constant at $30,000 and principal retains its million dollar value via the addition of 5 percent to the investment account each year.

These scenarios, remember, make certain assumptions about inflation, interest rates, taxes and stock market returns. Although based on historical relationships, they may be wide of the mark. For instance, they assume continuing inflation at the relatively modest rate of 5 percent, which seems to be the most probable outlook. However, others predict a 1930s-style deflation, in which case stock market investing could be disastrous. Still others forecast runaway inflation which would likely destroy all financial instruments except common stocks. If you can guard against the extremes of high inflation *and* deflation, via careful planning and wise investing, retirement should be a pleasant experience.

Stock market investing could cost many retirees sleepless nights as they watch their assets drop in value during the bear phases of market cycles. Although market sell offs should cause less anxiety than trying to live on money market interest rates, few people would put all their retirement funds in the stock-market basket—a high-risk strategy I do not advocate.

Although there are no easy answers, Chapter 2 will analyze a retirement portfolio using traditional stocks, bonds and money market strategies. But first let's take a closer look at the stock market itself to see what role it might play in building and preserving your wealth.

Standard & Poor's 500 Composite Stock Index

Long-term performance of the stock market is best represented by Standard & Poor's (S&P) Composite Stock Index. This index is a market-value weighted measure of common stock performance. Market-value

---

Table 1-3. Investing $1,000,000 in Retirement—A High-Performance Strategy

Assumptions

- Investment strategy: buy common stocks yielding 3.0 percent plus 9.0 percent growth
- Inflation is 5.0 percent
- Dividends are taxed at 33.3 percent
- Capital gains are taxed at 33.3 percent
- 37.5 percent of after-tax earnings are spent each year
- 62.5 percent of after-tax earnings are reinvested each year

	Years into Retirement		
	0	*10*	*20*
Investment Capital			
Investment in T-bills	$1,000,000	$1,630,000	$2,650,000
Adjusted for inflation	1,000,000	1,000,000	1,000,000
Annual Earnings			
Dividends	30,000	49,000	80,000
Capital gains	90,000	147,000	238,000
Total pre-tax return	120,000	196,000	318,000
Taxes	40,000	65,000	106,000
After-tax earnings	80,000	131,000	212,000
Earnings reinvested	50,000	82,000	132,000
Earnings spent	30,000	49,000	80,000
Purchasing power	30,000	30,000	30,000

---

weighting gives each stock in the index emphasis proportional to its price multiplied by its number of shares outstanding (market capitalization). Commonly referred to as the S&P 500, it includes 500 of our nation's largest companies. Valued at about $2.5 trillion, it encompasses roughly two-thirds of the total U.S. equity market capitalization.

Table 1-4 compares the long-term (1926-87) performance of the S&P 500 index to other financial strategies. It shows the index outperforming other high quality investments by wide margins—9.9 percent for the S&P versus 4.3 percent for 20-year government Treasury bonds and 3.5 percent for Treasury bills.

Exhibit 1-1 graphically establishes that the only financial strategies which create wealth are found in the stock market. As shown, a dollar invested in Treasury bills in 1926 would have grown to $8.37 by 1987, while a dollar invested in the S&P 500 (labeled *Common Stocks* on the graph) would have grown to $347.96 (both numbers are before any expenses associated with investing and income taxes).

The common stock graph of Exhibit 1-1 also demonstrates the stock market's high short-term volatility. It is unfortunate that most investors are averse to short-term price fluctuations—they often panic and sell after prices have dropped. If they were to approach the stock market with a long-term commitment, much like they do their real estate holdings, they might be surprised at how the volatility of their stock portfolio levels out after several years.

In addition to setting your sights on the long term, I urge you to let the broad market provide the growth you seek through well diversified portfolios. Don't try to outguess the market by picking individual stocks or market sectors which happen to be in favor at the time. Such trading activity only leads to disappointment. The following history lesson must be appreciated before you can become a successful investor.

Table 1-4. Annual Compounded Rates of Return, 1926-87

Small company common stocks	12.1%
Standard & Poor's 500 stock index	9.9
Long-term corporate bonds	4.9
Long-term government bonds	4.3
Treasury bills	3.5
Inflation	3.0

Source: Roger G. Ibbotson and Rex A. Sinquefield, *Stocks, Bonds, Bills, and Inflation: Historical Returns (1926-87)*, 1989, Dow Jones-Irwin.

Exhibit 1-1. Wealth Indexes of Investments in U.S. Capital Markets (1926-87)

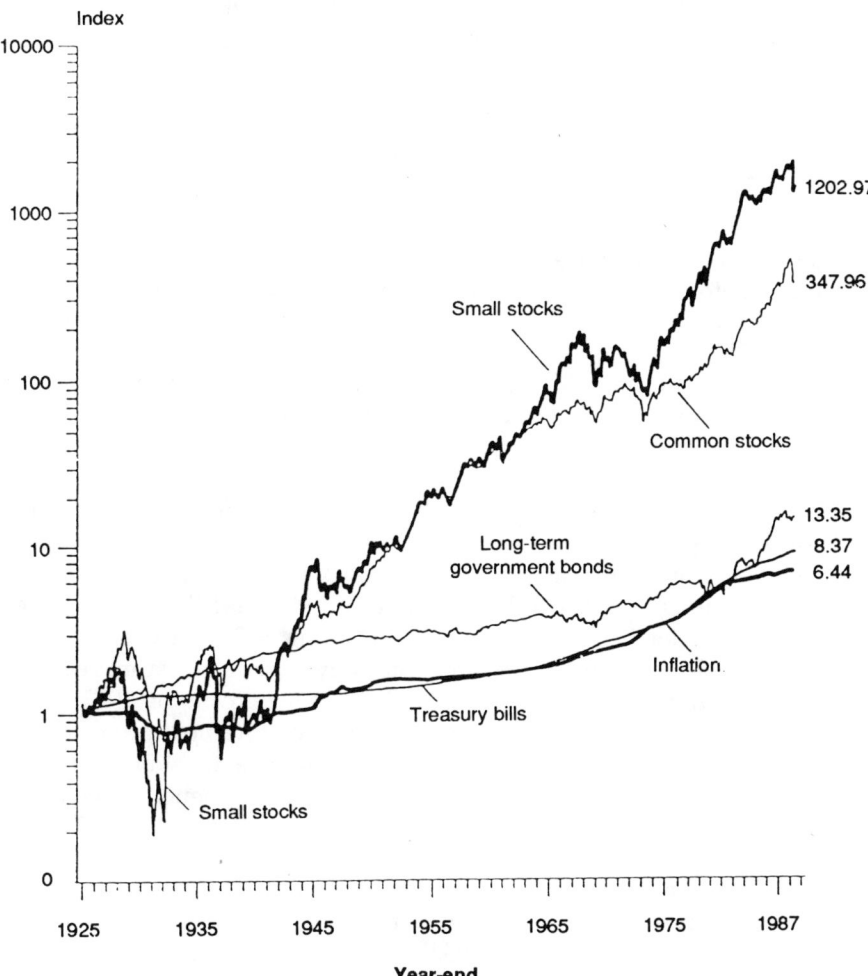

Source: Roger G. Ibbotson and Rex A. Sinquefield, *Stocks, Bonds, Bills, and Inflation: Historical Returns (1926-87)*, 1989, Dow Jones-Irwin.

Blue Chip Growth Stocks

Most people invariably turn to blue chip growth stocks when protecting their assets from the ravages of inflation. Is this a winning strategy?

Suppose that in 1973 you received the following ten-year forecasts for ABC Corp., the premier company in a dynamic, growing industry.

Sales growth	250%
Earnings growth	250%
Dividend growth	230%

These vital financial statistics were actually realized through unfaltering year-to-year increases. Can we view this as a true corporate success story? YES! Is it a sure path to stock market riches? Unfortunately, NO!

Replace the letters ABC with IBM and enter the real world of investing. The company accomplished the forecasts above, but its common stock took a rocky road with a lot of detours.

Exhibit 1-2 graphs the annual highs and lows for International Business Machine's common stock from 1973 through 1989. Starting from a $91 high in early 1973, IBM dropped below $40 in the 1973-74 bear market. It then rebounded to $81 in 1979 but sank to $50 in 1981, the eighth year of our ten-year scenario. It wasn't until 1982 that the stock moved decisively above its 1973 starting point, reaching $134 ten years later in 1983. Until the long-awaited advance, the only return investors received was the cash dividend, ranging from about 1.5 percent in 1973 to 3.0 percent in 1983—meager earnings from America's foremost growth company. How many early investors had the patience to stay with IBM through those disappointing years? And what has happened since 1983?

From its $134 high in 1983, IBM's stock moved sideways through 1986 then climbed to $176 going into the October 1987 crash. It then plummeted to the $100 range where it continues to languish in 1990. While I expect most IBM holders were not happy with these seventeen-year results, other large growth stocks did even worse, some losing more than half their values. What went wrong?

Back in the early 70s, the big nifty-fifty growth companies were considered to be "one decision" investments by institutional money managers. They believed these stocks could be bought at any price, since future earnings would more than make up for the high price/earnings multiples of the time. In retrospect, the nifty-fifty turned out to be a fad, as

Exhibit 1-2. Annual Price Data for IBM's Common Stock, 1973-89

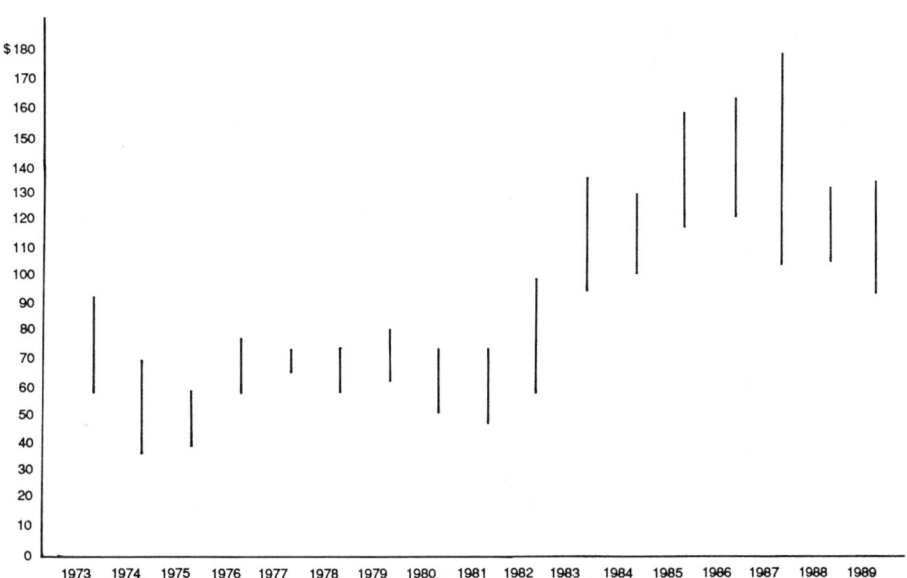

were conglomerates in the late 60s, small high-tech stocks in the early 80s, and, I venture to guess, the leveraged buyout craze in recent years.

Chasing the latest fad like the IBMs of the early 70s is a sure way to underperform in the markets. But, how are we to know what is faddish and what is prudent investing? Didn't the conventional wisdom of the time say to buy and hold IBM and the other big growth stocks? Haven't institutional "gunslingers" been winning recently at the leveraged buyout game?

I'm not suggesting that it's easy, or even possible, to identify and avoid fads. If you can, that's a plus, but fortunately, it's not necessary. I believe all stock portfolios should be widely diversified; large growth stocks as well as companies representing the broad market should be included. You will surely end up with a few stocks which turn out to be fads, but they won't have a serious impact on your overall portfolio. Remember, trying to outguess the markets is a sure road to failure.

One stock market strategy which I believe should be avoided by most retirees is the top-performing small-capitalization stocks listed in Table 1-4. Let's see why.

Small Capitalization Companies

Much has been published in recent years comparing the performance of small company stocks with the blue chips. Table 1-4 and Exhibit 1-1 show how the stocks making up the fifth quintile (smallest 20 percent) on the New York Stock Exchange performed, relative to other modes of investing. By compounding at 12.1 percent annually (versus 9.9 percent for the S&P 500), a theoretical dollar invested in the small stock category would have grown to $1,202.97 compared to $347.96 for the S&P 500 (1926-87).

Be aware that these small cap stocks were not all emerging growth companies that were newly listed on the big board. Many were non-dividend-paying "fallen angels" which had *dropped* into the lowest 20 percent category. Capitalization cut-off for this group is currently near $100 million, which includes all but about the largest 1,500 out of a universe of more than 5,000 actively traded stocks (including the American Stock Exchange and the Over-the-Counter Market).

Notice in Exhibit 1-1 how volatile small stocks have been and how their performance has frequently diverged from the blue chip market. For instance, small stocks dropped nearly 50 percent from 1969 through 1973 while the S&P 500, buoyed by the nifty-fifty, gained 10 percent (including dividends). Coming off the 1973-74 bear market, small caps advanced 1,500 percent by early 1983 versus 500 percent for the S&P 500. From this point through 1987 they drifted sideways while the blue chip S&P, hyped by the takeover game, trended sharply higher. And because the negative divergence has continued into 1990, their annual long-term advantage has narrowed from 2.2 to about 1.5 percent.

I believe that broad portfolio diversification is imperative when dealing with high-risk small stocks. A logical approach would be mutual funds specializing in this market sector; unfortunately, many such funds are not what they appear to be. A number of them, claiming to be "small cap," buy companies that far exceed $100 million (some go up to a billion dollars or more). These so-called small stock funds, aimed towards investors favoring small firms, find it difficult to take large positions in the true small-company market sector.

Although the long-term performance of small stocks has been modestly better than the S&P 500, I believe their lack of a steady dividend stream and high price volatility precludes their use in most retirement portfolios. I mention them to pave the way for small-cap *convertible bond strategies*, to be described later, which *can* be important retirement tools.

Building Wealth

I hope I have convinced retirees of the need for high-performance investing. The examples should also jolt into action anyone preparing for retirement. They should realize they will probably require a larger retirement estate than they are presently planning and that high-performance investing is crucial to their success. Building wealth should be given top priority during working years.

Most investment advisers counsel people to take big risks early in their careers as the best way to accumulate capital. Later, as they near retirement, they are advised to shift to conservative, fixed-income investments. There are two problems with this conventional wisdom. Risk takers usually wind up losing more than they win, thus becoming unable to accumulate the wealth they need to meet their retirement goals. And the lucky few who win do not acquire the investment skills needed for continued success. Both winners and losers are ill prepared for their retirement years.

Investors have two basic ways to build wealth, and both are *equally* important. First, save regularly, especially in tax-deferred programs such as Individual Retirement Accounts (IRAs). Second, invest wisely, by searching out superior, rather than popular, strategies.

I urge you to set aside as much as possible and as early as possible. Don't wait until you are fifty before planning for retirement. $2,000 invested each year in an IRA for 40 years can grow to a *real* million dollars if your earnings average 10 percent per year *above the rate of inflation*. A difficult task, but working toward that goal is a lot better than settling for money market rates of return.

Your company's tax-deferred pension or profit sharing plans are other excellent sources for building wealth, especially if they permit you to take a lump-sum distribution at retirement (for you to invest wisely). Unfortunately, many corporate plans convert your vested interest into an immediate annuity without giving you a choice. While the monthly check may look good at first, inflation can quickly destroy its real value—and an annuity leaves nothing to your heirs.

Recognize that any final sum accumulated in a tax-deferred plan will be fully taxable at the time it is withdrawn, either as a lump sum or in periodic payments. You must take these future income taxes into consideration.

Once you have done everything possible to save as much as you can, the next step is to select the best investment strategies for your particular goals.

The financial markets offer extensive choices. Most are acceptable, a few are exceptional, but some—usually the most widely touted—are certain losers. As an individual investor, or as a trustee for a pension or profit sharing plan, you must acquire the knowledge and skills necessary to sort through the innumerable alternatives. Select only those best meeting your carefully chosen objectives and offering above-average performance. As a reader of serious financial books, you are far ahead of the typical investor—as well as most advisers other investors might turn to for guidance.

As a knowledgeable investor, however, you run the risk of getting too close to the markets, a statement I do not make lightly. Did you know, for example, that the trading volume in most stocks results in about a 100 percent annual turnover of the company? And this is also true for most professionally managed accounts. Portfolio turnover of this magnitude can reduce annual returns by several percent through brokerage commissions and bid-ask price spreads; the winners in the trading game are stockbrokers, market makers and exchange specialists.

I strongly urge you to set your sights for the long term and avoid the short-term "excitement" of the markets. Recognize that any investment strategy will underperform your expectations from time to time (review Exhibit 1-1).

Keep in mind also that all investment strategies go through cycles. You *must* have the perseverance to ride through the down phases, some lasting for years (you'd need confidence in your strategy to do this). There isn't any way to get out at the top and back in at the bottom of a cycle. Professional money managers can't do it! You can't do it! Market timing receives far too much undeserved attention in the financial media; it doesn't work and it encourages people to jump in and out. It can lead only to unnecessary costs and poor performance.

I also encourage you to concentrate your time and attention on selecting *strategies*, not on picking individual securities. I'm told, for example, that it takes a skilled financial analyst three days to understand most annual reports. Even if you have the time and ability to do this yourself, as well as to study the many other factors that must be evaluated when making specific security selections, you will not have enough time to uncover the best investment strategies. Spend your time finding superior strategies (or weeding out those whose time has past). Then, via mutual funds or individual account management, hire skilled managers with qualifications to implement your chosen strategies.

Be aware that the best strategies may be brand new, therefore lacking a track record upon which to base a decision. As an example, when listed call options first began trading in 1973, their premiums were so high that writing them against common stock was a superior strategy. That was obvious to knowledgeable investors.

Understand also that strategies having good track records cannot necessarily be expected to perform well in the future. Institutions jumped on the covered-call-writing band wagon in 1977 and drove the premiums down to the point that any advantage disappeared. Again, that was obvious to knowledgeable investors as it occurred.

I must emphasize the importance of portfolio diversification—both the number of different securities within a given strategy as well as the number of different strategies within a portfolio. Some investment professionals advise people to own only three or four stocks and watch those stocks closely. *I cannot think of worse advice!* Nondiversified stock portfolios do not offer any long-term advantages and are riskier than the broad market over the short term. *There is nothing to be gained by watching your stocks closely.* The only beneficiary I can imagine would be your stockbroker when you nervously sell your stocks as negative news about your holdings becomes public.

There *are* strategies which require little or no diversification. T-bills and Treasury bonds are obvious examples, yet government-bond mutual funds have been one of the most popular investments in recent years. But why would anyone pay a sales commission plus ongoing management fees to invest in a portfolio of government securities when a single government bond or two would do the job?

The next chapter takes a closer look at strategy alternatives and how to combine good ones for optimum performance. Subsequent chapters will show how carefully selected convertible bond strategies can actually provide stock market performance at lowered risk levels most investors can accept.

Chapter 2
THE INVESTMENT DECISION

Chapter 1 proves that common stocks are better long-term investments than money market or fixed-income securities. Few investors, however, have the psychological stamina needed for exposing a large part of their capital to stock market volatility, even if it is through the use of broadly diversified, blue-chip portfolios. Hence, most people buy a mix of financial instruments for additional diversification.

How do investors choose their investment mix? The answer to this question should lie in their ability to handle risk, and leads to several related questions. What is the risk-reward posture for:

- individual securities?
- individual strategies?
- a total portfolio?

The Capital Market Line

There is a rather simple way to relate risk to reward for different financial strategies. The investment community uses the *capital market line*
(CML) to graphically display *long-term*, risk-reward relationships. Exhibit
2-1 plots the sixty-two year financial data from Chapter 1. It gives us a
straight-line graph comparing risk and return for the four basic strategies: Treasury bills, government bonds (Treasuries), S&P 500 stocks and
small-company stocks.

The vertical axis shows annualized, pre-tax returns. The horizontal
axis indicates risk (relative volatility). Notice that the CML intersects the
vertical axis at the zero risk level, represented by Treasury bills or CDs.
As risk increases, expected returns also increase. To place other strategies
in perspective, the S&P 500 stock index is assigned a risk level of 1.0. As
shown, Treasury bonds are placed well to the left of the S&P 500 on the
line—high-risk, small-company stocks are to the S&P's right, at a risk
level about 50 percent higher. Recognize that the volatility of a stock

Exhibit 2-1. The Capital Market Line (1926-87)

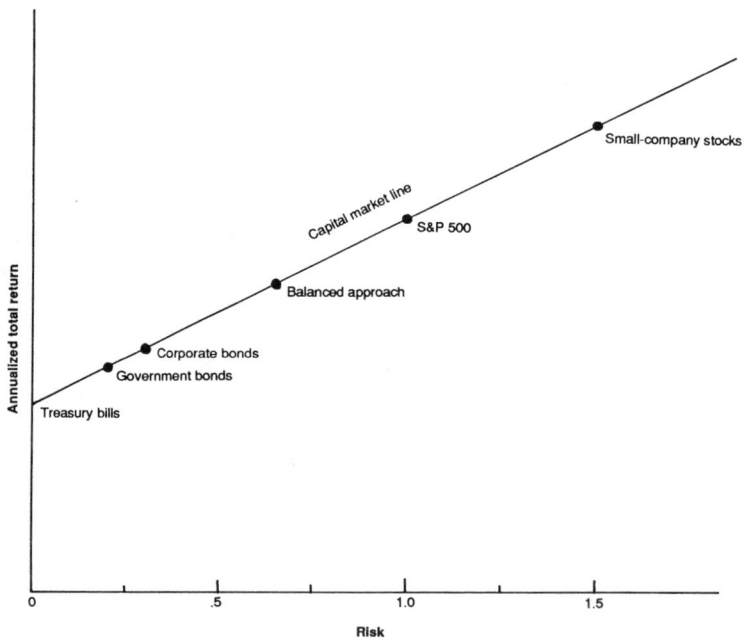

index, such as the S&P 500, is much lower than the individual volatilities of securities making up the index. *Thus, the capital market line is only indicative of broadly diversified portfolios.*

The capital market line is based on pre-tax performance, making it most useful when investing your IRA or other tax-deferred monies. Tax-paying investors, both individuals and corporations, should vary their strategy selections to optimize their after-tax returns. Individuals, for example, can purchase lower-yielding tax-exempt municipals instead of government or corporate bonds if there is an after-tax advantage. Companies can buy preferred stocks instead of bonds because dividends are chiefly exempt from corporate taxes.

Treasury bonds are shown as having a relative risk level slightly above T-bills. High-quality corporate bonds would be positioned at a modestly higher risk than Treasuries. Recently issued, heavily-leveraged junk bonds probably have a risk level near that of the stock market—time will tell. Municipal bonds also have risk levels ranging from high quality to junk (similar to corporates).

Balanced Investing

Professionally managed portfolios of large pension funds and other tax-exempt trusts generally consist of common stock and high-quality corporate (or government) bond combinations. Known as the *balanced approach* to investing, it falls near the middle of the capital market line. Although an equal mix is illustrated by Exhibit 2-1, most money managers fine-tune the blend based on their outlook for each of the two investment strategies. While individual investors often use T-bills or CDs (instead of bonds) to dampen the risk of their stock portfolios, professionals do not consider money market instruments to be investments. They use them primarily as a place to park excess cash. Individual investors should follow the lead of professionals and use money market securities as a temporary haven.

Your Retirement Portfolio

In Chapter 1, I urged you to protect yourself against the extremes of inflation *and* deflation. Your best inflation hedges are likely to be your personal residence and your common stock portfolio. The poorest investments during inflationary times are long-term bonds, with money market instruments following closely behind.

During periods of deflation, long-term (up to thirty years) Treasury bonds are, by far, the best investment strategy. Since interest rates can be expected to move down with deflation, T-bills or CDs must be rolled over at lower and lower rates. On the other hand, *long-term* Treasury bonds, *which are not callable*, would continue to provide the original high income. An additional benefit is that Treasuries would appreciate in value as interest rates fell, thereby offsetting probable stock market losses. Practically all corporate and tax-exempt bonds can be called in at or near par, well before their maturity dates. Callable bonds do not guarantee steady income or protection against falling stock prices during periods of declining interest rates.

In recent years, long-term government bond prices have fluctuated almost as widely as stocks. The worst five-year period for bonds since 1926, for example, was 1977-81 when 20-year Treasuries dropped over 40 percent. Investors had to pay taxes on the interest "earned" while watching their principal plummet. This loss was salt in the wound during soaring inflation (60 percent over the five years) which further washed away cherished principal. How many people, watching their equity being destroyed for five consecutive years by government-induced inflation, panicked near the bottom of the cycle, sold out, and replaced their bonds with historically high money market instruments, only to miss the bond market's five-year recovery back to near par?

My advice to most retirees is to hold a balanced portfolio of high quality common stocks and long-term (twenty to thirty years) Treasury bonds. If owning long-term bonds makes you uncomfortable, do not shorten maturity dates to only a few years as some advisers recommend. Rather, mix the long-term bonds with T-bills. With this approach, you will still have some assets which can dramatically rise in value during periods of deflation.

What To Avoid

While I recommend balanced investing for most retirees, this approach cannot be expected to totally protect both purchasing power and principal. Some may not like it because it does not offer the high income of bonds alone. Others may feel they need higher income than what T-bills or bonds provide, and succumb to the allure of packaged investments promising unrealistically high returns.

When an investment strategy is touted as one that will increase return while reducing risk, ask why and how the strategy is expected to produce returns *above the capital market line,* and why it hasn't been exploited by the professional community. There may be a logical answer, but usually the claims are extolled by someone seeking a high-commission sale.

Remember that the risk-free benchmark is the interest rate currently being paid on T-bills. Long-term Treasury bonds will usually yield more but they involve interest rate risk. The difference between T-bill and Treasury rates may be viewed as a window of opportunity for the conservative, fixed-income investor. No one should accept short-term investments offering less than T-bill rates. For the long-term investor, alternatives offering returns higher than Treasuries involve additional risk. Investors who don't take the time to find out what they are getting into—and to evaluate whether the potential returns justify the higher risks—are leaving themselves open for a rude awakening.

Mortgage-backed government securities such as Ginnie Mae certificates (GNMAs), for example, are often extolled as better investments than Treasury bonds simply because they offer slightly higher yields. In reality, GNMA investors assume all the downside price risk during times of rising interest rates yet receive little upside participation when interest rates fall. In the real world, when interest rates fall, underlying mortgages are refinanced and principal is returned to the investor at par value. That is not a good risk-reward relationship. Investors need to fully understand the inherent risks and rewards of any investment.

Above-the-capital-market-line performance is an attainable goal; but it's a goal that is very difficult to reach after deducting management fees and trading expenses (commissions *and* bid-ask price spreads). Professional equity managers, for instance, attempt to outperform the market by selecting stocks which they believe to be undervalued. Yet most have found it impossible to beat an appropriate market index. Professional fixed-income managers play the performance game by trying to outguess the interest rate cycle. They jump back and forth between short- and long-term bonds, or assume higher risks in the junk bond market, with no greater success than the stock pickers.

All caveats aside, there *are* conservative strategies that can truly improve long-term performance. They include a variety of low-risk techniques offering attractive risk-reward opportunities to noninstitutional investors. The next few pages preview the strategies you will learn about in the following chapters.

Superior Investment Alternatives

Investment alternatives can be superior to traditional investing only when they cannot accommodate institutional monies managed by banks, mutual funds and other large money managers. These professionals have the resources to analyze the strategies you are about to learn and to take advantage of them. However, it is not worth their time because the strategies aren't big enough to absorb the billions under their control.

A number of financial market niches *are* largely avoided by the big institutions. They include convertible bonds, convertible preferreds and warrants. Of these choices, sophisticated convertible bond strategies offer the conservative investor the best trade-offs between risk and reward.

Convertible bonds are hybrid securities that should be viewed as alternatives to a combination of common stocks and straight (nonconvertible) bonds, as in the balanced approach. Like a straight bond, a convertible provides guaranteed interest and a maturity date when the issuing company must redeem it at par value. In addition, the company issuing a convertible bond makes a third promise: at the bondholder's option, anytime during the life of the instrument, the company will exchange it for a pre-set number of common stock shares. Thus, a convertible will participate in future price advances by its underlying common stock while providing the safety and benefits of fixed income.

Many companies, from start up firms to blue chips, use convertible bonds to raise capital. Like investors who buy them, companies view convertibles as an alternative to issuing conventional stock or bond securities. Once issued, a convertible's price will rise or fall in the aftermarket (secondary market) in response to price changes in its underlying common, interest rate changes and other market variables.

Bought mostly by institutional managers when newly issued, convertible bonds are largely ignored by the institutions in the secondary market because of their relatively poor trading liquidity. It is here, in the secondary market, that smaller investors can gain a substantial edge by carefully monitoring price movements. *Undervalued* convertible bonds are *always* available to the smaller investor.

The Convertible Strategies Line

High-quality convertible bonds trading near par can generally be looked at as an alternative to the balanced approach. When their prices advance above par, they take on more of the risk-reward characteristics of common stock. When their prices decline, they become more like straight bonds. At all times, however, they retain hybrid characteristics. Additionally, since convertible bonds are issued by a wide cross section of companies, convertible bond portfolios can be designed for nearly any risk level an investor wishes to assume. They can also be hedged with various financial instruments as an alternative to the money markets or fixed income investing.

This portfolio management flexibility is illustrated by the *convertible strategies line* of Exhibit 2-2 which compares convertible bond investing with traditional investing. Notice that the convertible strategies line is placed well above the capital market line. This better performance represents carefully chosen *undervalued* issues having the most attractive risk-reward features (most convertibles would be placed *on* the capital market line and overpriced issues would fall *below* it).

Of the four basic strategies illustrated by the convertible strategies line, *Convertible Hedging* is the most conservative. The hedging strategy shown indicates returns well above T-bills, at only a slightly higher risk level. It may also be viewed as a low-risk alternative to fixed income investing as well as the balanced approach. Other more aggressive hedging strategies offer stock market returns at far less risk than owning stocks. Convertible hedging strategies are ideal investments for retirement portfolios.

Moving up the convertible strategies line we come to *Large-Cap Convertibles*. These are undervalued convertible bonds of large capitalization companies—they are a high-return alternative to the conventional balanced approach. They may also be viewed as a low-risk alternative to the blue chip stock market itself and are also recommended for retirement portfolios.

Next we come to *Medium-Cap Convertibles* and *Small-Cap Convertibles*. These two high-performance strategies involve undervalued issues of mid-size and small companies. They are best for investors able to assume stock market risk—those who are building their wealth in preparation for retirement.

Chapters 3 and 4 provide the basics needed to take advantage of these highly profitable market niches; but before proceeding, allow me to tell you about my own approach to the markets. I view each convertible strategy as an alternative to a traditional strategy; essentially all my financial-market assets are allocated to various convertible strategies.

However, I recognize that most investors look at convertible bonds as a separate asset class, to be used as part of a diversified portfolio which includes common stocks and straight bonds—not as replacements for all stocks and bonds. They would be uncomfortable having all their funds in convertible investing. Thus, if you are new to convertible investing, I suggest that as you read the book you examine each convertible strategy as if you could choose only one. Then decide later which approach appeals to you the most and how it would relate to your other financial investments. After you become comfortable with that single strategy, you may be ready to strengthen your portfolio with other convertible strategies.

Exhibit 2-2. The Convertible Strategies Line

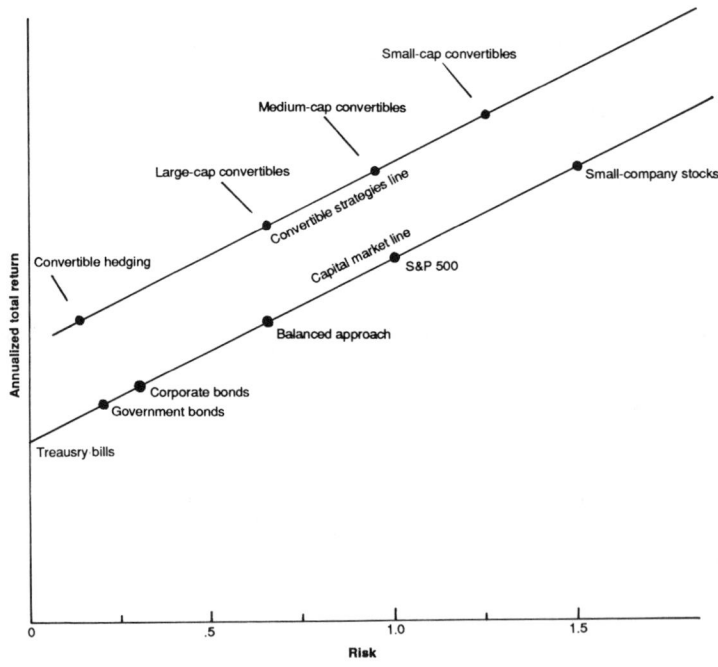

Chapter 3

UNDERVALUED CONVERTIBLE BONDS

onvertible bonds are issued by a wide variety of firms. International Business Machines, for example, acquired Rolm Corp. in 1984 via a AAA rated, $1.3 billion issue, the largest up to that time. In recent years, small growth companies have increasingly used convertibles to obtain additional working capital. A complete listing of the more than 600 convertible bonds trading in early 1990 is provided in Appendix A.

The New-Issue Convertible Bond Market

Table 3-1 presents data showing convertible bonds brought to the market during the 1980s representing both large- and small-capitalization companies. The large-cap issue typifies those of major, high-quality compa-

Table 3-1. Typical New Convertible Bond Issues

	Large-cap	Small-cap
Price	$1,000	$1,000
Issue size, $ million	100	20
Interest rate (coupon)	8%	10%
Underlying common stock yield	4%	0%
Yield advantage	4%	10%
S&P investment grade	A	B
Straight bond equivalent yield	12%	16%
Investment value	$700	$650
Investment value premium	43%	54%
Conversion premium	15%	25%

nies; the small-cap bond represents the mid-size and small company market sectors. (See the convertible strategies line of Chapter 2.)

Notice the difference in bond issue size—$100 million versus $20 million. Large company convertibles typically have much better market liquidity and, like their underlying stocks, are usually listed on the New York Stock Exchange. Some NYSE listed companies also have convertible bonds issued and traded in the Eurobond market based in London. Small firm convertibles may trade in these major markets as well, yet are more frequently found on the American Stock Exchange or the over-the-counter market.

Bond interest rates, 8 percent versus 10 percent, also help distinguish large from small (Table 3-1). As a result, the yield advantage (bond interest minus stock dividends) for the large cap convertible is 4 percent versus a very high 10 percent for the small cap issue. As compensation for the higher yield advantage, buyers of the small company issue had to accept a larger conversion premium (15 percent for the large cap versus the small cap's 25 percent). A large conversion premium means less potential price appreciation.

The following examples will analyze the small-cap convertible, first as it is newly issued and then trading in the aftermarket at a lower price. I chose this issue for my examples because three of the four basic convertible strategies, illustrated by the convertible strategies line of Chapter

2, involve mid-size and small companies. Additionally, these are the market sectors where the best convertible bargains can be found.

Anatomy of a Convertible Bond

A convertible's most important features are its investment value and its conversion value.

Investment value, the horizontal line of Exhibit 3-1 is the price at which the small-cap convertible bond (XYZ Corp.), would be expected to trade if it were a straight (nonconvertible) bond. Bond-rating services estimate a convertible's investment value (debt value) the same way they evaluate straight bonds: they consider inherent quality and prevailing interest rates for similar securities. Standard & Poor, for example, assigns a AAA rating to the highest-quality bonds and a D rating to those in default.

A Standard & Poor's investment grade of B for our example, in a 16 percent interest rate environment for B rated, nonconvertible bonds (the straight bond equivalent yield of Table 3-1), would result in a debt value of 65 ($650). Thus, 65 becomes a floor that supports the convertible in the event of a price decline by its common stock. However, the floor is not guaranteed; it moves down if interest rates rise or the company's fundamentals deteriorate. It rises if interest rates fall or the fundamentals improve. Independently, since the bond will be redeemed at par at maturity, the floor will rise with the passage of time. Priced at 100, the convertible bond is trading at a 54 percent premium above its investment value floor—(100 – 65)/65 = 54 percent.

Conversion value (equity value), the sloping straight line in Exhibit 3-1, would be the bond's worth if it were exchanged for common stock and the shares immediately sold. The graph's straight-line is determined by multiplying the conversion ratio (40 shares) by the common stock's price. At a current stock price of $20, the conversion value is 80 (40 shares X $20 per share = $800). Priced at 100, the convertible bond is trading at a 25 percent premium above its equity floor—(100 – 80)/80 = 25 percent. Unlike the floating debt floor, the equity floor is fixed.

The convertible price curve (track) in Exhibit 3-1 is a prediction of bond prices at any future stock price over the near term (assuming the bond may be called by the company). If the bond has call protection it would trade on a higher price track than shown. This forecast is necessarily limited to the near term since the convertible price curve assumes

---

Exhibit 3-1. The Convertible Price Curve

XYZ Corp. 10 percent, 20-year bond trading at 100

- Conversion Ratio = 40 shares
- Straight Bond Equivalent Yield = 16 percent

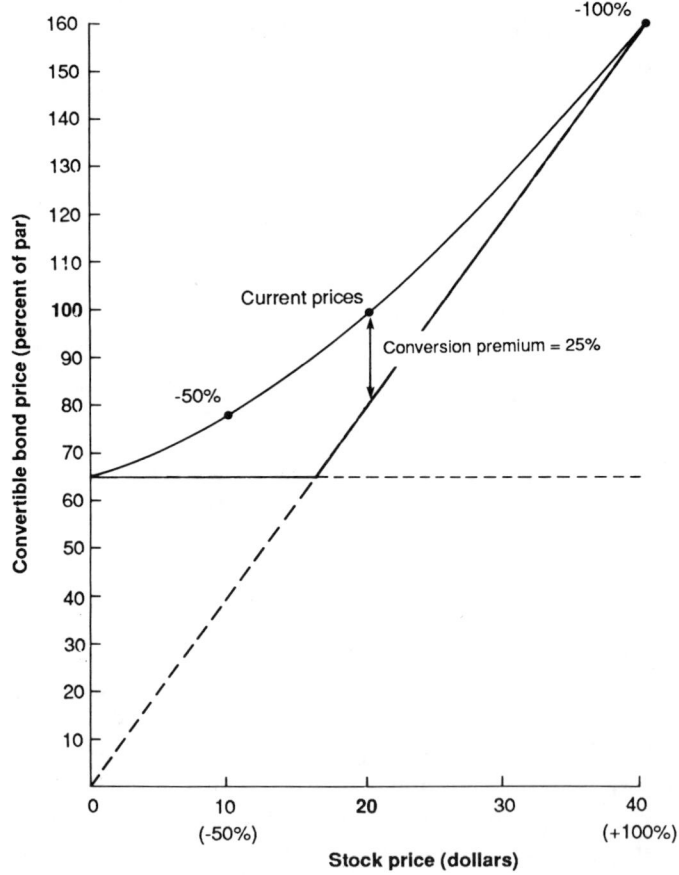

a constant investment floor. However, a large stock price decline would probably indicate deteriorating fundamentals—the price curve would naturally drop more quickly than predicted, if bankruptcy appeared likely.

As shown by the bond's price curve, it must advance at least 60 percent (from 100 to 160) if the common stock were to double to $40. Assume the company calls the bond at that point, causing it to lose its conversion premium. If the stock were to drop in half to $10, the curve predicts a 22 percent bond price decline to 78. The downside estimate, of course, is not as certain as the upside, which is based on a guaranteed equity floor.

These price projections allow us to prepare a risk-reward analysis which evaluates the convertible bond as *either* an alternative to a combination of stock and straight bonds or as a direct alternative to common stock.

New-Issue Risk-Reward Analysis

The XYZ Corp. 10 percent convertible bond is representative of new issues offered by mid-size and small companies at high interest rates that prevailed during the 1980s. How does the convertible compare with a 16 percent XYZ Corp. straight bond and/or its nondividend-paying common stock?

Table 3-2 compares the convertible bond with the balanced approach, 50 percent common stock and 50 percent straight bonds. The analysis assumes that long-term interest rates remain constant over the year. Thus, neither the convertible nor the straight bond need be adjusted for a changing interest rate for this analysis. (The impact of interest rate changes is evaluated in Appendix B.)

The analysis also considers the stock dropping in half to $10, remaining unchanged at $20, and doubling to $40. A range covering -50 percent to +100 percent should encompass most potential price movements in a twelve-month period.

The risk-reward analysis conclusively demonstrates the convertible bond's advantages over conventional securities. The convertible would be expected to provide higher returns than the balanced approach at any future stock price. The one-year advantage ranges from 2 percent in a flat market to 5 percent on the downside and 12 percent on the upside. These are substantial benefits.

Table 3-2. Risk-Reward Analysis for XYZ Corp. Convertible Bond Trading at 100 Versus Common Stock at $20 and Straight Bonds at 16 percent

Stock price in 12 months	10	20	40
Estimated convertible bond price	78	100	160
Balanced approach			
Common stock gain or loss	−50%	0%	+100%
Straight bond interest received	+16	+16	+16
50% stocks/50% straight bonds	−17%	+8%	+58%
Convertible bond			
Capital gain or loss	−22%	0%	+60%
Interest received	+10	+10	+10
Total return	−12%	+10%	+70%
Convertible advantage	+5%	+2%	+12%

How would the convertible bond compare directly with the common stock? This question is answered by the risk-reward analysis in Table 3-3. As shown, the convertible offers a total return of 70 percent of the stock's upside potential at only one-fourth the downside risk, while returning 10 percent more in a flat market. Managed portfolios of such convertibles would be expected to outperform their underlying stocks over a market cycle—an impossible ambition according to efficient market proponents.

The undervalued XYZ Corp. bond is, in fact, representative of newly-issued convertibles in the mid-size and small-company market sectors. Institutions buying them insist on risk-reward advantages as compensation for the expected poor trading liquidity in the secondary market. ("Poor" liquidity is primarily a result of these institutions' large size.) Individuals, however, can buy these new issues without being burdened by that problem. Savvy investors gain even greater benefits by searching out bargains in the secondary market.

Table 3-3. Risk-Reward Analysis for XYZ Corp. Convertible Bond Trading at 100 Versus Common Stock at $20

Stock price in 12 months	10	20	40
Estimated convertible bond price	78	100	160
Common stock gain or loss	–50%	0%	+100%
Convertible gain or loss	–22%	0%	+60%
Interest received	+10	+10	+10
Total return	–12%	+10%	+70%

The Secondary Trading Market for Convertible Bonds

Poor trading liquidity in the secondary market is a serious problem when large convertible bond positions must be sold. The public is not actively involved and most institutional managers routinely stay away from the secondary market. Thus, available buyers, large and small, are fewer than for most common stocks or straight bonds. When a large institutional holder does decide to sell, it hopes another institution is willing to buy at a price reasonably close to the current market price. If a swap cannot be arranged, the price must be lowered to attract buyers. That's how bargains are created.

Assume, for example, that XYZ Corp. convertible's price moves from 100 down to 90 with its common stock still at $20. As shown by the dashed curve in Exhibit 3-2, the ten-point price reduction cuts the conversion premium in half to only 12.5 percent. The lower convertible curve of Exhibit 3-2 passes through the new price of 90 and conservatively assumes the bond will remain on the lower price track. A stock price decline to $10 would find the convertible trading at 72, compared to 78 on the higher price track in our previous example. On the upside, the bond must advance to at least its 160 conversion value if the stock doubles, regardless of its price track.

Table 3-4 presents risk-reward calculations, compared to the common stock, for the bond at 90. Notice the improvement over the prior calculations at 100 (Table 3-3). Not only is current income increased from

Exhibit 3-2. The Convertible Price Curve

XYZ Corp. 10 percent, 20-year bond trading at 90

- Conversion Ratio = 40 shares
- Straight Bond Equivalent Yield = 16 percent

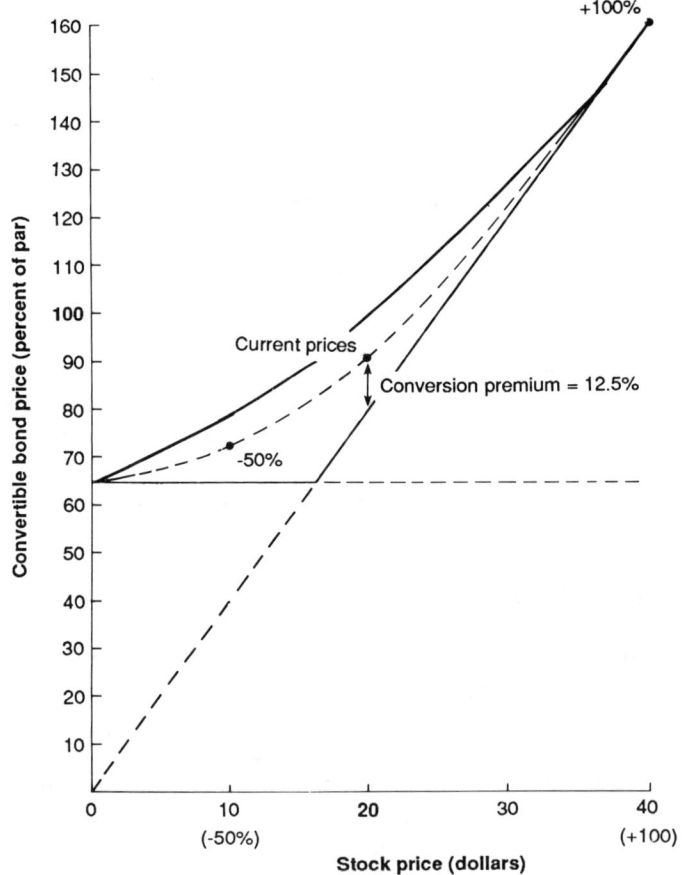

Table 3-4. **Risk-Reward Analysis for XYZ Corp. Convertible Bond Trading at 90 Versus Common Stock at $20**

Stock price in 12 months	10	20	40
Estimated convertible bond price	72	90	160
Common stock gain or loss	–50%	0%	+100%
Convertible gain or loss	–20%	0%	+78%
Interest received	+11	+11	+11
Total return	–9%	+11%	+89%

10 to 11 percent and risk reduced further, but the convertible now offers nearly the full upside potential of its common stock—89 percent versus 100 percent over the next twelve months. If we add another year's 11 percent interest, the bond's 100 percent total return will equal a stock doubling over a two-year period, while eliminating downside risk completely if the stock falls in half.

Profit Profiles

Exhibit 3-3 graphs the risk-reward calculations of Table 3-4 as *profit profiles*. Profit profiles permit a visual comparison of investment alternatives. They illustrate the relative merits of different strategies better than a risk-reward analysis table, since gains or losses can be quickly ascertained for any future stock price. Exhibit 3-3 shows the common stock providing greater profit for a twelve-month price advance above $25, while the convertible bond offers a higher return (or less risk) at any stock price below $25.

Looking at the profit profiles of Exhibit 3-3, most stock pickers would probably reject the convertible because it is destined to underperform its common at all prices above $25. Having been sold a tantalizing story, they may be convinced the stock will quickly rise to $40 a share or higher. They have forgotten (or never learned) that controlling risk is an important aspect of successful investing. Happiness may be a stock that doubles, but stocks are just as likely to go down. Suppose a portfolio

Exhibit 3-3. Profit Profiles: XYZ Corp. Convertible Bond Trading at 90 Versus Common Stock at $20

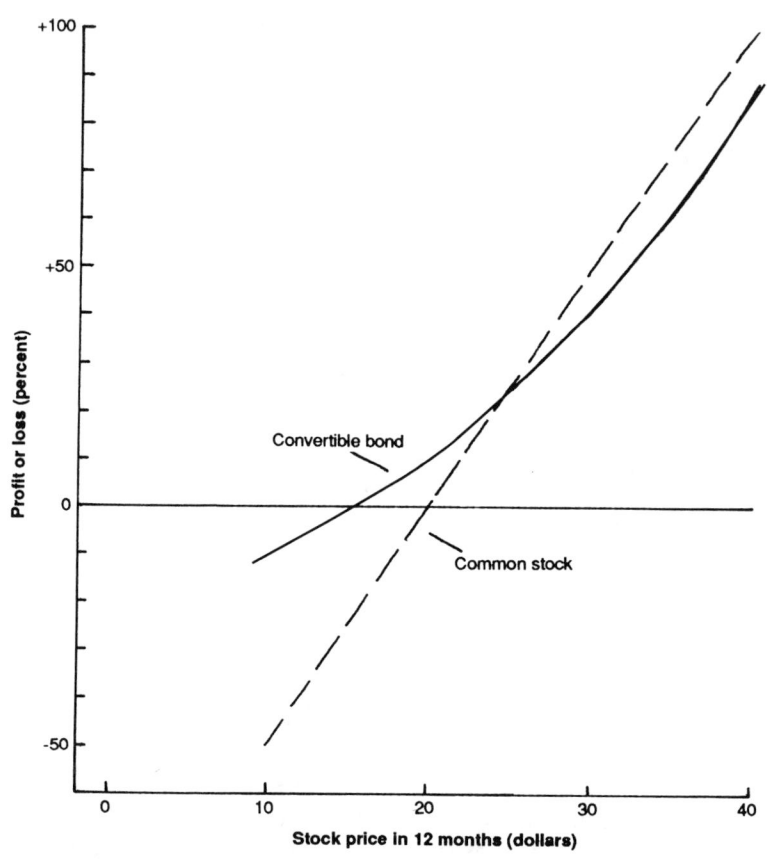

contained three stocks similar to XYZ Corp. and one doubled while the other two both dropped in half over the following year. The two 50 percent losers would cancel out the single 100 percent winner for a net break-even. On the other hand, a convertible specialist who owned three issues such as XYZ Corp. would wind up with a 24 percent profit (the average of +89%, –9% and –9%). *Which investor would you rather be?*

Newly issued at 100, the XYZ convertible bond is modestly under-valued relative to its stock, but priced at 90 in the secondary market it is *substantially* undervalued. Notice I am not passing judgment on the merits of the common stock itself. The mathematical relationships between the two securities are the primary focus of the risk-reward calculations. Whether to own any securities of XYZ Corp. is a separate decision. However, if given an undervalued opportunity (the bond trading at 90), I would certainly try to find some way to include the convertible in my portfolio (e.g., hedging strategies) even if I didn't like the company's fundamentals. This is what knowledgeable convertible investing is all about—taking advantage of undervalued opportunities while retaining a low-risk investment posture.

The next two chapters will describe portfolio management techniques and evaluate historical performance for large company convertibles. Later chapters will come back to small cap issues such as XYZ Corp.

Chapter 4

LARGE-CAP CONVERTIBLE BONDS

In Chapter 2, I encouraged individual investors to follow the professionals' lead through balanced investing, but I also stated that superior alternatives can be found in the convertible bond market. Few investors realize that selected convertible bonds can provide better returns than conventional stock/bond portfolios. Smaller investors can use them to gain an impressive advantage over the pros who typically avoid this market sector.

LARGE-CAP CONVERTIBLES VERSUS THE CAPITAL MARKET LINE

By my firm's definition, two essential criteria identify a convertible bond as a Large-Cap candidate: the company's capitalization and the bond's quality rating. For the first guideline, we have set $500 million as the minimum-capitalization cutoff. This number roughly encompasses the top 15 percent (800 firms) of actively traded companies. And because about 90 percent of S&P 500 companies are currently above $500 million, this capitalization guideline assures our working within the market's large-company sector.

A bond's quality rating, as appraised by Standard & Poor's or other bond rating services, comprises the second guideline. Many straight bond portfolios have established BBB as the minimum S&P quality standard. Yet this cutoff excludes a number of companies in the S&P 500 stock index. And since convertible bonds are usually subordinated to straight bonds in the same company, a minimum grade of BB for high-quality convertible bond portfolios is appropriate.

In addition, since undervaluation is also a qualification requirement for all of our convertible strategies, Large-Cap issues become a high-return alternative for conservative investors seeking income and growth.

Exhibit 4-1 compares Large-Cap risk-reward relationships with stocks and bonds on the convertible strategies line introduced in Chapter 2. Convertible portfolios are never identical, therefore risk-reward is shown as a range on the line, with the midpoint located above the balanced approach. Keeping in mind that both the capital market line and the convertible strategies line are based on diversified portfolios, not single securities, where can we place different Large-Cap portfolios within the range?

The lower sector of the Large-Cap's range in Exhibit 4-1 would include AA or AAA rated bonds of the largest companies. The upper sector of the range would include BBB or BB bonds of companies near the $500 million minimum.

Another factor to consider when identifying convertibles within the range, or recognizing others that fall outside the range, is the bond's price. Most convertibles trading at par fall near the range's midpoint. If their prices later decline, they move down the line and could drop below the range if they trade at deep discounts from par. At some low price level, they become direct alternatives to straight corporate bonds. As convertibles advance above par, they take on more of the risk-reward characteristics of their common stocks. At some high price level, they move out of the range and become direct alternatives to owning common stock.

The next few pages will show you how to build and manage a high-quality convertible bond portfolio, if you choose to do it yourself; and

Exhibit 4-1. Large-Cap Convertible Bonds Compared to the Capital Market Line

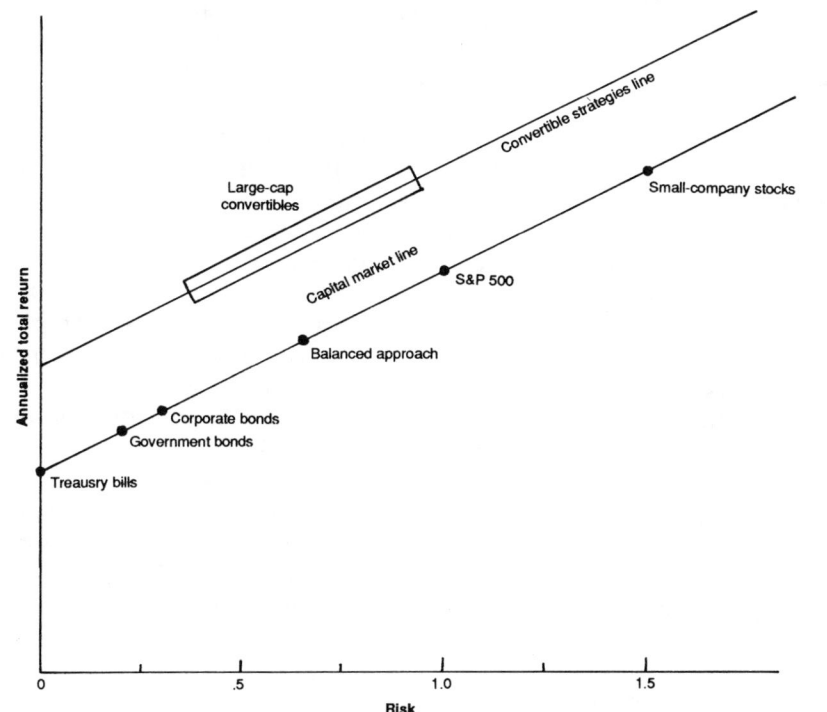

they provide the means for evaluating potential managers should you choose to hire them to do the job for you.

BUILDING A LARGE-CAP CONVERTIBLE BOND PORTFOLIO

This chapter introduces the guidelines we use to build and manage portfolios of Large-Cap convertibles.

Portfolio Diversification

As emphasized in Chapter 1, portfolio diversification is a cornerstone for successful investing yet, most individual portfolios contain only a few securities. Nondiversified portfolios not only lack long-term advantages over the market; they are far riskier, and ensure a *negative* risk-reward relationship. Furthermore, they cannot be expected to track market indexes. Hence, owners of such portfolios are unable to evaluate them against meaningful standards—they never know whether performance, good or bad, is the result of securities selection or luck. Others may diversify through a large number of different issues, but include securities in the same or closely related industries, thus defeating the purpose of diversification.

Diversification is essential to any successful investment program. For a portfolio of Large-Cap convertible bonds, we recommend a minimum of ten different issues in unrelated industries. Ten issues, however, should be considered only by investors willing to accept the high probability that year-to-year results will depart (diverge) widely from the performance of better-diversified portfolios or market indexes.

We prefer a minimum of twenty positions and consider broad diversification to mean about thirty issues. Our experience has shown that broadly diversified portfolios produce fairly consistent performance and can usually be compared with appropriate market indexes to evaluate performance. Yet even these larger portfolios will diverge from any given index from time to time, just as the S&P 500 and the nonweighted Value Line Composite of 1,700 stocks do not always track each other.

Fundamental Analysis

In the spring of 1990 there were approximately 800 firms having market capitalizations above $500 million. Stock pickers using this minimum capitalization cutoff should have been able to find thirty or so stocks they liked, representing only 4 percent of the available market. Convertible managers, on the other hand, had fewer issues to choose from. As shown in Appendix A, there were 176 companies capitalized at above $500 million having convertible bonds outstanding. Of their 213 issues, many would be rejected based on other factors (S&P rating below BB, call features, overpriced, and so on). Thus, there were only about 100 or so viable convertible bond candidates available for serious consideration by *any* convertible manager.

Convertible managers who accept fairly priced issues can usually apply a few fundamental criteria without screening out too many of the 100 entrants. Value-oriented managers following the tenets of this book, however, would find only ten or so underpriced candidates available at any given moment; they would plan on taking several months to build up to about thirty issues. These convertible veterans use fundamental analysis to sidestep the worst companies, not to find the best. This approach allows one to build a portfolio of the best convertibles the market has to offer.

Excess portfolio turnover is another reason to play down fundamental analysis. As indicated in Chapter 1, stock managers turn over their portfolios nearly every year as their fundamental screens shift between buy and sell. That is why most of them underperform market indexes. How can stock pickers gain an edge on the market by trading back and forth with their competitors? To avoid destroying a convertible portfolio through excessive trading, convertible buy and sell parameters should never be dependent on rigid fundamental screens of their underlying stocks. Fortunately, they need not be.

Technical Analysis

Technical analysis of individual securities should seldom (or never) be applied to convertible portfolios; it too would screen out many convertible candidates and lead to excessive trading.

Although I do not use any form of technical analysis when managing convertible bond portfolios, one such approach that may be appropriate for others is market timing. I am not suggesting that market timers sell out their convertible portfolios when they turn bearish on the market; it would be too costly. As detailed in my book *SuperHedging*, index put and call options can be used to effectively adjust a convertible portfolio's risk-reward characteristics. For example, someone turning bearish could buy a few index puts to profit from a correctly forecast bear market, without disrupting the underlying portfolio. This strategy will be reviewed in Chapter 9.

Event Risk Analysis

The ability to analyze and handle event risks is a major factor that distinguishes skilled convertible bond managers. Bankruptcy, of course, is the worst-case risk.

Fortunately, this peril can be largely avoided by following the minimum capitalization and S&P bond-rating guidelines for Large-Cap issues. (Bankruptcy considerations become important as we move up the convertible strategies line to the high-risk, Small-Cap bond sector—to be discussed in Chapter 6.)

Call features and company takeovers are event risks of a more timely nature. Keep in mind that when a bond is called, conversion is necessary in order to capture its equity value. Any premium and all accrued interest will be lost during the conversion process. Call risk is a serious matter and must therefore be continuously evaluated when selecting new positions and when monitoring portfolios.

A more difficult event risk to assess is what might happen if the company is taken over. Prior to the 1980s, acquisitions were normally consummated via an exchange of common stock. In that event, the convertible (in the company acquired) retained its conversion privileges; it became exchangeable into the acquiring company's stock. The junk bond market changed the rules. During the 80s, takeover artists used junk bonds to finance cash buyouts. Suddenly, many convertible bonds became exercisable into cash rather than common stock. They immediately lost their conversion premium and often were downgraded to a lower debt rating. Many of the takeovers would not have been economically viable without the harm inflicted upon convertible- and straight-debt holders. Although many professionals, including me, cautioned as far back as 1973 that this could become a serious problem, new issue buyers did not begin to insist on appropriate protection until the playing field became strewn with takeover victims. Now, new issues are commonly protected by poison puts which permit holders to return the bonds to the company for par value in the event of a takeover, but older issues still remain at risk. Convertible bond managers must carefully evaluate event risks such as these, as well as the inevitable new ones in the future.

Stock Beta Ratings

Beta is a popular tool for identifying stock market risk. It is defined as a measure of the past sensitivity of a stock's price to overall fluctuations in the prices of other stocks, as reflected in the S&P 500 or similar benchmark. A beta of 1.2, for example, indicates that a stock rose (or fell) on average in the past by 1.2 percent for each 1.0 percent rise (or fall) of the market. Most betas range between .75 and 1.5; highly market-sensitive and volatile securities, such as brokerage firm stocks, may have betas above 1.5; some utility stocks are below .75.

Beta can seriously mislead investors analyzing individual companies. They may view a stock having a 1.0 beta as no riskier than the
index which has a beta of 1.0 by definition. In reality, a single stock will
likely be two to three times more *volatile* (risky) than the index. I emphasize this point because portfolios containing only a handful of stocks are
far riskier than their average betas would indicate. In addition, some
high-risk stocks, such as gold mining shares, may have low betas because they do not correlate well with the market. However, while any
single beta could fail completely in forecasting its stock's future price
movements, a diversified portfolio's beta average is a useful tool for esti-
mating the portfolio's risk and reward relative to the overall market.

Recognizing that most Large-Cap convertible bonds are issued by
companies a tier or two below the biggest firms, the portfolio's underlying stock beta will probably fall within the 1.0 to 1.2 range. Portfolios
having beta averages above or below this range belong in different strategies.

Order Execution

Order execution is critical to the success of any convertible bond strategy, since the best bargains are usually found in the less liquid situa-
tions. Small investors dealing in odd lots (less than 100 bonds) should
probably restrict their selection universe to New York Exchange listed
issues, and always use carefully placed limit orders. Investors dealing in
100 or higher bond orders will find additional opportunities away from
the exchange (off board) and in the Eurobond market. Be aware that,
unlike those for stocks, large orders for listed bonds are usually executed
at the trading desks of major brokerage firms. Here it is extra important
to work with a knowledgeable and experienced broker.

Research

Successful investing in convertible bonds requires a systematic, thorough
evaluation of all possible candidates to cull the few offering exceptional
risk-reward characteristics. Other tools discussed in this chapter are important, but not nearly as crucial as finding the most attractive opportunities. Since a convenient source of statistical data is a must, three
information sources are presented and evaluated in Appendix A.

THE 80/40 PERFORMANCE ADVANTAGE

Suppose you were offered an investment strategy which promised to participate in 80 percent of the stock market's performance during rising quarters at only 40 percent of the loss during declining quarters. How might such a low-risk strategy succeed over the long run? How would it perform in a bull market?

Exhibit 4-2 graphs the S&P 500 stock index (including dividends) along with the hypothetical 80/40 portfolio from 1976 through 1989, a fourteen-year period representing the greatest bull market of the century. Despite the fact that there were only a few down quarters (sixteen out of fifty-six), the 80/40 portfolio produced the same total return as the S&P index: 15.2 percent annualized returns for both. A $100 investment in either would have grown to $725. (The 80/40 approach would have undoubtedly done better than the S&P during sideways or bear markets.) Is an 80/40 performance advantage possible in today's financial markets, which many investors believe are reasonably, if not totally, efficient?

A SAMPLE LARGE-CAP CONVERTIBLE BOND PORTFOLIO

Table 4-1 shows a sample portfolio of ten convertible bonds that fit my firm's purchase guidelines. The ten issues were selected from different industries and their underlying common stocks were rated average or higher for year-ahead performance by our research sources. To meet our risk-reward screens, each bond was required to offer at least 70 percent price appreciation if its stock doubled at half the risk or less if its stock dropped in half. Let's review the portfolio's characteristics.

Bond prices ranged from 95 to 118 with the average at 109. Undervalued issues are usually found when trading modestly above par. These bargains are made available by those new-issue buyers who quickly take profits upon a price advance. At an average price near 110, this sample portfolio would be placed in the upper area of the Large-Cap's range (Exhibit 4-1), making it more of a stock market alternative than an alternative to the balanced approach.

The average bond coupon was 7.0 percent, in line with new issues being brought to the market at the time. The portfolio's current yield was 6.5 percent versus 3.0 percent for the underlying common stocks (the S&P 500's yield was also 3.0 percent). Not only did the bonds offer a 3.5

Exhibit 4-2. The 80/40 Performance Advantage Growth of $100 14 Years Ended 12/31/89

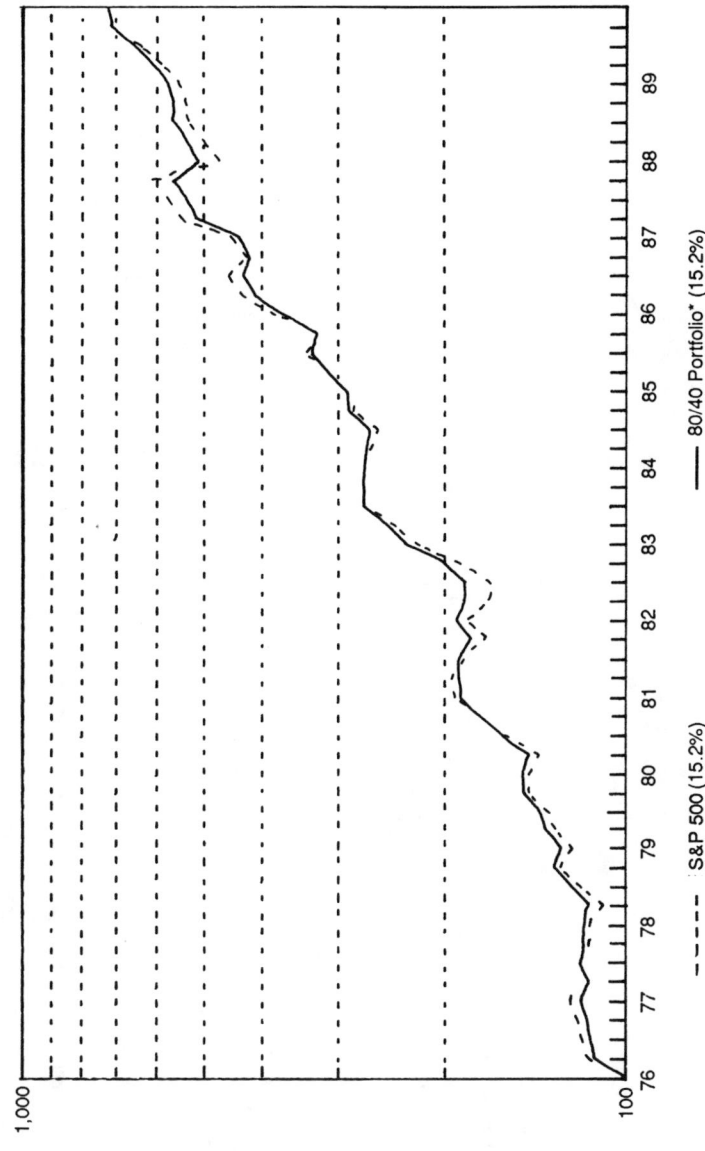

– – – – S&P 500 (15.2%) ——— 80/40 Portfolio* (15.2%)

*A portfolio that earned 80% of the S&P's "up quarter" returns and 40% of its "down quarter" returns.

Table 4-1. Large-Cap Convertible Bonds Available in April 1990

Company Name	Bond Description	Bond Price	Current Yield	Stock Beta	Leverage* -50%	Leverage* +100%
Alum. Co. of America	6.250-02	111.00	5.62	1.20	-22	90
American Brands	5.375-03	115.00	4.67	1.15	-10	95
Boise Cascade	7.000-16	100.00	7.00	1.20	-22	75
Browning-Ferris Ind.	6.250-12	104.50	5.98	1.20	-23	70
CBI Industries	7.000-11	112.00	6.25	1.00	-25	90
Enserch Corp.	10.000-01	107.00	9.35	1.05	-10	71
Humana Inc.	8.500-09	112.00	7.59	1.10	-16	84
International Paper	5.875-12	95.00	6.18	1.25	-22	75
Kerr-Mcgee	7.250-12	118.00	6.14	1.00	-24	90
Medco Containment	7.500-00	111.00	6.73	1.05	-21	72
Averages (10 positions)		108.61	6.55	1.12	-20	81

*The estimated percent change for the convertible for changes in the price of the underlying stock of -50 or +100 percent.

Source: Noddings & Associates' research.

percent yield advantage, but their interest payments were guaranteed by the companies—stock dividends are never guaranteed.

At 1.12, the average beta for the convertibles' underlying common stocks was in the middle of our 1.0 to 1.2 target range, again indicating that the convertible portfolio was essentially a stock market alternative.

Similar to the hypothetical 80/40 strategy, the convertible portfolio offered 81 percent price potential if the stocks were to double at only 20 percent loss if the stocks were to drop in half (-20 versus -50 equals 40 percent of the stocks' downside). The 81/40 risk-reward and 3.5 percent-yield advantages virtually assured that such a convertible portfolio would *outperform* the S&P 500 index over a market cycle, if managed properly. Above-market (above-the-line) performance would be near certain if we could build on the ten-issue sample portfolio to achieve optimum diversification at thirty issues or more.

The convertible bond market, which is efficiently priced on average, has always contained deep pockets of pricing inefficiencies. I frequently wonder why this is allowed to happen, especially in the big name companies as represented by our Large-Cap selection criteria.

MONITORING A LARGE-CAP CONVERTIBLE BOND PORTFOLIO

Convertible bond portfolios require active management for maximum long-term performance. Selected on the basis of risk-reward relationships, convertibles should be monitored along the same lines. (They must also be monitored to sidestep the event risks previously discussed.)

As the underlying common stock rises, and the convertible bond advances to the 140 to 160 area, profits should be taken; the convertible no longer offers the downside safety (or yield) originally provided. By replacing high-priced issues with bonds trading near par, profits are protected through the purchase of issues meeting the original selection criteria. *Holding convertibles which have advanced to well above par is the same as changing one's investment objective to the higher-risk posture of the stock market.* (See Appendix C for alternate methods for closing a convertible position after a major price advance.)

When the common stock drops, the convertible will resist further decline as it approaches its investment floor—it should be replaced with another issue trading near par. The convertible has fulfilled its downside protection function; it has decreased less than the common and now takes on more of the risk-reward characteristics of a straight debt instrument. Because the conversion premium has increased, the convertible will now trail well behind its stock on any future price advance. *Holding convertibles when they trade at deep discounts is the same as changing one's investment objective to the lower-return posture of the fixed-income market.*

Other sell guidelines include: downgrading of fundamentals, the convertible issue becoming overvalued, an approaching event risk and the replacing of a marginal issue with an exceptional alternative.

These procedures provide a systematic framework for continually monitoring a convertible bond portfolio. They allow one to maintain the most advantageous risk-reward posture for participation in advancing markets and for protection in declining markets. This is one of the few sure ways to invest unemotionally while increasing the odds in the investor's favor.

In the next chapters, I will show how diligently managed convertible bond portfolios have performed in the past.

Chapter 5

HISTORICAL PERFORMANCE DATA

To be superior, an investment strategy must be built on a common-sense foundation. Superior strategies should also be verifiable by proven track records. Do meaningful track records exist for undervalued convertible bonds?

CONVERTIBLE FUNDS

I referenced performance data for the seven funds then specializing in convertible securities in my book, *SuperHedging*. Covering an eleven-year period, 1974-84, the data showed convertible funds outperforming the S&P 500 stock index by nearly four percentage points per year—14.1 percent versus 10.2 percent annualized. Taking portfolio management and order execution costs of about three percent into account meant the funds had achieved the extraordinary feat of a seven percent above-the-market performance.

As a result of this stellar performance, the financial community responded with an outpouring of new convertible funds. Like their predecessors, most are closed-end and load mutuals although a few no-loads have also been brought out. Unlike the earlier funds, which seemed to have value-oriented management styles similar to those described in Chapter 4, a number of the new convertible managers, buying the popular but often overpriced new issues, act more like stock pickers.

The investment objectives of today's convertible funds are quite diverse. Some stress income while others emphasize growth. Some specialize in large capitalization issues while others are in the small-cap sector. Some use hedging tactics to further reduce risk. Others are not invested solely in convertibles. Considering all the differences, today's convertible funds cannot be viewed as a single group. Each fund should be evaluated against its own specific investment objectives.

Following the broad stock market's peak in mid-1983, the best-performing funds have been working within the large-capitalization market sector. At the other end of the convertible fund spectrum, those investing in securities of small companies have been underachievers. Needless to say, a fund's performance (good or bad) during those seven years of extraordinary market divergences would give little indication of how it might do in the future. All investors should fully understand a convertible fund's investment objectives, management style and relevant performance data—the same factors used when selecting stock or fixed-income funds.

CONVERTIBLE INDEXES

Riding the mid-80s popularity surge in convertible funds, the institutional community "discovered" convertibles as a separate asset class and began hiring convertible managers. Suddenly, plan sponsors and their consultants believed they needed new tools to evaluate these hybrid managers. In response, a number of major brokerage firms developed convertible indexes designed to represent "the convertible market."

The indexes vary in their construction; differences include the number of securities, capitalization, the convertible issue size and quality ratings. Further differences may include or exclude convertible preferred stocks, Euro convertibles and zero-coupon convertibles.

Frankly, the performance of convertible portfolios—managed in accordance with specific investment objectives—cannot be accurately evaluated by the popular convertible indexes. Any convertible index will most likely include securities having characteristics that are vastly different from managed portfolios. Furthermore, near the peak of a bull market most convertibles would be trading above par; convertible indexes would be more stock market sensitive than usual. Conversely, near the bottom of a bear market those same convertible indexes, containing many deeply discounted issues, would act more like fixed-income. Managed convertible portfolios should not be judged by such different and vacillating standards.

A better approach would be to truly understand (and approve of) the convertible manager's security selection and portfolio management procedures—then monitor buy and sell decisions to make sure that the procedures are effectively implemented. In other words, get involved. Don't take the easy way out by turning to an index for performance evaluation when it may be ill-suited for the job.

THE NODDINGS CONVERTIBLE BOND INDEXES

The three convertible indexes currently maintained by my firm represent undervalued convertible bonds as *low-risk alternatives to their common stocks*, as in the 80/40 performance advantage. Named *Large-Cap, Medium-Cap* and *Small-Cap*, they also represent specific market sectors based on company capitalization.

First introduced in my book, *The Investor's Guide to Convertible Bonds* (1982), our initial two indexes supported favorable theories with actual market experiences covering the six-year period from 1976 through 1981. *Low Risk Strategies for the High Performance Investor* and *SuperHedging* updated the data through 1984. This book takes the data through 1989. The following criteria have been used to construct and maintain the indexes over the fourteen-year time span (1976-89).

Account Selection

Our most diversified account, determined quarterly, was used to select issues for both the Large- and Medium-Cap indexes from 1976 through 1982; beginning in 1983, we used a different account for each index. In January 1987, the selection group was expanded to include several accounts and we started a third index covering small-company convertibles.

It should be noted that actual account returns do not correspond directly with the indexes because our clients normally use a combination of different convertible strategies with the mix dependent on market opportunities. Therefore, the indexes should be viewed as representative returns for specific subgroups of convertibles selected from a larger universe, not as track records of actual account performance.

Security Selection

The original parameters for the Large-Cap index were convertible bonds and preferreds having underlying common stocks ranked B+ or higher by Standard & Poor's. Most were listed on the New York Stock Exchange, but occasionally a more speculative American Exchange or Over-the-Counter company would receive a B+ rating and be included. Originally, Medium-Cap index parameters were convertibles with underlying common stocks ranked below B+.

Our selection criteria were refined in 1984 to exclude stocks not listed on the NYSE from the Large-Cap, and to limit the Medium-Cap group to stock ratings below B+ on the NYSE and up to B+ on the AMEX or OTC. Additionally, the rapidly expanding convertible bond market enabled us to upgrade the indexes by deleting convertible preferreds.

In January 1987, the indexes were once again refined to include an equity capitalization requirement and the quality rating was changed to the S&P *bond* rating. Our Large-Cap index currently contains convertible bonds that are rated BB or better by Standard & Poor's (or an equivalent rating by Moodys or Value Line) and whose companies have equity market capitalization above $500 million. The Medium-Cap includes convertible bonds rated CCC or better that are issued by companies from $100 to $500 million capitalization. The Small-Cap index includes convertibles issued by companies below $100 million capitalization not in default on interest payments, and rated C or higher if covered by Standard & Poor's.

As shown by Appendix A, the round-number capitalization-ranges of below $100 million, $100 to $500 million and above $500 million for Small, Medium and Large roughly divide the 600 plus convertible bond market into thirds, with about 200 issues in each group.

Weighting

Equal representation is given to each convertible security. Thus, gains or losses can be readily computed using percentage price changes plus income earned.

Pricing

Actual purchase and sale prices are used to calculate results. Basing performance records on last-traded exchange prices may lead to incorrect results. There is always a bid-ask price spread for any security which can distort results. In addition, a convertible may not trade for several days while its stock may be making a large price move—the last traded convertible price can quickly become meaningless.

Management and Trading Expenses

All convertible portfolios must be actively managed to maintain their desired risk-reward characteristics. Management expenses include custodial, administrative and portfolio management fees. Trading expenses include bid-ask price spreads and brokerage commissions. These expenses will total about 2 to 4 percent annually depending on portfolio size, trading activity and such. Except for the impact of bid-ask price spreads, they are not calculated into our indexes.

THE NODDINGS LARGE-CAP CONVERTIBLE BOND INDEX

Appendix D provides a complete listing of all 373 convertibles employed in the Large-Cap index over the fourteen-year period, including purchase and sale prices. Table 5-1 shows the bonds held as of January 1, 1990. In accordance with the index's selection criteria, each convertible bond was rated BB or higher and company capitalizations exceeded $500 million. The index contained forty issues and provided an average current yield of 6.5 percent.

Table 5-1. The Noddings Large-Cap Convertible Bond Index—Positions Held on January 1, 1990

Company Name	Bond Description	S&P Bond Rating	Bond Price	Current Yield %	Capital-ization ($mil)
Aluminum Co. of America	6.250-02	A-	120.00	5.21	6652
American Brands	5.375-03	A-	121.50	4.42	6685
Aanadarko Petroleum	7.000-04	A-	124.00	5.65	1932
Avnet Inc.	6.000-12	A+	91.00	6.59	1109
Berkshire Hathaway	0.000-04	AA+	44.50	0.00	9942
Boise Cascade	7.000-16	BBB	108.00	6.48	1805
Bruno's, Inc.	6.500-09	BBB+	110.50	5.88	1203
CBI Industries	7.000-11	BB+	100.50	6.97	628
CBS Corp.	5.000-02	A	102.00	4.90	4446
Comsat International	7.750-98	A-	97.00	7.99	596
Dana Corp.	5.875-06	BBB	78.00	7.53	1407
Enserch Corp.	6.375-02	BBB	107.25	5.94	1712
Federal Express	5.750-11	A+	92.00	6.25	2411
Fleming Company	6.500-96	BBB	92.00	7.07	880
Freeport McMoran	8.750-13	BBB-	118.50	7.38	1698
General Instrument	7.250-12	BBB	109.50	6.62	1086
Grace, W.R.	7.000-01	BB+	115.50	6.06	2786
Hechinger Company	5.500-12	BBB+	66.50	8.27	721
HomeFed Corp.	6.500-11	BBB+	90.50	7.18	671
Humana Inc.	8.500-09	BBB+	117.00	7.26	4322
Int'l. Lease Finance	5.750-01	BBB+	118.75	4.84	828
International Paper	5.875-12	BBB+	101.75	5.77	6147
Kerr-McGee	7.250-12	BBB+	120.00	6.04	2454
Lafarge Corp.	7.000-13	BBB+	98.12	7.13	857
Leggett & Platt	6.500-06	BBB	96.00	6.77	518
Loral Corp.	7.250-01	BBB	88.75	8.17	756
Masco Corp.	5.250-12	A-	78.00	6.73	3806
Mead Corp.	6.750-12	BBB+	91.50	7.38	2323
Medco Containment	7.500-00	BBB-	107.00	7.01	837
Noble Affiliates	7.250-12	BBB-	102.00	7.11	733
Norton Co.	7.750-12	A-	115.50	6.71	1232
Ogden Corp.	6.000-02	BBB	97.00	6.19	1270
Omnicom Group	7.000-13	BBB	110.50	6.33	638
Oryx Energy Company	7.500-14	BBB	125.00	6.00	4664
Potlatch Corp.	5.750-12	BBB+	95.38	6.03	1058
Prime Motor Inns	6.625-11	BB+	73.00	9.08	781
Primerica Corp.	7.250-06	BBB	97.75	7.42	3213
Trinity Industries	6.750-12	BBB-	102.00	6.62	544
Union Carbide	7.500-12	BBB-	88.25	8.50	3238
USX Corp.	5.750-01	BB+	74.75	7.69	9206
Averages (40 securities)				6.53	2445

Performance Measurement

Table 5-2 provides annual total returns since the index's inception in 1976 compared with three market indexes: Salomon Brothers' high-grade corporate bond index, Standard & Poor's 500 stock index and Value Line's composite index of 1,700 stocks. Quarterly performance data are provided in Table 5-3 along with statistical measurements of risk and return.

The convertible index's fourteen-year cumulative return was 1,080 percent compared to 625 percent for the S&P 500 and 798 percent for the

Table 5-2. The Noddings Large-Cap Convertible Bond Index Versus Market Indexes—Annual Total Returns

Year	Corporate Bonds*	S&P 500 Stocks	Value Line Stocks**	Large-Cap Convertibles
1976	18.7	23.6	36.2	45.9
1977	1.7	-7.4	3.8	8.1
1978	-0.1	6.5	7.7	16.8
1979	-4.2	18.5	28.3	24.2
1980	-2.7	32.5	22.0	35.3
1981	-1.2	-5.0	-1.3	17.5
1982	42.5	21.6	18.9	21.5
1983	6.3	22.5	34.8	28.6
1984	16.9	6.2	0.4	6.9
1985	30.1	31.7	32.2	28.3
1986	19.9	18.6	16.2	15.7
1987	-0.3	5.2	1.8	-0.9
1988	10.7	16.5	25.8	15.8
1989	16.2	31.6	20.7	14.3
Cumulative return	293	625	798	1080
Annualized return	10.3	15.2	17.0	19.3

*Salomon Brothers high grade corporate bond index.
**Value Line's geometric index (1976-82) and arithmetic index (1983-89) of 1,700 stocks—estimated dividends included.
Note: The indexes do not include management fees or trading expenses.

Table 5-3. The Noddings Large-Cap Convertible Bond Index Versus Market Indexes—Quarterly Total Returns

Year	Corporate Bonds	S&P 500 Stocks	Value Line Stocks	Large-Cap Convertibles
1976	4.2	15.0	25.8	19.2
	0.3	2.4	0.2	6.6
	5.6	1.9	-0.4	6.7
	7.5	3.1	8.5	7.6
1977	-2.3	-7.5	-2.5	-0.5
	3.9	3.2	5.8	7.3
	1.1	-2.8	-3.1	-1.0
	-0.8	-0.3	3.8	2.3
1978	0.0	-4.9	1.9	3.1
	-1.1	8.5	10.5	13.2
	3.1	8.7	10.7	10.3
	-2.0	-5.0	-13.6	-9.3
1979	1.6	7.1	12.5	10.3
	4.5	2.7	5.0	8.1
	-2.0	7.6	8.8	6.8
	-7.9	0.1	-0.2	-2.5
1980	-13.2	-4.1	-12.1	-5.8
	24.2	13.5	17.3	22.2
	-10.7	11.2	15.0	15.7
	1.0	9.5	2.9	1.6
1981	-1.0	1.4	6.5	8.4
	-2.0	-2.3	2.5	6.3
	-8.9	-10.3	-15.5	-9.1
	11.7	6.9	7.0	12.2
1982	4.9	-7.3	-8.3	-4.7
	0.9	-0.6	-3.0	-2.5
	21.3	11.5	10.2	13.8
	10.9	18.2	21.3	14.9
1983	4.0	10.0	16.3	15.4
	1.6	11.1	16.8	14.5
	-0.3	-0.2	-0.6	-0.8
	0.8	0.4	-0.2	-1.9

Table 5-3. (continued)

Year	Corporate Bonds	S&P 500 Stocks	Value Line Stocks	Large-Cap Convertibles
1984	-1.4	-2.4	-4.1	-1.1
	-3.6	-2.6	-3.0	-1.3
	12.5	9.7	8.2	6.9
	9.4	1.8	-0.2	2.4
1985	1.2	9.2	11.7	9.6
	12.3	7.3	5.2	6.8
	2.1	-4.1	-3.5	-1.8
	12.1	17.2	16.6	11.6
1986	10.8	14.1	15.6	11.6
	0.7	5.9	3.7	3.7
	1.9	-7.0	-7.0	-1.9
	5.5	5.6	4.2	1.9
1987	1.9	21.3	21.5	10.8
	-4.0	5.0	2.7	0.7
	-6.1	6.6	6.4	2.4
	8.6	-22.5	-23.3	-13.3
1988	4.6	5.7	16.2	10.0
	1.7	6.6	7.4	4.3
	2.7	0.3	-0.3	-0.7
	1.4	3.1	1.2	1.6
1989	1.3	7.1	7.9	5.6
	10.2	8.8	7.2	4.9
	0.5	10.7	8.1	5.2
	3.5	2.1	-3.4	-1.9
Cumulative return	293	625	798	1080
Quarterly return	2.7	3.9	4.4	4.8
Standard deviation	6.8	7.8	9.5	7.3
Coefficient of variation	252	200	215	153
Sharpe measure	0.10	0.24	0.26	0.38

broader based Value Line. Corporate bonds lagged far behind stocks at 293 percent.

Performance Evaluation

The Large-Cap index's 1,080 percent cumulative return was certainly impressive. Compounding at 19.3 percent annually it easily beat both the S&P's 15.2 percent annualized return and Value Line's 17.0 percent. The quarterly returns, plotted by Exhibit 5-1, indicate a high correlation between the convertibles and the stock indexes, as would be expected. Yet, investors entering the convertible market in recent years have not seen above-market performance—convertibles underperformed common stocks each of the last five years (1985-89).

Since the broad stock market's top in 1983, the largest capitalization companies have dominated the market. This was especially conspicuous in 1989 when the S&P 500 returned 31.6 percent versus 14.3 percent for Large-Cap convertibles. Although the convertible index contains companies capitalized above $500 million, it is not representative of the biggest companies which drive the capitalization-weighted S&P. The top fifty companies in the S&P account for more than 50 percent of its performance. Looking at Table 5-1, there were only two convertible bonds in the convertible index whose companies were at about the top fifty cutoff (Berkshire Hathaway and USX Corp.), and only three others at about the top one hundred cutoff.

Table 5-3 provides popular risk-reward evaluation measurements including standard deviation, coefficient of variation and the Sharpe measure. Each confirms the superior risk-reward advantages of undervalued convertible bonds. In addition, the S&P 500 experienced forty positive quarters and sixteen negative quarters over the fourteen-year period. During the positive quarters, the S&P averaged +7.6 percent versus +7.7 percent for the convertibles; during the negative quarters the S&P averaged –5.2 percent versus only –2.6 percent for convertibles. Compared to the 80/40 advantage target over its underlying stocks, the Large-Cap convertible index produced an even better—101/50—advantage over the S&P 500.

Exhibit 5-1. The Noddings Large-Cap Convertible Performance Advantage 14 Years Ended 12/31/89

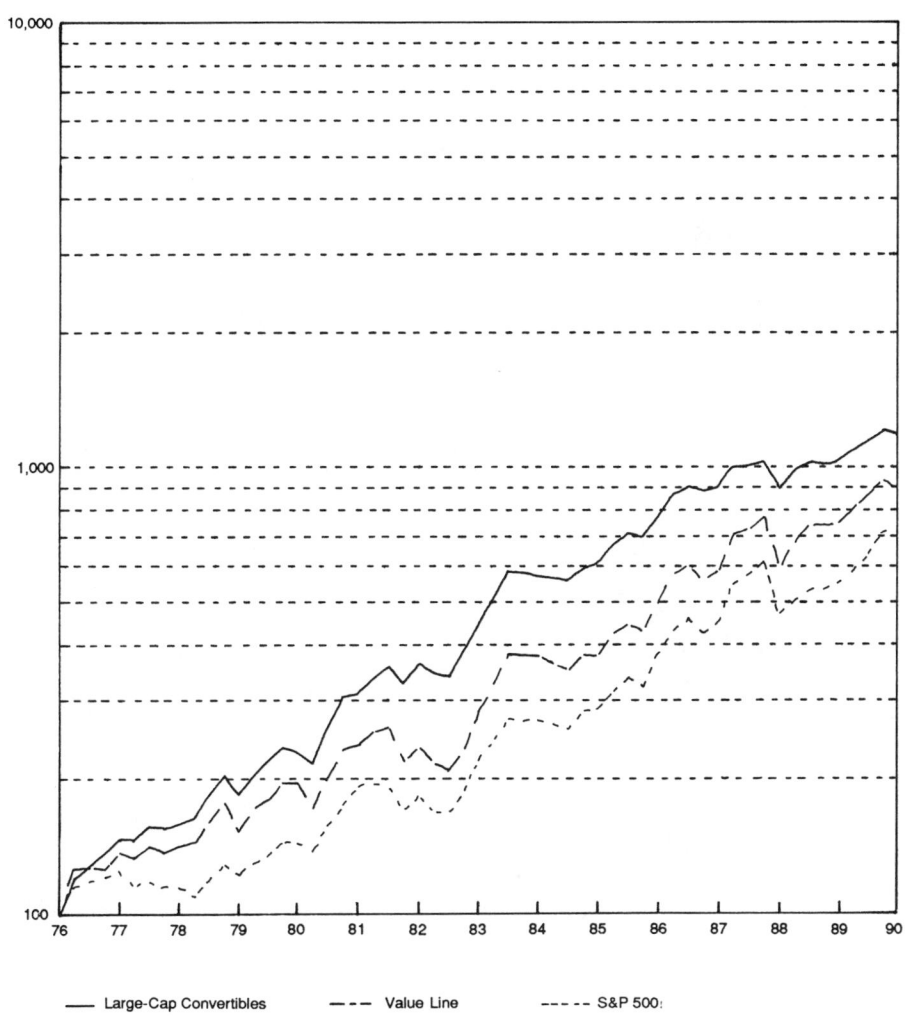

— Large-Cap Convertibles   — – – Value Line   – – – – S&P 500:

Chapter 6

MEDIUM- AND SMALL-CAP CONVERTIBLE BONDS

By my firm's definition, "Medium-Cap" describes convertible bonds rated CCC or higher by Standard & Poor's, issued by companies having capitalization between $100 and $500 million. And since the bonds must also be mathematically undervalued, Medium-Cap convertible bond portfolios become a low-risk, high-return alternative for investors seeking capital appreciation.

"Small-Cap" describes undervalued convertible bonds issued by companies with capitalization below $100 million and not in default on their interest payments. They should be viewed as low-risk alternatives for aggressive investors seeking the long-term advantages offered by the small-company sector of the financial markets.

Exhibit 6-1 compares risk-reward relationships for Medium- and Small-Cap convertible bonds utilizing the convertible strategies line. Like the characteristics for Large-Cap convertibles, risk-reward is shown as a range on the line. And if placed on the convertible strategies line of Exhibit 4-1, it would overlap the range for Large-Cap issues. In other words, some Medium- or Small-Cap convertible bonds are safer than some Large-Cap convertibles, depending on such factors as relative prices and quality ratings. A convertible security cannot be categorized by a single criterion.

THE 80/40 PERFORMANCE ADVANTAGE

The guidelines of Chapter 4 for building and managing Large-Cap portfolios essentially apply to Medium- and Small-Cap convertible bond portfolios as well. The most important difference is that these smaller issues tend to be more undervalued than the institutionally-followed larger issues. Additionally, Medium- and Small-Cap convertible bonds usually provide more income than Large-Cap issues; this extra income means greater safety.

Another difference is that small firms are more likely to run into financial difficulties. Thus, we can expect portfolios of these smaller companies to experience more bankruptcy or near-bankruptcy occurrences. Although greater income and better risk-reward relationships tend to offset the higher probability of bankruptcy, I believe that broad portfolio diversification becomes even more important when dealing with riskier companies.

In any case, Medium- and Small-Cap convertible bonds should be looked at as 80/40 alternatives to their higher-risk, underlying common stocks. Keeping that relationship in perspective at all times will allow savvy investors to achieve the long-term performance results they are seeking through undervalued securities.

MEDIUM- AND SMALL-CAP CONVERTIBLE BOND INDEXES

Appendix E provides a complete listing of the 329 convertibles employed in the Noddings Medium-Cap convertible bond index since its inception in 1976. Appendix F provides a similar listing for our newer, Small-Cap convertible bond index covering 104 issues (1987-1989). Tables 6-1 and 6-2 show the bonds held as of January 1, 1990, thirty-six issues in each index.

Exhibit 6-1. Medium- and Small-Cap Convertible Bonds Compared to the Capital Market Line

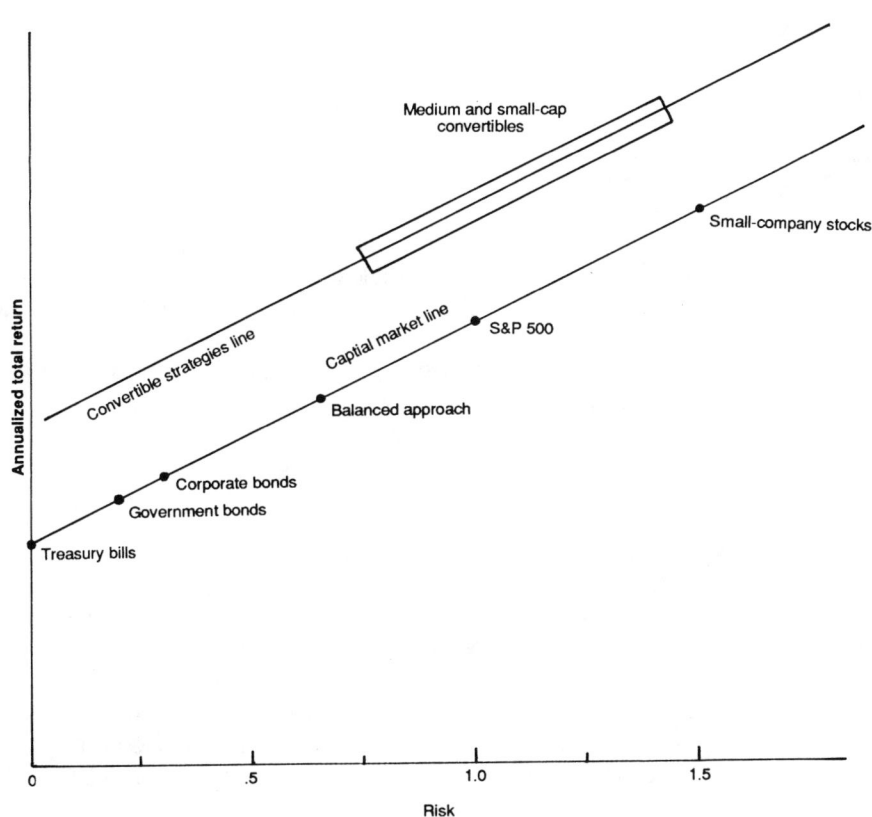

Notice from the tables that the current yields for the Medium- and Small-Cap indexes were 9.1 and 10.7 percent respectively compared to 6.5 percent for the Large-Cap (Table 5-1). Convertible bonds are an unusual way to participate in the long-term growth potential of smaller companies while simultaneously enjoying high income. The high yields also help cushion the adverse impact of an occasional bankruptcy on the overall portfolio.

Notice also that the tables include Value Line's bond rating when available, because these convertibles are often not rated by Standard & Poor's (or Moodys). Value Line will rate them if they are covered in their convertible service (Appendix A).

Performance Measurement

Table 6-3 provides annual total returns since the Medium-Cap index's inception in 1976 compared with two stock market indexes: Value Line's index of 1,700 stocks and Value Line's low-cap stock index based on the smallest 10 percent of the companies in their 1,700 stock universe. Data for the Small-Cap convertible bond index was added beginning in 1987. Quarterly performance data are provided in Table 6-4.

Performance Evaluation

Once again we see that undervalued convertibles have produced remarkable returns over the years. Compounding at 20.8 percent for a cumulative return of 1,317 percent over fourteen years, the Medium-Cap index outpaced all stock market indexes including the best-performing Value Line index's 798 percent.

Table 6-4 also includes the popular risk-reward evaluation standards which again confirm the advantages of undervalued convertibles. Also, looking at the up and down quarters experienced by the S&P 500 (Table 5-3) we find the Medium-Cap index averaging +8.0 percent in the forty positive quarters (versus +7.6 percent for the S&P) and only –1.9 percent in the 16 negative quarters (versus –5.2 percent for the S&P). The Medium-Cap index at –1.9 percent performed surprisingly better than its high-quality Large-Cap colleague at –2.6 percent.

The single best stock market proxy for the Medium-Cap convertible bond index is probably the Value Line 1,700 stock index. Exhibit 6-2 graphically depicts a high correlation between it and the convertibles.

Table 6-1. The Noddings Medium-Cap Convertible Bond Index—Positions Held on January 1, 1990

Company Name	Bond Description	Bond Ratings S&P	VL	Bond Price	Current Yield %	Capitalization ($mil)
Alaska Air Group	6.875-14	BB+	E	89.25	7.70	341
America West Airlines	11.500-09	NR	I	109.75	10.48	172
Atari Corp.	5.250-02	B-	I	66.00	7.95	497
Bally Manufacturing	6.000-98	B	G	66.38	9.04	421
Burnup & Sims	12.000-00	NR	H	100.00	12.00	213
CML Group	7.500-12	B-	F	76.00	9.87	132
Conner Peripherals	9.000-14	B-	G	135.00	6.67	510
Copperweld	9.920-08	B+	H	100.00	9.92	107
Diasonics Inc.	6.500-01	NR	F	104.00	6.25	288
Environmental Systems	6.750-11	B-	H	53.00	12.74	179
Graphic Scanning	10.000-01	NR	J	108.00	9.26	335
Grow Group	8.500-06	CCC+	F	81.25	10.46	86
Guilford Mills	6.000-12	BBB-	E	75.12	7.99	233
Hadson Corp.	7.750-06	NR	G	69.00	11.23	99
Horn & Hardart	7.500-07	NR	H	74.00	10.14	96
Hudson Foods	14.000-08	B-	H	110.00	12.73	137
Immunex Corp.	7.500-11	CCC	H	110.00	6.82	149
Ingles Markets	9.000-08	B+	E	103.00	8.74	165
Inspiration Resources	8.500-12	B	F	94.00	9.04	406
Jamesway	8.000-05	B+	F	74.00	10.81	97
JP Industries	7.250-13	B+	F	78.00	9.29	134
Kaman Corp.	6.000-12	BBB-	E	63.00	9.52	234
Kirby Exploration	7.750-14	BBB-	D	100.00	7.75	210
Mark IV Industries	7.000-11	B-	H	108.00	6.48	206
Mentor Corp.	6.750-02	NR	F	90.00	7.50	147
Midway Airlines	8.500-02	NR	G	94.00	9.04	125
Olsten Corp.	7.000-13	BB+	D	89.50	7.82	257
PHM Corp.	8.500-08	BB+	G	74.00	11.49	279
Ranger Oil Ltd.	6.500-02	NR	E	106.00	6.13	497
RPM Corp.	5.750-01	NR	E	112.00	5.13	428
Sunshine Mining	8.875-08	CCC	I	83.00	10.69	300
Talley Industries	9.000-05	NR	NR	88.00	10.23	93
Universal Health Syste	7.500-08	NR	I	60.50	12.40	136
Vishay Intertechnology	4.750-03	NR	D	95.50	4.97	200
Watts Industries	7.750-14	BBB+	D	118.50	6.54	463
Webb, Del E.	10.375-09	CCC+	H	87.00	11.93	78
Averages (36 securities)					9.08	235

Table 6-2. The Noddings Small-Cap Convertible Bond Index—Positions Held on January 1, 1990

Company Name	Bond Description	Bond Ratings S&P	Bond Ratings VL	Bond Price	Current Yield %	Capital-ization ($mil)
AST Research	8.500-13	B-	G	88.00	9.66	121
Ben & Jerry's	9.500-07	NR	NR	110.00	8.64	41
Carmike Cinemas	8.000-07	B	G	126.50	6.32	70
Chock Full O'Nuts	7.000-12	B-	G	69.00	10.14	52
Conquest Exploration	9.500-14	CCC	I	107.00	8.88	96
Data-Design Labs	8.500-08	B-	I	70.50	12.06	36
Data Switch	9.000-96	NR	NR	65.00	13.85	40
Ducommun Inc.	7.750-11	NR	J	55.50	13.96	12
Foothill Group	9.500-03	B+	I	100.00	9.50	68
Giant Group	7.000-06	B-	H	83.00	8.43	60
Graphic Industries	7.000-06	BB-	G	60.50	11.57	67
Health Images	6.500-98	NR	NR	134.00	4.85	61
Howtek Inc.	9.000-01	NR	NR	75.00	12.00	70
Intermark	7.375-07	B-	I	85.00	8.68	63
Jackpot Enterprises	8.750-14	B+	F	87.00	10.06	47
Lionel Corp.	8.000-07	B	G	64.00	12.50	68
LTX Corp.	10.500-09	CCC-	I	80.25	13.08	25
Lynch Corp.	8.000-06	NR	H	95.00	8.42	34
Mgt. Co. Entertainment	14.000-09	NR	NR	121.00	11.57	60
Marcade Group	12.500-99	NR	NR	90.00	13.89	40
Medalist Industries	7.500-01	NR	NR	72.00	10.42	21
Metro Airlines	8.500-12	CCC+	I	88.00	9.66	45
Nasta International	12.000-02	NR	NR	82.00	14.63	19
O'Brien Energy Systems	7.750-02	CCC+	G	142.50	5.44	71
Porta Systems	9.250-00	B-	H	107.50	8.60	75
Recognition Equipment	7.250-11	B-	H	58.00	12.50	67
Renaissance GRX	9.000-96	NR	NR	100.00	9.00	7
Salick Health	7.250-01	NR	G	91.50	7.92	60
Spartech	9.000-99	CCC+	J	57.00	15.79	10
Sterling Electronics	10.750-09	NR	NR	83.50	12.87	9
Thermo Environmental	6.000-96	BB-	NR	96.00	6.25	71
Traditional Industries	9.500-07	CCC-	NR	41.25	23.03	10
Transcisco	9.000-96	NR	H	101.00	8.91	40
Trans-Lux	9.000-05	NR	NR	80.00	11.25	11
Tridex	10.250-96	NR	NR	72.00	14.24	8
Wyle Laboratories	6.250-02	NR	F	81.00	7.72	115
Averages (36 securities)					10.73	49

Table 6-3. The Noddings Medium- and Small-Cap Convertible Bond Indexes Versus Market Indexes—Annual Total Returns

Year	Value Line*	Value Line Low-Cap**	Medium-Cap Convertibles	Small-Cap Convertibles
1976	36.2	62.3	39.5	——
1977	3.8	36.1	14.2	——
1978	7.7	37.5	38.1	——
1979	28.3	43.5	41.7	——
1980	22.0	32.2	37.4	——
1981	-1.3	9.3	8.0	——
1982	18.9	31.3	34.8	——
1983	34.8	40.6	27.3	——
1984	0.4	-20.6	0.3	——
1985	32.2	13.2	25.2	——
1986	16.2	-2.8	19.7	——
1987	1.8	-25.1	-9.9	-13.1
1988	25.8	18.2	20.7	12.4
1989	20.7	-13.0	9.2	8.2
Cumulative return	798	682	1317	——
Annualized return	17.0	15.8	20.8	——

*Value Line's geometric index (1976-82) and arithmetic index (1983-89) of 1,700 stocks—estimated dividends included.
**The smallest 10 percent of the companies making up the Value Line index of 1,700 stocks—dividends not included.

Note: The indexes do not include management fees or trading expenses.

The Noddings Small-Cap convertible bond index can probably best be compared with the Value Line low-cap stock index, and, although the convertible index is only three years old, it is already showing good correlation with, and outperforming, the Value Line low-cap quarterly data of Table 6-4. Three-year cumulative returns are +5.7 percent for small-company convertibles versus –23.0 percent for small-company stocks; convertibles are again proving their advantages.

Table 6-4. The Noddings Medium- and Small-Cap Convertible Bond Indexes Versus Market Indexes—Quarterly Total Returns

Year	Value Line	Value Line Low-Cap	Medium-Cap Convertibles	Small-Cap Convertibles
1976	25.8	53.4	10.3	——
	0.2	-1.7	10.5	——
	-0.4	-1.3	6.1	——
	8.5	9.0	7.9	——
1977	-2.5	13.4	3.0	——
	5.8	8.2	7.2	——
	-3.1	0.8	0.7	——
	3.8	10.1	2.7	——
1978	1.9	15.2	10.9	——
	10.5	24.9	12.1	——
	10.7	23.0	17.7	——
	-13.6	-22.2	-5.6	——
1979	12.5	23.0	14.9	——
	5.0	7.1	9.1	——
	8.8	11.2	9.4	——
	-0.2	-2.1	3.3	——
1980	-12.1	-10.4	-3.5	——
	17.3	16.4	17.2	——
	15.0	29.1	11.9	——
	2.9	-1.8	8.6	——
1981	6.5	18.4	13.2	——
	2.5	10.4	2.8	——
	-15.5	-20.5	-11.7	——
	7.0	5.1	5.1	——
1982	-8.3	-1.6	-0.1	——
	-3.0	-1.4	2.6	——
	10.2	8.3	9.6	——
	21.3	24.9	20.0	——
1983	16.3	24.2	13.1	——
	16.8	22.7	21.7	——
	-0.6	-3.1	-6.5	——
	-0.2	-4.7	-1.1	——

Table 6-4. (continued)

Year	Value Line	Value Line Low-Cap	Medium-Cap Convertibles	Small-Cap Convertibles
1984	-4.1	-4.4	1.9	——
	-3.0	-7.5	-6.9	——
	8.2	2.2	4.4	——
	-0.2	-12.2	1.3	——
1985	11.7	12.0	13.4	——
	5.2	-3.7	5.8	——
	-3.5	-4.1	0.8	——
	16.6	9.4	3.5	——
1986	15.6	10.4	8.6	——
	3.7	-4.2	9.0	——
	-7.0	-11.6	-2.6	——
	4.2	3.9	3.8	——
1987	21.5	14.0	13.7	11.4
	2.7	-3.6	-1.5	-1.5
	6.4	4.7	0.1	1.6
	-23.3	-34.9	-19.6	-22.0
1988	16.2	23.0	10.7	11.3
	7.4	4.8	6.4	3.5
	-0.3	-2.3	1.0	1.1
	1.2	-6.1	1.5	-3.4
1989	7.9	3.6	3.1	8.5
	7.2	3.7	5.9	1.7
	8.1	-0.8	6.6	3.8
	-3.4	-18.4	-6.2	-5.5
Cumulative return	798	682	1317	——
Quarterly return	4.4	4.7	5.1	——
Standard deviation	9.5	14.6	7.8	——
Coefficient of variation	215	308	151	——
Sharpe measure	0.26	0.19	0.41	——

Exhibit 6-2. The Noddings Medium-Cap Convertible Performance Advantage
14 Years Ended 12/31/89

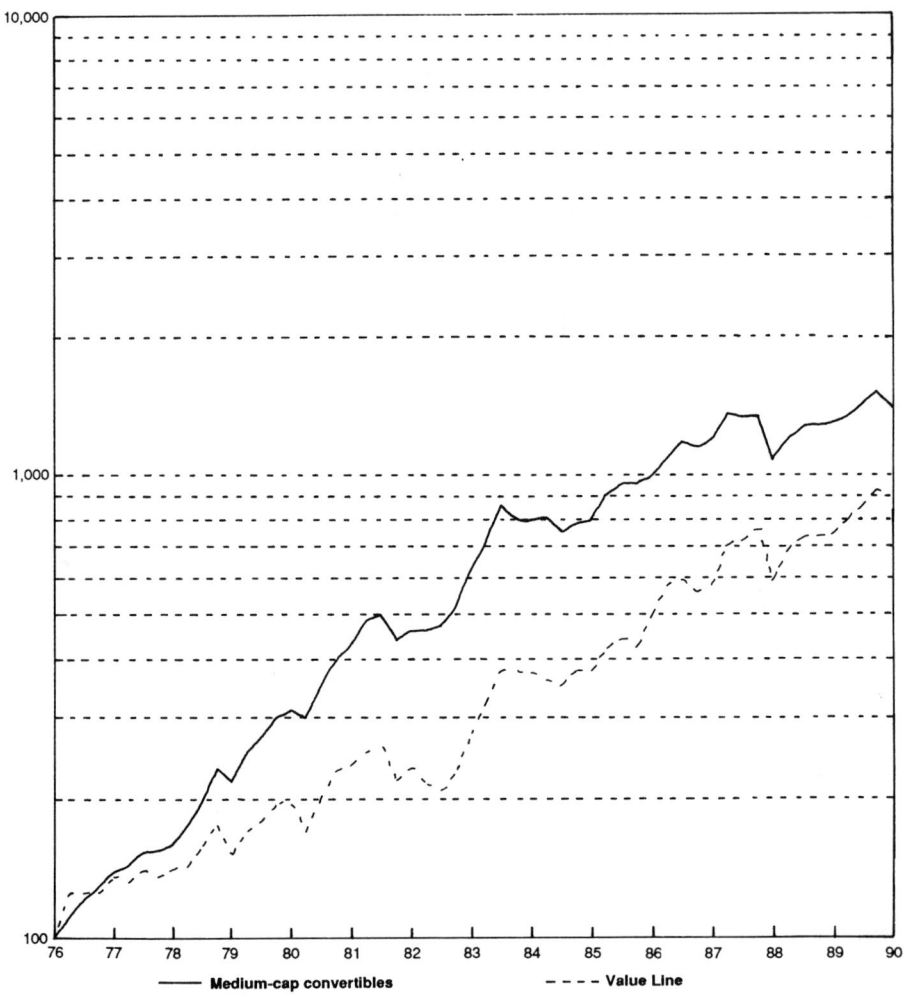

Chapter 7

HEDGING CONVERTIBLE BONDS WITH COMMON STOCK

Convertible-bond hedging permits conservative investors to take advantage of undervalued opportunities, regardless of how speculative they may be, and do so safely. By selling common stock short against carefully selected convertibles, the conservative investor can retain much of the stock market's potential while eliminating most of its risk.

Although any undervalued convertible may be hedged by shorting stock, the strategy is best suited to the more speculative issues. These issues tend to be more undervalued than higher-quality convertibles. Also, they usually provide greater yields; and since their underlying stocks pay little or no dividends, the payment of the short sale dividend is not a serious burden. The ideal convertible hedge candidate is a high-yielding bond trading at its conversion value, with a volatile underlying common stock paying no dividend. While the ideal candidate can be found on occasion, we must usually accept compromises on these selection parameters. Let's evaluate a typical attractive situation.

CONVERTIBLE/STOCK HEDGING

Chapter 3 illustrated the risk-reward characteristics for the XYZ Corp.'s 10 percent convertible bond brought to the market at 100 when its stock was at $20. Let's assume that XYZ Corp. common stock advances from $20 up to $30 after the convertible was issued. At a $30 stock price, the convertible is worth 120 if exchanged for common. Assuming that the convertible was callable in a year or so, its normal price should be near 130, but suppose it could be purchased for only 122, as shown in Exhibit 7-1.

Although mathematically undervalued at a price of 122, the convertible would probably be considered too risky for most conservative investors—XYZ Corp. is still a speculative company, and the bond is trading at nearly twice its $650 investment floor. In fact, those who purchased the bond at 100 might be selling at 122. They may be perfectly satisfied with a 22 percent capital gain in addition to the 10 percent coupon and may be seeking the safety of a replacement issue at 100. However, other conservative investors, who have the ability to employ hedging strategies can take advantage of such an attractive opportunity via the convertible/stock hedge.

THE BULLISH HEDGE

The risk-reward calculations and profit profile of Exhibit 7-2 illustrate a bullish hedge position. For this, and for the neutral and bearish positions to follow, I make these assumptions:

- Ten bonds are purchased at 122 for a cash investment of $12,200.
- The common stock at $30 pays a 2 percent annual dividend, or $15 each quarter per 100 shares.

Exhibit 7-1. Convertible Price Curve for XYZ Corp.

10 percent, 20-year bond trading at 122 with the common stock at $30

- Conversion Ratio = 40 shares
- Straight Bond Equivalent Yield = 16 percent

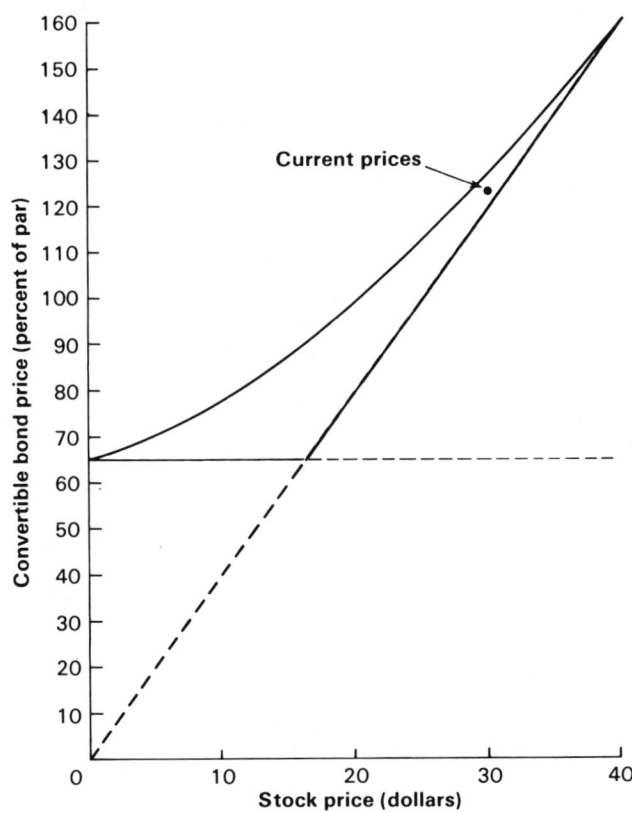

Exhibit 7-2. XYZ Corp. Convertible Bonds Hedged by the Short Sale of Stock— Bullish Posture

	Price	Prices in Six Months			
Stock	$ 30.00	$ 15	$ 30	$ 45	$ 60
Convertible	122.00	85	122	180	240

Strategy: Buy 10 bonds and short 200 shares of stock ($6000)*

Profit or (loss) on bonds	(3700)	0	5800	11800
Profit or (loss) on stock	3000	0	(3000)	(6000)
Bond interest received	500	500	500	500
Stock dividends paid	(60)	(60)	(60)	(60)
Total profit or (loss)	(260)	440	3240	6240
Return on investment	– 2.1%	+ 3.6%	+ 26.6%	+ 51.1%
Annualized return	– 4.2%	+ 7.2%	+ 53.2%	+102.2%

*Investment = $1220 per bond X 10 bonds = $12200

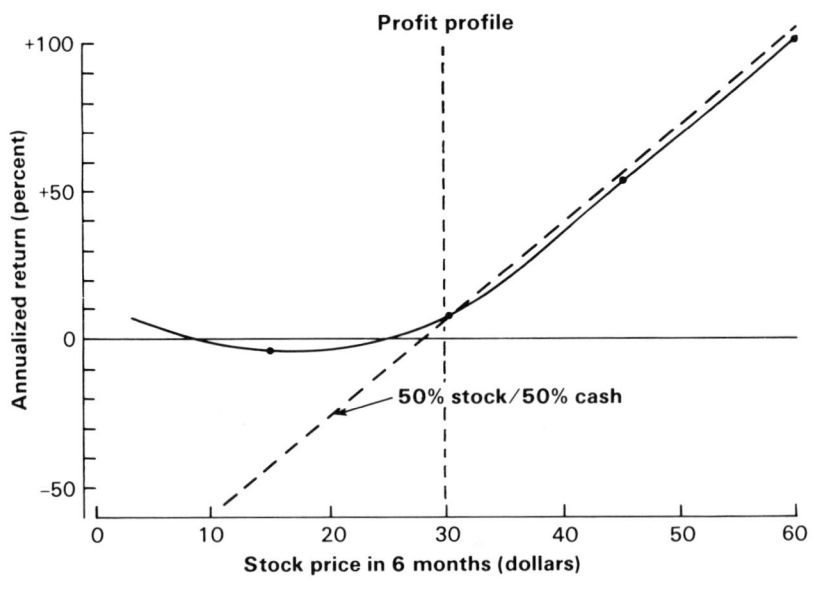

- Short sale proceeds are credited to a special short account and held by the brokerage firm until the stock is bought back. These funds are not available for use by the short seller.
- Risk-reward calculations are based on a six-month holding period. Whereas most hedge positions are held longer, six months permits a direct comparison with the option strategies to be presented in Chapter 8.
- Commissions are excluded for ease of illustration.

As shown by the risk-reward calculations of Exhibit 7-2, the bullish hedge assumes the short sale of 200 common shares. Since ten bonds represent 400 shares, this amounts to a half hedge and is designed to reduce downside risk to about break-even. If the common were to drop in half to $15 over the ensuing six months, the $3,700 loss on the ten-bond position would be largely offset by the short sale's $3,000 profit plus the $440 net interest earned ($500 received for ten bonds minus $60 in stock dividends paid). The six-month total loss of $260 equals -2.1 percent on the $12,200 investment, or -4.2 percent annualized. If the 50 percent stock decline occurred more rapidly, the loss would be greater; if it took longer than six months, the additional interest earned would ultimately produce downside profits.

In a static market, the hedge position provides a net interest income of 7.2 percent annually, well above that of the typical common stock. The desired outcome, however, is for the stock to make a strong advance. Here, the bond profits would exceed short sale losses, providing significant capital appreciation. If the stock were to gain 50 percent to $45, for instance, the hedge's annualized return would be 53 percent; a stock doubling to $60 would produce a 102 percent annualized return.

Bullish hedges are designed to participate in upward market moves at reduced risk. Since their underlying common stocks are more volatile than high-quality stocks, diversified portfolios of such conservative hedges can be expected to perform nearly as well as an index like the S&P 500 during market advances, while minimizing losses during market declines.

Hedgers who disregard short-term price movements should remain in a bullish posture throughout a market cycle. A bullish stance is not only more compatible with the stock market's long-term upward bias, it will also produce greater profits during volatile sideways movements than neutral or bearish strategies. The odds are roughly equal that a stock will either drop in half or double. A bullish hedge offers much higher profits if the stock doubles than a bearish hedge does if the stock halves; the neutral hedge falls in between. Thus, hedgers lacking forecasting ability will reap greater profits over the long run by keeping their portfolio in a bullish posture.

NEUTRAL AND BEARISH HEDGES

Investors desiring greater safety than bullish hedging provides, or downside profits, can short additional common shares (up to 400) against a ten-bond XYZ position. Exhibit 7-3 presents a neutral hedge involving 300 shares short. Exhibit 7-4 shows a bearish hedge involving a full 400 share short position.

Neutral strategies are recommended for very conservative investors. Bearish tactics are recommended for investors employing market timing and who believe XYZ Corp. is about to experience a price decline. Technicians can quickly shift from a bullish to a bearish stance by adding to the shares sold short instead of liquidating their entire positions and incurring large trading expenses. When they turn bullish once again, they can cover a portion of the stock held short.

Investors who do not employ market timing, however, may also have use for neutral or bearish hedges if they have unhedged convertibles in their portfolios. The net result can produce a low-risk posture for the total portfolio, as if each convertible security were individually protected. Convertibles and their related hedging strategies provide portfolio management flexibility unavailable to investors using conventional stocks, bonds and money market instruments.

MANAGING THE HEDGE PORTFOLIO

Hedging convertible bonds via the short sale of common stock is a relatively passive investment strategy, since large price movements are usually necessary before action need be taken.

This strategy's ideal market environment is a bull market in secondary stocks such as the six-year period from the end of the 1974 bear market through 1980, and again from mid-1982 through mid-1983. Under such favorable conditions, profits are taken when bonds advance to well above par, and the funds are reinvested in new positions priced closer to

Exhibit 7-3. XYZ Corp. Convertible Bonds Hedged by the Short Sale of Stock— Neutral Posture

	Price	Prices in Six Months			
Stock	$ 30.00	$ 15	$ 30	$ 45	$ 60
Convertible	122.00	85	122	180	240

Strategy: Buy 10 bonds and short 300 shares of stock ($9000)*

Profit or (loss) on bonds	(3700)	0	5800	11800
Profit or (loss) on stock	4500	0	(4500)	(9000)
Bond interest received	500	500	500	500
Stock dividends paid	(90)	(90)	(90)	(90)
Total profit or (loss)	1210	410	1710	3210
Return on investment	+ 9.9%	+ 3.4%	+14.0%	+26.3%
Annualized return	+19.8%	+ 6.8%	+28.0%	+52.6%

*Investment = $1220 per bond X 10 bonds = $12200

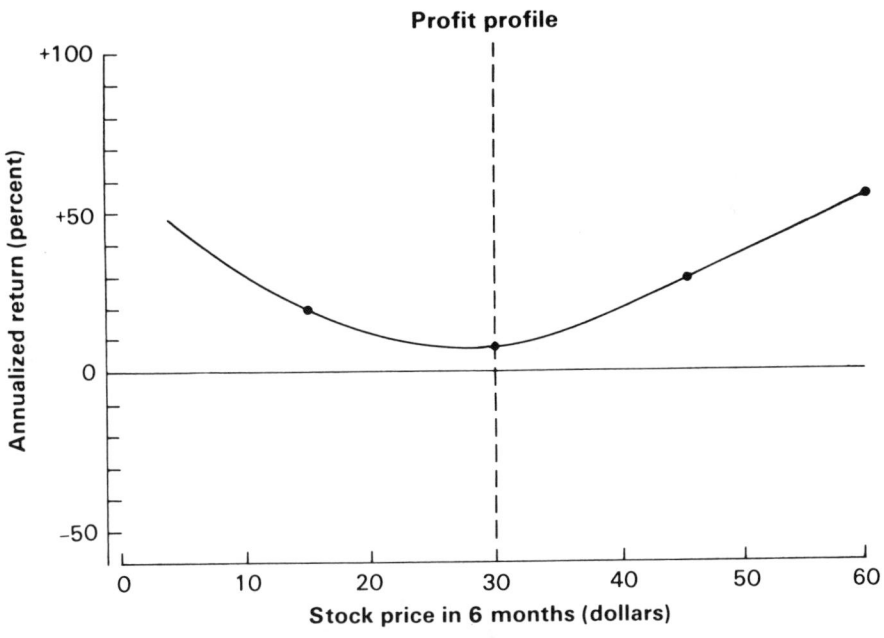

Profit profile

Exhibit 7-4. XYZ Corp. Convertible Bonds Hedged by the Short Sale of Stock— Bearish Posture

	Price	*Prices in Six Months*			
Stock	$ 30.00	$ 15	$ 30	$ 45	$ 60
Convertible	122.00	85	122	180	240

Strategy: Buy 10 bonds and short 400 shares of stock ($12000)*

Profit or (loss) on bonds	(3700)	0	5800	11800
Profit or (loss) on stock	6000	0	(6000)	(12000)
Bond interest received	500	500	500	500
Stock dividends paid	(120)	(120)	(120)	(120)
Total profit or (loss)	2680	380	180	180
Return on investment	+22.0%	+ 3.1%	+ 1.5%	+ 1.5%
Annualized return	+44.0%	+ 6.2%	+ 3.0%	+ 3.0%

*Investment = $1220 per bond X 10 bonds = $12200

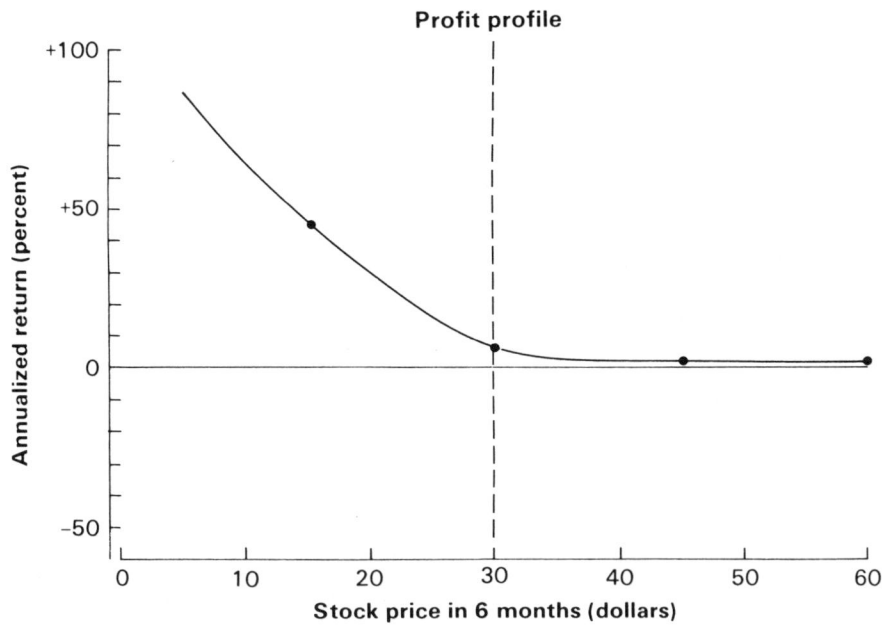

Profit profile

par. Maintaining the portfolio in a low-risk posture in preparation for the next market advance is the hedger's objective.

While managing a convertible hedge portfolio during advancing markets is not too difficult, bear markets can present unforeseeable problems. Although bullish hedges, for example, are designed to break-even during bear markets, rising interest rates and/or panic sell-offs can push the bonds well below the theoretical investment floors assigned at time of purchase. Thus, hedgers are sometimes faced with losing positions when the short sale profits cease to protect bonds driven to deeply discounted price levels. My advice is: don't panic. Let's look at the bullish hedge in XYZ Corp. as an illustration of what one can expect to experience on occasion.

Originally established at prices of 122 and $30 for the XYZ Corp. bonds and stock, the hedge, involving 200 shares sold short against ten bonds, was intended to roughly break-even on the downside, including interest earned. If the stock plummeted from $30 to $5 over the next twelve months, as an extreme example, the ten bonds were expected to lose no more than $5,700 as they approached their $650 investment floor. In theory, this loss would have been more than offset by short sale profits of $5,000 plus $880 net interest earned. But suppose that the decline was accompanied by large corporate losses and rising fears that the company was headed into bankruptcy. In that event, the market might drop the convertible's price to well below 65. At a price of 40, for instance, a net position loss of $2,300 would exist, representing nearly 20 percent on the original investment.

Studies have shown that deep-discount bonds, like XYZ Corp. at 40, significantly outperform the markets, on average.[1] Thus, it would make little sense to close out the entire position. Rather, I would normally cover the shorted stock for profits and hold the bond unhedged. At 40, its current yield is 25 percent, and the ten-bond position, worth only $4,000, now makes up but a small portion of the total portfolio. (Note that much of the original $12,200 investment was returned during the twelve-month decline through the process of marking the short account to the market.)

Recognize that although some deep-discount bonds will experience further declines, others that turn around should offset the additional losses of those that do not recover. In fact, the unhedged XYZ Corp. bond at 40 is probably no riskier, and potentially just as profitable, as the

---

1. *Low Risk Strategies for the High Performance Investor*, Chapter 6.

original hedge position. Hence, over time, a convertible hedge portfolio can be expected to include unhedged bonds trading at deep-discount levels as well as hedged bonds trading above par.

Chapter 8

HEDGING CONVERTIBLE BONDS WITH PUTS AND CALLS

Shorting stock was the primary strategy for protecting undervalued convertibles until the introduction of listed equity call options in 1973. This widely heralded event on the new Chicago Board Options Exchange (CBOE) opened the floodgates to an ever expanding grab-bag of financial instruments useful in hedging market risk. Put options were added later and the number of stocks with listed puts and calls has increased to over 600 companies. Other derivative securities, such as index options, have also been introduced throughout the world's financial markets.

Equity puts and calls offer additional portfolio-management flexibility and may be potentially more profitable than shorting stock. Therefore, all convertible hedgers must be able to deal effectively with option strategies if they are to successfully compete. (Basic put and call option strategies are covered in Appendix G for your review.)

THE UNIVERSE OF CONVERTIBLE BONDS WITH LISTED OPTIONS

Undervalued convertible bonds should constitute the base holdings of any hedging program seeking above-average performance. Hedging is profitable when the securities purchased are undervalued and/or those sold are overpriced. One of these conditions must exist or stockbrokers and marketmakers will be the only winners—as they are when investors write (sell) fairly priced covered call options against fairly priced common stocks. Since the option market is reasonably efficient, hedgers must turn to undervalued convertibles in order to capitalize on the profitable advantages hedging can offer.

Of the more than 600 companies having listed puts and calls in 1990, 150 also had one or more convertible bonds within their financial structure (totaling about 200 issues). Of the 200 convertible bonds to choose from, some were undervalued (as defined in previous chapters) and were therefore superior alternatives to their underlying common stocks. They were also candidates for setting up profitable convertible/option hedges.

PUTS AND CALLS VERSUS SHORTING STOCK

Basic option Strategy 4 (Appendix G) illustrates how a simultaneous purchase of an at-the-money put and sale of an at-the-money call is analogous to selling stock short. The primary differences between the two tactics are that the price spread between the put and call becomes a net credit to the account, and there are no short-sale dividends to be paid. In actuality, the long-put/short-call combination permits hedgers to capture the value of risk-free money whereas short-sale proceeds are frozen.

Portfolio management flexibility is another advantage. Hedgers may utilize either a put or a call to adjust their portfolio's risk-reward characteristics or to take advantage of under- or overpriced opportunities. The price spread between the two options, for example, might properly reflect the value of money, yet both options may be undervalued or over-valued. If both are undervalued, one should hedge convertibles with long puts only; if both are overvalued, call writing would be the favored strategy.

Table 8-1 analyzes six-month at-the-money puts and calls trading at various premium levels on XYZ Corp. stock, which is trading at $30. The center column shows the same percentages used for the basic option strategies of Appendix G: put and call premiums of 7.1 and 10 percent respectively. We can assume that a $2.125 put and a $3.00 call represent normal values since they are reasonably close to real-world premiums for options on similar stocks. The $0.875 price difference reflects risk-free money at 8 percent when XYZ Corp. stock yields 2 percent.

The outer columns of the table present possible prices, assuming both options are either underpriced or overpriced. Studying the under-valued options in the first column tells us that hedgers would buy puts trading at $1.375 and avoid selling calls at $2.25. From the overvalued options in the right-hand column, we know hedgers would sell calls at $3.75 and avoid buying puts at $2.875. The $0.75 price differences from normal values mean extra profits every time such transactions are executed.

Let's move on and evaluate various option-hedging strategies using the XYZ Corp. convertible bonds priced at 122, as in the convertible/stock hedging strategies of Chapter 7. The risk-reward calculations are based on certain assumptions that simplify the arithmetic:

Table 8-1. Various Premium Levels for Put and Call Options on XYZ Corp. Common Stock Trading at $30

| | Option premium levels | | |
	Undervalued	Normally valued	Overvalued
Call option premiums	7.50%	10.00%	12.50%
Put option premiums	4.58%	7.08%	9.58%
Call option price	$2.250	$3.000	$3.750
Put option price	$1.375	$2.125	$2.875
Price difference	$0.875	$0.875	$0.875

- Ten bonds are purchased at 122 for a cash investment of $12,200.
- The common stock is trading at $30.
- A normally valued six-month call option, having a $30 exercise price, is trading at $3.00.
- A normally valued six-month put option, having a $30 exercise price, is trading at $2.125.
- Each position is held until the options expire in six months.
- Options are assumed to be trading at their intrinsic values at expiration.
- Net premiums received from option transactions are placed in Treasury bills yielding 8 percent.
- Premiums for puts purchased are assumed to be borrowed at 8 percent.
- Commissions are excluded.

HEDGING UNDERVALUED CONVERTIBLES WITH PUT OPTIONS

Ten XYZ Corp. convertible bonds are exchangeable into 400 shares of common stock. Thus, the purchase of four puts represents a full hedge position. Exhibit 8-1 provides the risk-reward calculations and profit profile. As shown, the puts protect the bonds in a declining market; furthermore, the hedge begins to produce profits if the stock drops below $27.50. At a stock price of $15, for instance, a net six-month profit of 15.7 percent is anticipated. If the stock ends up unchanged at $30, the bond interest earned offsets most of the put-option acquisition costs; the net loss is 3.1 percent. Protecting convertibles with put options is a bullish strategy. If the stock were to double, the net profit would be 94 percent.

Exhibit 8-1 also includes the profit profile for protecting common stock with puts (Strategy 2 of Appendix G). Once again, we can observe the advantages of dealing with undervalued convertible securities. Not only does the convertible/put-option hedge offer downside profits, it even provides higher returns than the stock/put-option combination upon a price advance. By overlooking the undervalued convertible bond, anyone hedging XYZ Corp. common stock at the time made a serious investment error. Sadly, most option investors are unaware that attractive convertibles might be available on stocks they are evaluating.

Exhibit 8-1. XYZ Corp. Convertible Bonds Hedged by Put Options

	Price	*Prices at Expiration (6 months)*			
Stock	$30.00	15	30	45	60
Convertible	122.00	85	122	180	240
Put	2.125	15	0	0	0

Strategy: Buy 10 bonds and buy 4 at-the-money puts*

Profit or loss on bonds	−3700	0	5800	11800
Profit or loss on puts	5150	−850	−850	−850
Bond interest received	500	500	500	500
Interest paid on $850 (puts)	−34	−34	−34	−34
Total profit or loss	1916	−384	5416	11416
Return on investment - %	15.7	−3.1	44.4	93.6
Annualized return - %	31.4	−6.3	88.8	187.1

*Investment = $1,220 per bond x 10 bonds = $12,200

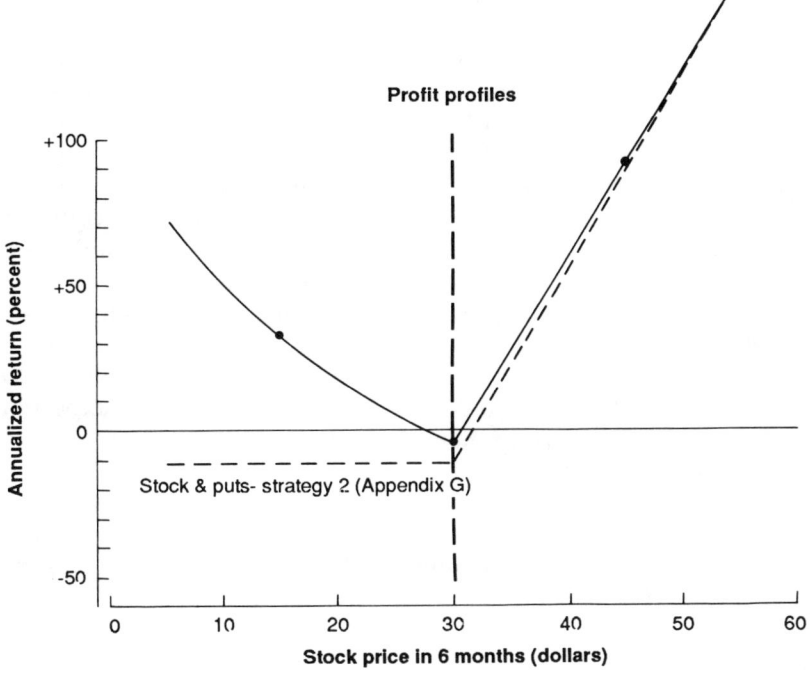

Profit profiles

Stock & puts- strategy 2 (Appendix G)

Annualized return (percent)

Stock price in 6 months (dollars)

Bullish investors might reduce the number of puts to a partial hedge; they recognize that protecting undervalued convertibles requires fewer puts than protecting common stock. If two puts were purchased to hedge the ten-bond position, the six-month loss for a 50 percent stock price decline would be only about 5 percent. Furthermore, the cost saving by purchasing only two puts increases the hedge-position returns in stable or rising markets.

HEDGING UNDERVALUED CONVERTIBLES WITH CALL OPTIONS

Exhibit 8-2 presents risk-reward calculations and the profit profile for writing covered call options against the ten XYZ Corp. convertible bonds. Like selling calls against common stocks, this modestly bullish strategy produces small returns most of the time. However, by comparing the convertible hedge results with the stock position results, we can again recognize the advantages offered by undervalued securities. Not only does the convertible's higher yield provide additional profits in stable or rising markets, its investment floor cushions downside losses.

Break-even price, the common stock's price at which losses begin to accrue at the call's expiration, is a popular tool for evaluating option-writing strategies. The convertible bond hedge has a lower break-even price of $24.00 versus $26.50 for the stock hedge; but more important, potential losses on the convertible hedge are much lower than on the stock position. For example, if the stock dropped to $15, the convertible hedge would be expected to lose 16.0 percent for the six-month period, compared to 38.5 percent when writing calls against stock.

If both the put and call options are efficiently priced, we can assume that a call-writing strategy's expected rate of return over the long run will be the same as when hedging convertibles with put options. Recognize also that both strategies reduce risk but neither can be expected to increase returns, as some proponents of covered call writing against common stocks falsely claim.

Option premiums should be evaluated before deciding whether to sell calls or buy puts. Hedgers should look for the occasional inefficiencies in the option market, meaning underpriced puts and overpriced calls. They should not lock themselves into a single strategy.

Exhibit 8-2. XYZ Corp. Convertible Bonds Hedged by Call Options

	Price	*Prices at Expiration (6 months)*			
Stock	$30.00	15	30	45	60
Convertible	122.00	85	122	180	240
Call	3.00	0	0	15	30

Strategy: Buy 10 bonds and sell 4 at-the-money calls*

Profit or loss on bonds	−3700	0	5800	11800
Profit or loss on puts	1200	1200	−4800	−10800
Bond interest received	500	500	500	500
Interest received on $1,200 (calls)	<u>48</u>	<u>48</u>	<u>48</u>	<u>48</u>
Total profit or loss	−1952	1748	1548	1548
Return on investment - %	−16.0	14.3	12.7	12.7
Annualized return - %	−32.0	28.7	25.4	25.4

*Investment = $1,220 per bond x 10 bonds = $12,200

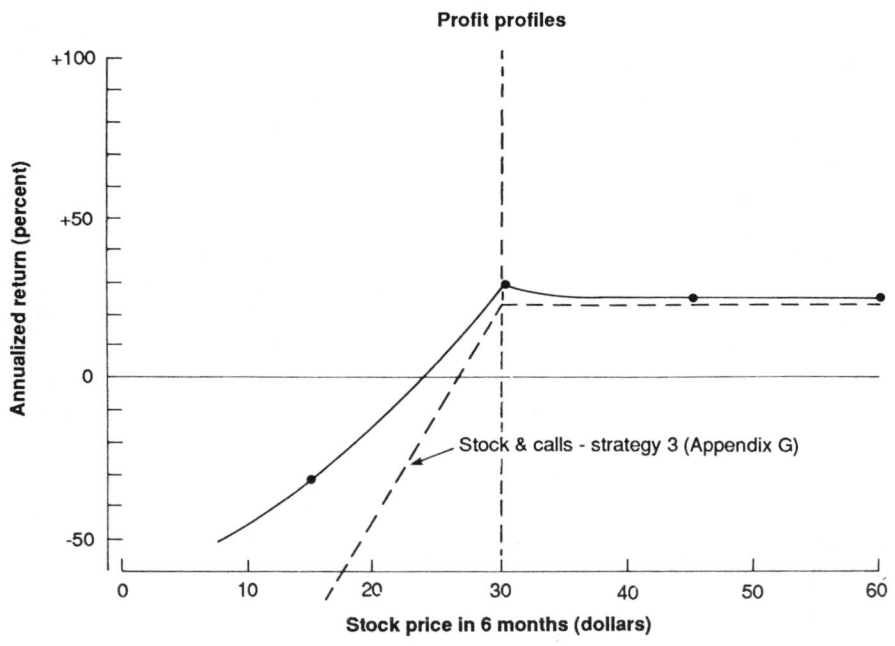

Profit profiles

Stock & calls - strategy 3 (Appendix G)

Annualized return (percent)

Stock price in 6 months (dollars)

HEDGING UNDERVALUED CONVERTIBLES WITH BOTH PUTS AND CALLS

Hedging convertible bonds with put or call options are conservative low-risk strategies. When put options are used, however, little or no profits can be expected in dull, sideways market movements. Selling calls, on the other hand, produces profits most of the time, but loses during bear markets. Hedgers not wanting to expose their capital to bear market losses, but still desiring some profits during static markets, can go long puts and short calls simultaneously. Analogous to the convertible/stock hedges of Chapter 7, Exhibits 8-3, 8-4 and 8-5 show bullish, neutral and bearish hedge postures.

Look first at the bullish hedge of Exhibit 8-3. A purchase of two puts combined with the sale of two calls is similar to shorting 200 shares of stock against the ten-bond position (Exhibit 7-2). There are two major advantages when using options: the premium differential between the put and call, which is credited to the account, provides additional profit, and no short sale dividends are paid. As a result, the put-call combination adds 4 percent to the convertible/stock hedge yearly returns of Exhibit 7-2. Also included in Exhibit 8-3 is the profit profile for the traditional balanced approach using half common stock and half cash. The lower-risk convertible hedge is expected to outperform the balanced approach at all possible outcomes. It's a heads-you-win, tails-you-don't-lose investment opportunity.

The neutral and bearish strategies of Exhibits 8-4 and 8-5 are even more conservative. They are expected to produce profits regardless of the price the stock closes at on the options' expiration date.

When comparing the option strategies with shorting stock, one may conclude that stocks should never be shorted when hedging convertibles. However, not all attractive convertibles have listed options, especially high-performance, small-company convertible bonds like XYZ Corp. The put and call option strategies illustrated are always available when dealing with larger company convertibles as represented by those in the Noddings Large-Cap convertible bond index.

Chapter 9 will show how diversified portfolios, having both large and small company convertibles, can be hedged with index options. This strategy, used skillfully, offers one of the most sophisticated and profitable use of convertible securities.

Exhibit 8-3. XYZ Corp. Convertible Bonds Hedged by Put and Call Options—Bullish Posture

	Price	*Prices at Expiration (6 months)*			
Stock	$30.00	15	30	45	60
Convertible	122.00	85	122	180	240
Call	3.00	0	0	15	30
Put	2.125	15	0	0	0

Strategy: Buy 10 bonds, buy 2 puts, and sell 2 calls*

Profit or loss on bonds	−3700	0	5800	11800
Profit or loss on puts	2575	−425	−425	−425
Profit or loss on calls	600	600	−2400	−5400
Bond interest received	500	500	500	500
Interest received on $175	7	7	7	7
Total profit or loss	−18	682	3482	6482
Return on investment - %	−0.1	5.6	28.5	53.1
Annualized return - %	−0.3	11.2	57.1	106.3

*Investment = $1,220 per bond x 10 bonds = $12,200

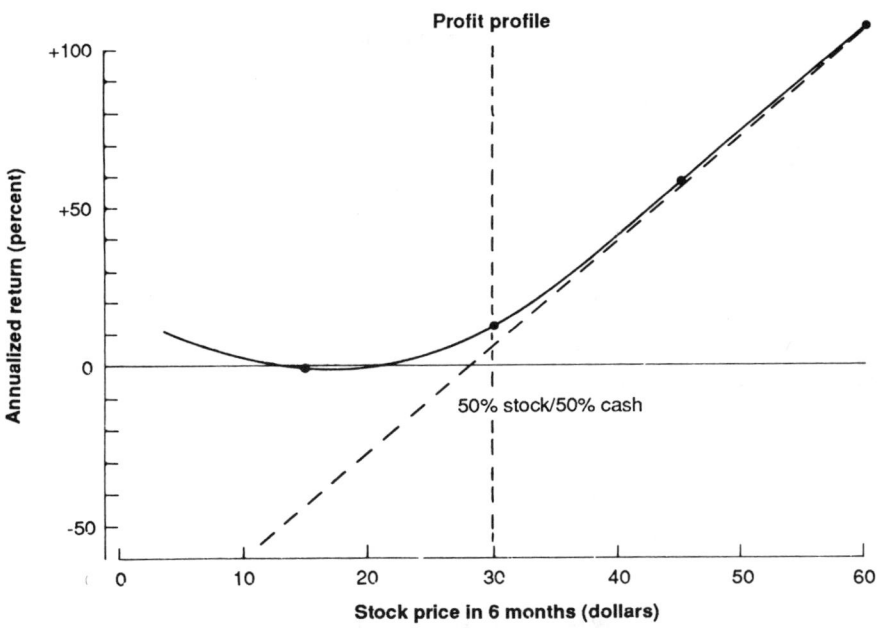

Exhibit 8-4. XYZ Corp. Convertible Bonds Hedged by Put and Call Options— Neutral Posture

	Price	*Prices at Expiration (6 months)*			
Stock	$30.00	15	30	45	60
Convertible	122.00	85	122	180	240
Calls	3.00	0	0	15	30
Put	2.125	15	0	0	0

Strategy: Buy 10 bonds, buy 3 puts, and sell 3 calls*

Profit or loss on bonds	−3700	0	5800	11800
Profit or loss on puts	3862	−638	−638	−638
Profit or loss on calls	900	900	−3600	−8100
Bond interest received	500	500	500	500
Interest received on $262	10	10	10	10
Total profit or loss	1572	772	2072	3572
Return on investment - %	12.9	6.3	17.0	29.3
Annualized return - %	25.8	12.7	34.0	58.6

*Investment = $1,220 per bond x 10 bonds = $12,200

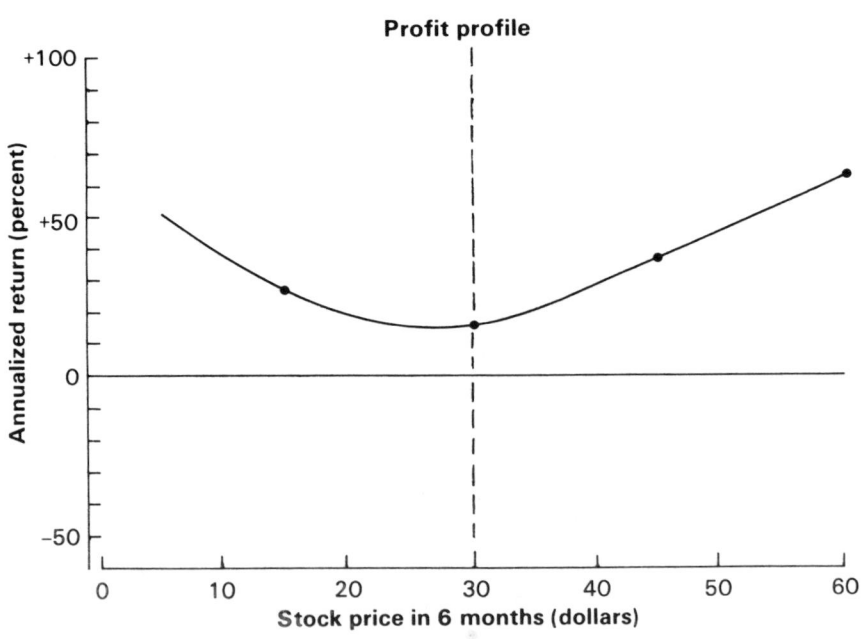

Exhibit 8-5. XYZ Corp. Convertible Bonds Hedged by Put and Call Options— Bearish Posture

	Price	*Prices at Expiration (6 months)*			
Stock	$30.00	15	30	45	60
Convertible	122.00	85	122	180	240
Call	3.00	0	0	15	30
Put	2.125	15	0	0	0

Strategy: Buy 10 bonds, buy 4 puts, and sell 4 calls*

Profit or loss on bonds	−3700	0	5800	11800
Profit or loss on puts	5150	−850	−8850	−850
Profit or loss on calls	1200	1200	−4800	−10800
Bond interest received	500	500	500	500
Interest receivid on $350	14	14	14	14
Total profit or loss	3164	864	664	664
Return on investment - %	25.9	7.1	5.4	5.4
Annualized return - %	51.9	14.2	10.9	10.9

*Investment = $1,220 per bond x 10 bonds = $12,200

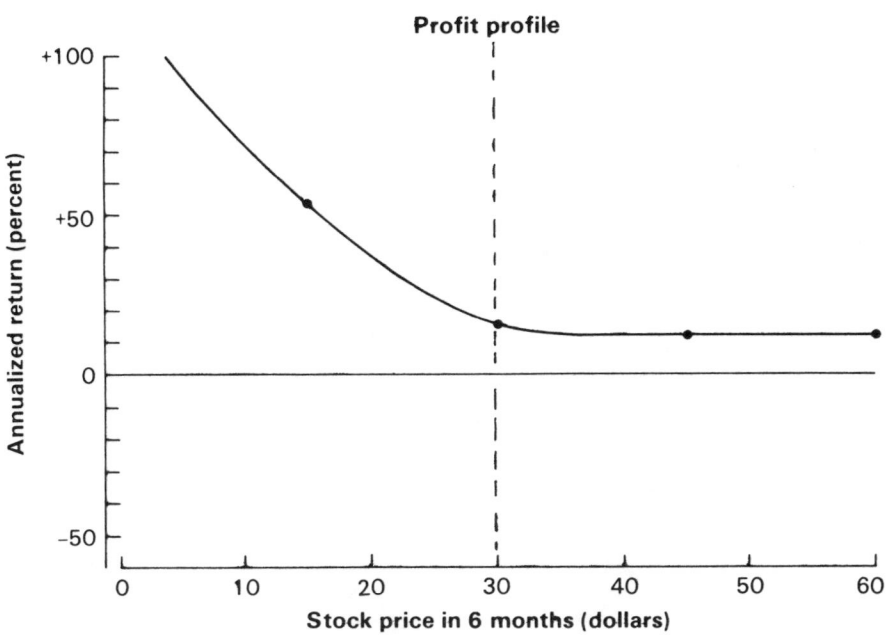

Profit profile

Chapter 9
SUPERHEDGING

Convertible hedging strategies can play important roles in conservative investment programs aimed at above-average performance. By hedging undervalued convertible bonds, conservative investors can place a larger portion of their investment capital in equity-related strategies. Chapters 7 and 8 showed how to take advantage of attractive market opportunities via traditional hedging tactics. However, as profitable as traditional hedging can be for sophisticated investors, there exists an even better strategy for large, diversified portfolios—SuperHedging.

I coined the term "SuperHedging" in 1975 when working with a client on an unusual investment concept. Initially, SuperHedging involved the purchase of dual-purpose fund capital shares—trading at large discounts from their net asset values—in combination with the sale of listed call options on a diversified selection of common stocks.[1] As a result, we protected the highly leveraged fund shares with carefully selected (overpriced) calls on unrelated securities. The strategy earned more than 100 percent over a two-year period as the funds' discounts evaporated. .

---

1. *How the Experts Beat the Market*, Thomas C. Noddings. Homewood, Illinois, Dow Jones-Irwin, 1976.

In 1978, I expanded the concept to include well diversified portfolios of undervalued convertible securities hedged by the sale of unrelated call options and/or the purchase of unrelated puts.[2] In 1986, I broadened the concept further by hedging convertible bond portfolios with index puts and/or calls.[3] Because it employs unrelated securities, Super-Hedging may appear to be speculative; however, as I will soon demonstrate, the markets effectively tie both sides of the hedge portfolio together.

Taking advantage of market inefficiencies on both sides of the hedge is the driving force behind SuperHedging. Buying underpriced securities while selling overpriced securities makes SuperHedging the ultimate hedging strategy. Not only does it reduce risk, it can simultaneously enhance returns—the best of both worlds.

EFFICIENTLY PRICED INDEX OPTIONS

As with equity put and call options, index option premiums are influenced by a number of variables including prevailing interest rates, the index's yield and anticipated future market volatility. Interest and dividend rates over the near term are usually not expected to change significantly. Future volatility is, at best, an educated guess. Rather than guess, our evaluation of current option premiums begins with a determination of fair-market values based on historical data.

Table H-1 in Appendix H presents a back-tested, quarterly analysis of three-month put and call options on the S&P 500. Although index option trading began later, I assumed a 1976 starting point to coincide with the Noddings convertible bond indexes. For ease of illustration, I assumed a constant T-bill rate of 8.0 percent and index dividends at 4.0 percent. Both are rounded figures, close to their averages for that fourteen-year time frame (1976-89). Since each strategy is expected to produce similar results over the long run, I adjusted the put and call premiums until the fourteen-year cumulative returns were about the same whether the index was hedged with long puts or short calls (or a put/call combination which was the average of the other two strategies). The theoretical fair-market premiums came out to be 2.75 percent for

---

2. *Advanced Investment Strategies*, Thomas C. Noddings. Homewood, Illinois, Dow Jones-Irwin, 1978.
3. *SuperHedging*, Thomas C. Noddings. Chicago, Illinois, Probus Publishing, 1986.

puts and 3.75 percent for calls, numbers close to actual S&P 500 option premiums in recent years.

The yearly performance data is presented in Table 9-1. Notice how, at about 12 percent, the annualized returns for each of the three hedging strategies came in well below the 15.2 percent return from the index itself. As would be expected, the 12 percent figures are about the same as a 50/50 mix of stocks and T-bills (near the middle of the capital market line). Hedging reduces risk but *the use of efficiently priced options does not enhance returns.* In fact, hedging stocks with fairly priced options virtually guarantees a return well below the capital market line after portfolio management and order execution expenses are taken into account.

I strongly urge you to carefully study Tables H-1 and 9-1 if you plan to employ index options. Notice from Table H-1 how quarterly performance figures for each strategy vary widely under different market conditions. Protecting a stock portfolio with index puts, for example, performs best in volatile markets; selling calls performs best in static markets. Although the put/call combination produces more consistent results, and did not experience a losing year (Table 9-1), all three strategies would be expected to produce similar results over a market cycle.

Tables H-2 and 9-2 present similar data for the more volatile, unweighted Value Line index of 1,700 stocks. Here the fair-market put and call premiums would have come in higher than the S&Ps at 3.3 and 4.5 percent respectively. Since actual premiums for Value Line options were running below these figures in recent years, the market was reflecting lower volatility for this index in the later years of the study.

These theoretical S&P 500 and Value Line option premiums allow us to back-test various strategies for hedging the Noddings Large-Cap and Medium-Cap convertible bond indexes over that same fourteen-year time frame. They will also help us identify underpriced and overpriced opportunities in the future.

HEDGING LARGE-CAP CONVERTIBLE BONDS WITH INDEX OPTIONS

Since most large companies currently have listed puts and calls trading on their stocks, why not simply use these equity options for hedging their convertible bonds instead of index options? The answer lies in the cost of managing a diversified hedge portfolio.

Table 9-1. Annual Returns for the S&P 500 Index if Hedged by 3-month At-the-Money, Normally Valued Index Puts and Calls—1976-89

Reference: Appendix H, Table H-1

Assumptions:

- T-bill rate = 8.00 percent
- Index yield = 4.00 percent
- Put premium = 2.75 percent
- Call premium = 3.75 percent
- Hedge ratio = 1.00

Year	S&P 500 Index	Hedging Strategy Long Puts	Short Calls	Puts & Calls*
1976	23.7	11.3	20.4	15.9
1977	-7.5	-4.7	5.3	0.2
1978	6.6	8.2	7.1	7.6
1979	18.5	7.4	19.4	13.3
1980	32.5	26.0	14.5	20.2
1981	-5.0	-0.8	4.0	1.7
1982	21.4	21.2	9.2	15.2
1983	22.5	12.2	18.3	15.3
1984	6.2	2.3	12.5	7.3
1985	31.7	25.1	14.5	19.8
1986	18.7	16.1	11.2	13.7
1987	5.2	23.7	-6.6	8.2
1988	16.5	5.4	19.6	12.4
1989	31.7	18.7	20.4	19.6
Cumulative return	625	381	380	389
Annualized return	15.2	11.9	11.9	12.0

*Equivalent to a 50 percent short position.

Table 9-2. Annual Returns for the Value Line Index if Hedged by 3-month At-the-Money, Normally Valued Index Puts and Calls—1976-89

Reference: Appendix H, Table H-2

Assumptions:

- T-bill rate = 8.00 percent
- Index yield = 3.20 percent
- Put premium = 3.30 percent
- Call premium = 4.50 percent
- Hedge ratio = 1.00

		Hedging Strategy		
Year	VLE Index	Long Puts	Short Calls	Puts & Calls*
1976	36.2	22.5	20.9	22.2
1977	3.8	-2.1	14.7	6.1
1978	7.7	10.7	6.1	8.5
1979	28.3	14.2	21.8	18.1
1980	22.0	23.7	7.9	15.7
1981	-1.3	3.5	3.9	3.9
1982	18.9	19.9	8.3	14.2
1983	34.8	21.9	20.2	21.4
1984	0.4	-2.8	11.9	4.4
1985	32.2	21.9	18.0	20.1
1986	16.2	11.0	13.9	12.5
1987	1.8	18.0	-5.2	6.5
1988	25.8	12.1	21.6	17.0
1989	20.7	11.0	18.0	14.5
Cumulative return	798	449	434	456
Annualized return	17.0	12.9	12.7	13.0

*Equivalent to a 50 percent short position.

Assuming a $250,000 portfolio containing twenty-five convertible bonds, the traditional hedging strategies described in Chapter 8 would require twenty-five or fifty different options, depending on the strategy employed. Brokerage commissions and bid-ask price spreads for large numbers of small option orders could quickly destroy the advantages offered by the undervalued convertible bonds. As a low-cost alternative, this same $250,000 convertible portfolio could be hedged with only one or two different index options. In addition, each index option represents about $30,000 in market value versus $3,000 for an option on a typical $30 stock—a single order for about eight index puts or calls (or two orders, each for four puts and four calls) would suffice. Index options provide substantial savings in order execution costs; they also reduce the time required for portfolio management.

The fact that the chosen index will diverge negatively from a convertible portfolio from time to time is the main disadvantage of using index options. This annoyance could frustrate investors who do not understand a strategy's intricacies or who lack a long-term outlook. To place these problems in perspective, let's see how the Noddings Large-Cap convertible bond index would have performed over its fourteen-year life if it had been hedged by S&P 500 or Value Line puts and calls.

Tables H-3 and H-4 present back-tested studies for the convertible index assuming puts were purchased or calls sold on 100 percent of the portfolio. The third strategy, which is the average of the other two, is the same as shorting the stock market against 50 percent of the long positions, a neutral market posture for the Large-Cap convertible bond index. Option premiums were assumed to be fairly priced as previously calculated. Yearly data are presented in Tables 9-3 and 9-4.

Although quarterly variations were significant, the long-term results were surprisingly consistent. Using S&P 500 options, for example, would have produced annualized returns for the SuperHedge strategies ranging from 15.5 to 15.7 percent, compared to 19.3 percent for the convertible index and 15.2 percent for the venerable S&P 500 (Table 9-3). The worst-performing year was 1989, when the S&P 500 gained 31.7 percent while the convertible bond index lagged far behind, along with the broad stock market, at 14.3 percent. As would be expected for such negative divergence, hedge strategies using S&P 500 index puts and calls underperformed even more severely than the unhedged convertibles (hedge returns ranged from 2.6 to 4.1 percent).

Note that the S&Ps would have been the optimal index options for hedging the convertibles during the initial eight years when the blue

Table 9-3. Annual Returns for the Noddings Large-Cap Convertible Bond Index if Hedged by 3-month At-the-Money, Normally Valued S&P 500 Index Puts and Calls—1976-89

Reference: Appendix H, Table H-3

Assumptions:

- T-bill rate = 8.00 percent
- Index yield = 4.00 percent
- Put premium = 2.75 percent
- Call premium = 3.75 percent
- Hedge ratio = 1.00

Year	S&P 500 Index	Convert. Index	Hedging Strategy Long Puts	Hedging Strategy Short Calls	Hedging Strategy Puts & Calls*
1976	23.7	45.9	31.8	42.1	37.0
1977	-7.5	8.1	11.0	22.5	16.7
1978	6.6	16.8	18.6	17.5	18.0
1979	18.5	24.2	12.8	25.1	18.9
1980	32.5	35.3	28.8	17.6	23.1
1981	-5.0	17.5	22.9	28.1	25.6
1982	21.4	21.5	21.0	8.9	15.0
1983	22.5	28.6	17.9	24.9	21.5
1984	6.2	6.9	2.9	13.0	7.9
1985	31.7	28.3	21.7	10.8	16.3
1986	18.7	15.7	12.6	7.9	10.3
1987	5.2	-0.9	13.3	-13.9	-0.6
1988	16.5	15.7	4.7	18.9	11.6
1989	31.7	14.3	2.6	4.1	3.4
Cumulative return	625	1081	658	654	669
Annualized return	15.2	19.3	15.6	15.5	15.7

*Equivalent to a 50 percent short position.

**Table 9-4. Annual Returns for the Noddings Large-Cap Convertible Bond Index
if Hedged by 3-month At-the-Money, Normally Valued Value Line
Index Put and Calls—1976-89**

Reference: Appendix H, Table H-4

Assumptions:

- T-bill rate = 8.00 percent
- Index yield = 3.20 percent
- Put premium = 3.30 percent
- Call premium = 4.50 percent
- Hedge ratio = 1.00

| | | | *Hedging Strategy* | | |
| | | *Convert.* | *Long* | | *Puts &* |
Year	*VLE Index*	*Index*	*Puts*	*Short Calls*	*Calls**
1976	36.2	45.9	31.4	27.3	29.9
1977	3.8	8.1	2.0	19.3	10.4
1978	7.7	16.8	19.5	14.9	17.3
1979	28.3	24.2	10.5	17.8	14.2
1980	22.0	35.3	36.4	19.9	28.1
1981	-1.3	17.5	22.5	23.3	23.1
1982	18.9	21.5	22.2	9.6	16.0
1983	34.8	28.6	16.2	14.4	15.6
1984	0.4	6.9	3.4	18.6	10.8
1985	32.2	28.3	18.2	13.6	16.0
1986	16.2	15.7	10.0	12.7	11.5
1987	1.8	-0.9	11.5	-9.7	0.9
1988	25.8	15.7	2.9	11.1	7.1
1989	20.7	14.3	4.9	11.5	8.1
Cumulative return	798	1081	578	548	580
Annualized return	17.0	19.3	14.7	14.3	14.7

*Equivalent to a 50 percent short position.

chips underperformed the broader market. During the last six years of the studies, the Value Lines were the best options as the broader market lagged the blue chips.

Notice also that unlike using index options with common stocks, each of the three convertible/option strategies enhanced returns by outperforming a 50/50 mix of convertibles and T-bills. Risk reduction through the use of fairly priced options permits conservative investors to place all their capital in undervalued convertibles. And inefficiently priced options offer additional enhancement. It is seldom, if ever, advantageous to combine convertibles with money market instruments.

HEDGING MEDIUM-CAP CONVERTIBLE BONDS WITH INDEX OPTIONS

As when hedging large-company convertibles, SuperHedging strategies using undervalued convertible bonds in smaller companies offer low-cost alternatives to traditional hedging. Also, most companies capitalized at below $500 million do not have equity puts and calls trading on their stocks (Chapter 8). And since many of the stocks underlying the convertibles are unavailable for shorting (Chapter 7), index option strategies become the choice approach for sophisticated investors.

Using studies similar to those analyzing the Noddings Large-Cap convertible bond index, let's see how the Noddings Medium-Cap convertible bond index would have performed if hedged by S&P 500 or Value Line options. Tables H-5 and H-6 (Appendix H) present quarterly calculations and Tables 9-5 and 9-6 show the annual data. Again, the results were unexpectedly consistent over the long run; annualized hedge returns ranged from 15.6 to 17.2 percent versus 20.9 percent for the Growth convertible index. Quarterly returns varied more widely than with the Core convertible index—an expected event since convertibles on smaller companies will not track these major stock indexes as well.

Again, each of the three convertible/option strategies enhanced returns by outperforming a 50/50 mix of convertibles and T-bills.

Table 9-5. Annual Returns for the Noddings Medium-Cap Convertible Bond Index if Hedged by 3-month At-the-Money, Normally Valued S&P 500 Index Puts and Calls—1976-89

Reference: Appendix H, Table H-5

Assumptions:

- T-bill rate = 8.00 percent
- Index yield = 4.00 percent
- Put premium = 2.75 percent
- Call premium = 3.75 percent
- Hedge ratio = 1.00

Year	S&P 500 Index	Convert. Index	Long Puts	Short Calls	Puts & Calls*
1976	23.7	39.5	25.9	34.8	30.5
1977	-7.5	14.2	17.0	29.1	23.0
1978	6.6	38.1	40.0	38.7	39.3
1979	18.5	41.7	29.0	42.7	35.8
1980	32.5	37.4	30.7	19.1	24.8
1981	-5.0	8.0	13.2	17.7	15.5
1982	21.4	34.8	34.0	20.8	27.4
1983	22.5	27.3	16.8	24.2	20.5
1984	6.2	0.3	-3.5	6.1	1.3
1985	31.7	25.2	18.5	7.1	12.8
1986	18.7	19.7	16.7	11.5	14.1
1987	5.2	-9.9	4.6	-21.1	-8.5
1988	16.5	20.7	9.3	24.0	16.5
1989	31.7	9.2	-2.1	-0.4	-1.2
Cumulative return	625	1318	820	793	822
Annualized return	15.2	20.9	17.2	16.9	17.2

*Equivalent to a 50 percent short position.

Table 9-6.   Annual Returns for the Noddings Medium-Cap Convertible Bond Index if Hedged by 3-month At-the-Money, Normally Valued Value Line Index Puts and Calls—1976-89

Reference: Appendix H, Table H-6

Assumptions:

- T-bill rate = 8.00 percent
- Index yield = 3.20 percent
- Put premium = 3.30 percent
- Call premium = 4.50 percent
- Hedge ratio = 1.00

			Hedging Strategy		
Year	*VLE Index*	*Convert. Index*	*Long Puts*	*Short Calls*	*Puts & Calls**
1976	36.2	39.5	25.5	19.6	23.1
1977	3.8	14.2	7.8	25.7	16.5
1978	7.7	38.1	41.3	35.7	38.6
1979	28.3	41.7	26.5	34.5	30.6
1980	22.0	37.4	38.2	20.5	29.3
1981	-1.3	8.0	12.8	13.5	13.3
1982	18.9	34.8	35.2	21.8	28.5
1983	34.8	27.3	15.0	14.0	14.8
1984	0.4	0.3	-3.0	11.5	4.1
1985	32.2	25.2	15.1	10.0	12.7
1986	16.2	19.7	14.0	16.2	15.2
1987	1.8	-9.9	3.0	-17.1	-7.1
1988	25.8	20.7	7.4	16.0	11.8
1989	20.7	9.2	0.2	6.6	3.4
Cumulative return	798	1318	726	661	714
Annualized return	17.0	20.9	16.3	15.6	16.2

*Equivalent to a 50 percent short position.

FINDING INEFFICIENTLY PRICED INDEX OPTIONS

Even though the option market became dominated by institutional investors in the late 1970s, there have been an ongoing number of mispriced opportunities over the years. An obvious case is when the price spread between puts and calls becomes greater than the fair-value price spread based on T-bill and index yields (see Appendix H). Nimble hedgers can take advantage of the resulting underpriced puts or overpriced calls, or the favorable long-put/short-call combination.

An unbelievable situation was found during the days following the October 19, 1987 crash. Both put and call premiums went through the roof and put premiums actually exceeded call premiums for a period of several weeks. Fortunate hedgers who had long-put positions going into the crash received outlandish profits and were given the opportunity to switch to a more attractive short-call hedge posture.

Although opportunities like those seen after the crash may never happen again, I expect that index option markets will always contain pockets of pricing inefficiencies. It should be well worth the time and effort of convertible hedgers to search them out.

THE NODDINGS CONVERTIBLE HEDGE INDEX

Since my firm began managing portfolios in 1976, we have used a variety of different convertible strategies depending on market opportunities. Of these different strategies, the one which has always provided optimum risk-reward relationships is bullishly-biased *Convertible Hedging*. To document long-term performance results for this strategy, we maintained quarterly performance data for our largest hedge accounts. Hence, we are able to introduce an index similar to those previously shown for large-, medium- and small-cap convertible bonds. The primary difference in constructing the various indexes is that the Convertible Hedge index is based on actual account performance, with the last eight years represented by the same account. Consistent with the convertible bond indexes, portfolio management and order execution costs (estimated at 1.0 percent per quarter) have been added back to the accounts' net performance data.

As shown in Tables 9-7 and 9-8, convertible hedging strategies, at an 18.3 percent compounded annual rate of return, also outperformed con-

Table 9-7. The Noddings Convertible Hedge Index Versus Market Indexes—Annual Total Returns

Year	Corporate Bonds*	Value Line Stocks**	Value Line Low-Cap***	Convertible Hedge
1976	18.7	36.2	62.3	32.1
1977	1.7	3.8	36.1	25.3
1978	-0.1	7.7	37.5	21.7
1979	-4.2	28.3	43.5	19.5
1980	-2.7	22.0	32.2	18.2
1981	-1.2	-1.3	9.3	12.2
1982	42.5	18.9	31.3	38.4
1983	6.3	34.8	40.6	22.7
1984	16.9	0.4	-20.6	-6.6
1985	30.1	32.2	13.2	24.2
1986	19.9	16.2	-2.8	23.2
1987	-0.3	1.8	-25.1	10.4
1988	10.7	25.8	18.2	12.0
1989	16.2	20.7	-13.0	10.3
Cumulative return	293	798	682	956
Annualized return	10.3	17.0	15.8	18.3

*Salomon Brothers high grade corporate bond index.
**Value Line's geometric index (1976-82), arithmetic index (1983-89)—estimated dividends included.
***The smallest 10 percent (by capitalization) of companies making up the Value Line index—dividends not included.

ventional modes of investing over the fourteen-year period. Hedging performed especially well during the early years when the small-stock market sector was doing well, since the best hedging opportunities are usually found in this sector. And if the hedge accounts were margined during the early years, as was the account used in the index the past eight years, the fourteen-year annualized return would have exceeded twenty percent.

Table 9-8. The Noddings Convertible Hedge Index Versus Market Indexes— Quarterly Total Returns

Year	Corporate Bonds	Value Line Stocks	Value Line Low-Cap	Convertible Hedge
1976	4.2	25.8	53.4	3.4
	0.3	0.2	-1.7	5.5
	5.6	-0.4	-1.3	9.7
	7.5	8.5	9.0	10.4
1977	-2.3	-2.5	13.4	7.1
	3.9	5.8	8.2	4.3
	1.1	-3.1	0.8	8.2
	-0.8	3.8	10.1	3.7
1978	0.0	1.9	15.2	6.2
	-1.1	10.5	24.9	5.7
	3.1	10.7	23.0	9.4
	-2.0	-13.6	-22.2	-0.9
1979	1.6	12.5	23.0	6.2
	4.5	5.0	7.1	9.8
	-2.0	8.8	11.2	4.5
	-7.9	-0.2	-2.1	-1.9
1980	-13.2	-12.1	-10.4	-7.8
	24.2	17.3	16.4	17.3
	-10.7	15.0	29.1	7.0
	1.0	2.9	-1.8	2.1
1981	-1.0	6.5	18.4	9.4
	-2.0	2.5	10.4	3.6
	-8.9	-15.5	-20.5	-7.0
	11.7	7.0	5.1	6.4
1982	4.9	-8.3	-1.6	4.7
	0.9	-3.0	-1.4	-0.3
	21.3	10.2	8.3	12.3
	10.9	21.3	24.9	18.1
1983	4.0	16.3	24.2	18.6
	1.6	16.8	22.7	12.7
	-0.3	-0.6	-3.1	-5.2
	0.8	-0.2	-4.7	-3.2

Table 9-8. (continued)

Year	Corporate Bonds	Value Line Stocks	Value Line Low-Cap	Convertible Hedge
1984	-1.4	-4.1	-4.4	0.4
	-3.6	-3.0	-7.5	-6.8
	12.5	8.2	2.2	4.3
	9.4	-0.2	-12.2	-4.3
1985	1.2	11.7	12.0	14.3
	12.3	5.2	-3.7	3.1
	2.1	-3.5	-4.1	2.5
	12.1	16.6	9.4	2.8
1986	10.8	15.6	10.4	18.1
	0.7	3.7	-4.2	5.4
	1.9	-7.0	-11.6	-1.8
	5.5	4.2	3.9	0.8
1987	1.9	21.5	14.0	11.8
	-4.0	2.7	-3.6	-1.2
	-6.1	6.4	4.7	2.5
	8.6	-23.3	-34.9	-2.5
1988	4.6	16.2	23.0	3.5
	1.7	7.4	4.8	3.4
	2.7	-0.3	-2.3	1.2
	1.4	1.2	-6.1	3.4
1989	1.3	7.9	3.6	4.8
	10.2	7.2	3.7	5.0
	0.5	8.1	-0.8	2.4
	3.5	-3.4	-18.4	-2.1
Cumulative return	293	798	682	956
Quarterly return	2.7	4.4	4.7	4.5
Standard deviation	6.8	9.5	14.6	6.3
Coefficient of variation	252	215	308	140
Sharpe measure	0.10	0.26	0.19	0.40

SOME FINAL THOUGHTS

The question is often raised about the likelihood of all financial markets ultimately becoming efficient. In that event, the kinds of attractive convertible bond strategies you have learned about would cease to exist. However, I don't believe that will happen. I've been using convertible securities for more than twenty years, and although strategies change from time to time, the opportunities for the *noninstitutional investor* are greater today than at any time during my investment career.

All successful investors have a common trait: *knowledge.* Knowledgeable investors know how to evaluate financial investments, pick the best strategies, allocate their assets among those strategies, select investment advisors to manage the strategies and evaluate performance using appropriate measurement standards. It is indeed unfortunate, but few people have such knowledge.

I must again emphasize my strong belief that investing is a long-term endeavor. Few investment strategies should be entered into with a time horizon of less than five years and sometimes a successful outcome takes longer; it depends so much on events over which we have no control.

There is no finer way to invest than to take advantage of market inefficiencies. The rewards are not just monetary; I have tremendous satisfaction from developing new strategies and watching them unfold. However, since few people will understand, or even care about your investments, there may be no one you can turn to for guidance. You must become your own expert. You may feel quite alone at times, but that's the price you must pay for doing anything unconventional. Highly profitable investments will always be unconventional.

Appendix A

CONVERTIBLE BONDS/ INFORMATION SOURCES

I t is extremely difficult for convertible bond investors, professional and nonprofessional, to be aware of unusual convertible terms and to stay abreast of such rapidly occuring events as mergers and acquisitions. Access to one or more convertible bond services is mandatory.

The right hand column of the following table identifies convertible bonds mainly covered by three information sources as of January 1, 1990: Value Line, R.H.M. Associates, and Standard & Poor's. Other sources include brokerage firms whose coverage is not extensive.

Value Line Convertibles is published weekly by Value Line, Inc., 711 Third Avenue, New York, NY 10017 (subscription rate: $445 per year). Providing basic data plus risk-reward estimates for the most actively traded convertible bonds and convertible preferreds, this service is a must for most convertible bond investors. As a by-product, it also includes SCORES and actively traded warrants. This service is available at a few public libraries and brokerage offices.

The R.H.M. Convertible Survey is published weekly by R.H.M. Associates, Inc., 172 Forest Avenue, Glen Cove, NY 11542 (subscription rate: $235 per year). This service covers most of the issues in Value Line plus a number of less actively traded bonds and preferreds. It provides most basic data but not investment floors or risk-reward estimates. Having relatively limited circulation, it probably won't be available for inspection at your library or brokerage office.

Standard & Poor's monthly bond guides are also included as a reference source because they are readily available from one's stockbroker. However, by avoiding important bond terms and conditions, risk-reward estimates, current events, buy/sell recommendations and all Euroconvertibles, these guides cannot be viewed as a meaningful information source.

In some cases the name of the bond is different than the stock into which it converts. The table lists the stocks to be received while the footnotes identify the bonds' trading descriptions when they are different. Value Line is consistent with this approach while R.H.M. and Standard & Poor's highlight the name of the bond first and footnote the stock to be received.

Convertible Bonds Available in January 1990
(excluding companies in bankruptcy and bonds convertible into cash)

Company	Descript.	Company size, $millions*<100	100-500	>500	Source	FN
Advest Group	9.000-08	X			a b c	
Air Wisconsin Services	7.750-10	X			a b c	
A.L. Labs	7.750-14		X		a b c	
Alaska Air Group	6.875-01		X		a b c	
Alaska Air Group	7.750-10	-			a b c	
Alco Health	6.250-01	X			- - -	
Alexander & Alexander	11.000-07			X	a b c	
Alex Brown	5.750-01		X		a b -	
Alliant Computer Systems	7.250-12	X			a b c	
Allwaste	7.250-14		X		a b c	
Aluminum Co. of America	6.250-02			X	a b -	
ALZA	5.500-02			X	a b -	
AMDURA	5.500-93	X			- b c	
Amedco	7.500-98	X			- b -	
Ameribanc	8.000-05	X			- b c	
America West Airlines	11.500-09		X		a b c	
America West Airlines	7.750-10	-			a b c	
America West Airlines	7.500-11	-			a b c	
Amer. Bankers Insurance	9.750-04		X		a b c	
Amer. Bankers Insurance	5.750-01	-			a b -	
American Brands	7.750-02			X	a b -	
American Brands	5.375-03			-	a b -	
American Express	6.500-14			X	a b c	1
American General	6.875-00			X	a b -	
AMGEN	8.000-04			X	a b -	
Amoco	7.375-13			X	a b c	2
Amvestors Financial	8.500-12	X			- b -	
Anacomp	9.000-96		X		- - -	
Anacomp	13.875-02	-			a b c	
Anadarko Petroleum	7.000-04			X	a b -	3
Anadarko Petroleum	6.250-14			-	a b c	
Anadarko Petroleum	5.750-12			-	a b c	
Andal	5.500-97	X			- b c	
Andersen Group	10.500-02	X			a b c	
Anthony Industries	11.250-00		X		a b c	

Company	Descript.	Company size, $millions*			Source	FN
		<100	100-500	>500		
Apache Corp.	9.500-96			X	- - -	
Arrow Electronics	9.000-03	X			a b c	
Ashland Oil	6.750-14			X	a b c	
Ashland Oil	4.750-93			-	- b c	
AST Research	8.500-13		X		a b c	
Astrex	9.500-00	X			- b c	
Astrex 'B'	9.500-00	-			- b c	
Atalanta/Sosnoff	7.125-01	X			a b c	
Atari	5.250-02		X		a b c	
Atlantic American	8.000-97	X			a b c	
Atlantic Financial Federal	7.750-11	X			a b c	
Audiotronics	10.250-02	X			- b c	
Autodie	7.000-11	X			a b c	
Avalon	7.000-92	X			- b c	
Avnet	8.000-13			X	a b c	
Avnet	6.000-12			-	a b c	
AVX Corp.	8.250-12		X		a b c	
Axiom Systems	10.000-98	X			- - c	
Baker Hughes	9.500-06			X	a b c	4
Bally Manufacturing	6.000-98		X		a b c	
Bally Manufacturing	10.000-06		-		a b c	
Baltimore Bancorp	6.750-11		X		a b c	
BankFlorida Financial	9.000-03	X			a b c	
Bank of Boston	7.750-11			X	a b c	
Bard (C.R.)	4.250-96			X	- b c	5
Baxter International	4.375-91			X	- b c	
Baxter International	4.750-01			X	- b c	
BayBanks	5.000-94			X	- - c	
Bay Financial	6.750-91	X			- - c	
BB&T Financial	8.750-05		X		a b c	
Ben & Jerry's Homemade	9.500-07	X			- b c	
Bergen Brunswig	0.000-04			X	a b c	
Berkshire Hathaway	0.000-04			X	- b c	
Beverly Enterprises	7.625-03		X		a b c	
Beverly Enterprises	0.000-03		-		a b c	
Bindley Western	8.625-10	X			a b c	
Biotechnica International	8.750-96	X			a b c	
BlockBuster	0.000-04			X	a b c	
Blocker Energy Int'l.	8.250-95	X			- - -	
Boise Cascade	7.000-16			X	a b c	

Company	Descript.	<100	100-500	>500	Source	FN
			Company size, $millions*			

Company	Descript.	<100	100-500	>500	Source	FN
Bolt Beranak & Newman	6.000-12		X		a b c	
Bonneville Pacific	7.750-09		X		a b c	
Bowmar Instrument	13.000-95	X			- b c	
BRE Properties	9.500-00		X		- b c	
BRE Properties	9.500-08		-		a b c	
BRintec	7.500-11	X			- - c	
Brown & Sharpe Mfg.	9.250-05	X			a b c	
Brown (Robert C.) & Co.	7.500-11	X			a b c	
Browning-Ferris	6.250-12			X	a b c	
Bruno's	6.500-09			X	a b c	
Builders Transport	8.000-05	X			a b c	
Builders Transport	6.500-11	-			a b c	
BSN Corp.	7.750-01	X			a b c	
Burham Pacific Properties	8.500-12		X		- b c	
Burnup & Sims	12.000-00		X		a b c	
Businessland	5.500-07		X		a b c	
CalFed	6.500-01			X	a b -	
Canandaigua Wine	7.000-11	X			a b c	
Carmike Cinemas	8.000-07	X			a b c	
Carolina Freight	6.250-11		X		a b c	
Casey's General Stores	6.250-12		X		a b c	
CBI Industries	7.000-11			X	a b c	
CBS	5.000-02			X	a b -	
CCB Financial	8.750-10		X		a b c	
Cellular	6.750-09		X		a b c	
Central Jersey Bancorp	7.625-12		X		a b c	
Cetus Corp.	5.250-02		X		a b -	
Cetus Corp.	6.000-11		-		a b c	6
Chambers Development	6.750-04			X	a b c	
Champion International	6.500-11			X	a b c	
Chartwell Group	7.000-12	X			a b c	
Chemical Waste	0.000-12			X	a b c	7
Chesapeake Utilities	8.250-14	X			- - c	
Chili's	6.250-12		X		a b c	
Chock Full O'Nuts	8.000-06	X			a b c	
Chock Full O'Nuts	7.000-12	-			a b c	
Chubb Corp.	5.500-93			X	a b -	
Church & Dwight	6.500-11		X		a b c	
CIGNA	8.200-10			X	a b c	
Cincinnati Financial	9.375-05			X	- b c	

Company	Descript.	Company size, $millions*			Source	FN
		<100	100-500	>500		
Circle K Corp.	8.250-05		X		a b c	
Circle K Corp.	7.000-12		-		a b c	
Citicorp	5.750-00			X	- b c	
Citizens First Bancorp	6.750-01		X		- b -	
Clayton Homes	7.750-01		X		a b c	
Clayton Homes	6.000-07		-		a b c	
CML Group	7.500-12		X		a b c	
Coeur d'Alene	6.000-02		X		a b -	
Colonial BancGroup	7.500-11	X			- b c	
Columbia First Federal	7.500-11	X			a b c	
Columbia Savings & Loan	7.000-11		X		a b c	
Columbia Savings & Loan	7.250-11		-		a b c	
Comcast	7.000-14			X	a b c	
Comcast	0.000-95			-	a b c	
Comcast 'A'	2.750-03			-	a b -	
Comarco	9.750-00	X			- - c	
Comerica	10.000-93	-			- b -	
Comerica	9.000-92	-			- b c	
Commtron	6.875-11	X			a b c	8
COMPAQ Computer	6.500-13			X	a b c	
Computer Products	9.500-97	X			a b c	
Comsat International	7.750-98			X	a b -	
Conner Peripherals	9.000-14		X		a b c	
Conquest Exploration	9.500-14	X			a b c	
Consul Restaurants	13.000-92	X			- b c	
Consul Restaurants	10.000-03	-			- b c	
Continental Medical Sys.	7.750-12		X		a b c	
Control Data	8.500-11			X	a b c	
Convex Computer	6.000-12		X		a b c	
Cooper Cos	10.625-05	X			a b c	9
Copperweld	9.920-08		X		a b c	
Corning Glass	6.500-06			X	a b c	10
Cornerstone Financial	7.000-99	X			- b c	
Cornerstone Financial	8.750-97	-			- b -	
Corroon & Black	7.500-05			X	a b c	
Countrywide Credit	7.000-11		X		a b c	
Covington Development	12.500-94	X			- b c	11
CPT Corp.	10.000-01	X			a b c	
Crane Co. 'B'	5.000-94			X	- b c	
Cray Research	6.125-11			X	a b c	

Company	Descript.	Company size, $millions*			Source	FN
		<100	100-500	>500		
Creative Medical Systems	8.000-92	X			- b -	
CUC International	0.000-96		X		- - c	
Cummins Engine	0.000-05			X	a b c	
Customedix	15.000-97	X			- b c	12
Damson Oil	14.625-93	X			- b c	
Damson Oil	12.875-93	-			- b c	
Damson Oil	14.000-93	-			- b c	
Dana Corp.	5.875-06			X	a b c	
Data-Design Labs	8.500-08	X			a b c	
Datapoint	8.875-06	X			a b c	
Data Switch	8.250-02	X			a b c	
Data Switch	9.000-96	-			- b c	13
DBA Systems	8.250-10	X			a b c	
Deere & Co.	5.500-01			X	a b c	
Delmed	10.500-97	X			- - c	
Delmed	10.500-02	-			- - c	
DEP Corp.	7.375-01	X			- b c	
Deposit Guarantee	8.750-10		X		a b c	
Derwood Investment Trust	8.000-91	X			- - c	
Diagnostic/Retrieval	8.500-98	X			a b c	
Diasonics	6.500-01		X		a b -	
Diceon Electronics	5.500-12	X			a b c	
Digicon	9.350-97	X			- - c	
Dixie Yarns	7.000-12		X		a b c	
Dreyers Grand Ice Cream	6.500-11		X		a b c	
Drug Emporium	7.750-14		X		a b c	
DSC Communications	8.000-03			X	a b c	14
DSC Communications	7.750-14			-	a b c	
Ducommun	7.750-11	X			a b c	
Dupont	7.000-01			X	a b -	15
DWG Corp.	5.500-94		X		- - c	
Eastman Kodak	6.375-01			X	a b -	
Ecolab	5.125-91			X	- - c	
EDO Corp.	7.000-11	X			a b c	
Empire Gas	9.000-98	X			- - c	
Emerson Electric	5.000-92			X	- b c	16
Emerson Electric	8.000-10			-	a b c	17
ENSERCH	10.000-01			X	a b c	
ENSERCH	6.375-02			-	a b -	
Entertainment Marketing	8.500-06	X			a b c	

Company	Descript.	Company size, $millions*			Source	FN
		<100	100-500	>500		
Entertainment Marketing	6.000-07	-			a b c	
Environmental Systems	6.750-11		X		a b c	
Enzo Biochem	9.000-01	X			- - -	
Equitable Resources	9.500-06			X	- b c	18
Equitec Financial Group	10.000-04	X			a b c	
Esterline	8.250-95	X			- b -	
E'town Corp.	6.750-12	X			- - c	
Evans & Sutherland	6.000-12		X		a b c	
Executone Info Systems	7.500-11		X		a b c	
Falcon Products	12.000-95	X			- b c	
Farah Inc.	5.000-94	X			- b c	
Fedders	5.000-96		X		a b c	19
Fedders	5.000-92		-		- b -	
Federal Express	5.750-11			X	a b c	20
Federal Nat'l. Mortgage	4.375-96			X	a b c	
Federal Realty Inv. Trust	8.750-10		X		a b c	
Federal Realty Inv. Trust	5.250-02		-		a b -	
Fieldcrest Cannon	6.000-12		X		a b c	
Fin. Corp of Santa Barbara	9.000-12	X			a b c	
First Amarillo Bancorp	10.000-08	X			- b c	
First Central Financial	9.000-00	X			- - c	
First Financial Management	7.000-13			X	a b c	
First Florida Banks	6.875-96			X	- - c	
First Interstate Iowa	9.000-98	X			- b c	
First-Knox Banc Corp	8.500-09	X			- - c	
First Liberty Financial	8.250-05	X			a b c	
First Security	9.500-06		X		a b c	
First Union RE Equity	10.250-09		X		a b c	
Firstcorp	8.250-05	X			a b c	
Fleet/Norstar Financial	8.500-10			X	a b c	
Fischbach	4.750-97	X			- b c	
Fischbach	8.500-05	-			- b c	
Fleming Cos	6.500-96			X	a b c	
Flowers Industries	8.250-05			X	a b c	
Foothill Group	9.500-03	X			a b c	
Ford Motor Co.	4.500-96			X	- b c	21
Ford Motor Co.	4.875-98			-	- b c	21
Foremost Corp. America	4.000-92		X		- b c	
Forest Oil	5.500-94		X		- b c	
Fortune Financial Group	10.000-10	X			a b c	

Company	Descript.	<100	100-500	>500	Source	FN
			Company size, $millions*			
Forum Group	6.250-11	X			a b c	
Freeport-McMoRan	8.750-13			X	a b c	
Fremont General	7.250-11		X		a b c	
Fries Entertainment	7.500-06	X			a b c	
Fruit of the Loom	6.750-02			X	a b c	
Fuqua Industries	6.500-02			X	a b -	
Furon	8.000-11	X			a b c	
Galactic Holdings/Newmont	7.000-95			X	- - -	
General Devices	13.500-95	X			- b c	
Genetech	5.000-02			X	a b -	
General Instrument	7.250-12			X	a b c	
GenRad	7.250-11	X			a b c	
GIANT Group	7.000-06	X			a b c	
GLENFED	7.750-01			X	a b -	
Goodyear Tire	6.875-03			X	a b -	
Goulds Pumps	9.875-06		X		a b c	
Grace, W.R.	6.250-02			X	a b -	
Grace, W.R.	7.000-01			-	a b -	
Grace, W.R.	4.250-90			-	a b c	
Grace, W.R.	6.500-96			-	a b c	
Graham-Field Health Prod.	7.500-99	X			- b -	22
Graphic Industries	7.000-06	X			a b c	
Graphic Scanning	10.000-01		X		a b c	
Great Amer. Communications	7.500-92		X		- b c	23
Great American First	8.500-11		X		- b -	
Great Lakes Bancorp	7.250-11	X			a b -	
Greenery Rehab Group	6.500-11	X			a b c	
Greyhound	6.500-90			X	- b c	
Grow Group	8.500-06	X			a b c	
Grumman	9.250-09			X	a b c	
GTECH	12.750-05		X		a b c	
Guilford Mills	6.000-12		X		a b c	
Gulf States Utilities	7.250-92			X	- b c	
Hadson	7.750-06		X		a b c	24
Hallwood Group	6.750-91	X			- b c	
Harland (John H.)	6.750-11			X	- b c	25
HCC Industries	12.500-00	X			- - c	
Health-Chem	10.375-99	X			a b c	
Healthco International	7.000-11		X		a b c	
Health Images	6.500-98	X			- b -	

Company	Descript.	Company size, $millions*			Source	FN
		<100	100-500	>500		
Healthsouth Rehab	7.750-14		X		a b c	
Hechinger	5.500-12			X	a b c	
Hecla Mining	0.000-04			X	a b c	
Heldor Industries	9.000-91	X			- b c	
Hercules	6.500-99			X	a b c	
Hercules	8.000-10			X	a b c	
Hexcel	7.000-11		X		a b c	
Hills Department Stores	11.000-02		X		a b c	
Home Depot	6.750-14			X	a b c	
HomeFed Corp.	6.500-11			X	a b c	
Home Shopping Network	5.500-02		X		- b -	
Horn & Hardart	7.500-07	X			a b -	
Howtek	9.000-01	X			- b -	
Hudson Foods	14.000-08		X		a b c	
Hudson Foods	8.000-06	-			- b c	
Hudson General	7.000-11	X			a b c	
Huffy	7.250-14		X		a b c	
Hughes Supply	7.000-11	X			a b c	
Humana	8.500-09			X	a b c	
ICN Pharmaceuticals	6.750-01	X			a b -	
IMC Fertilizer	0.000-05			X	a b c	26
Immunex	7.500-01		X		a b c	
Independence Bancorp	7.000-11		X		a b c	
Informix	7.750-12		X		a b c	
Ingles Markets	9.000-08		X		a b c	
Inspiration Resources	8.500-12		X		a b c	
Insteel Industries	7.750-06	X			- b c	
Instrument Systems	7.000-91	X			- - c	
Interface	8.000-13		X		a b c	
Intermark	7.375-07	X			a b c	
Inter-Regional Financial	11.500-02	X			a b c	
Inter-Regional Financial	10.000-03	-			a b c	
Int'l. Business Machines	7.875-04			X	a b c	
Int'l. Lease Finance	5.750-01			X	a b -	
Int'l. Minerals & Chemical	4.000-91			X	- b c	
International Paper	5.875-12			X	a b c	27
International Paper	5.750-02			-	a b c	
International Rectifier	9.000-10	X			a b c	
Int'l. Totalizer Systems	10.000-03	X			- b c	
Interstate Securities	7.750-11	X			a b c	

Company	Descript.	Company size, $millions*			Source	FN
		<100	100-500	>500		
ITT Corp.	8.625-00			X	- b c	
IRT Property	2.000-02		X		- - -	
Iverson Technology	8.250-02	X			- - c	
Jackpot Enterprises	8.750-14	X			a b c	
Jacobson Stores	6.750-11		X		a b c	
Jamesway	8.000-05	X			a b c	
Jefferies Group	8.500-10	X			a b c	
Jones Intercable	7.500-07		X		a b c	
J.P. Industries	7.250-13		X		a b c	
Kaman Corp.	6.000-12		X		a b c	
Kasler Corp.	9.000-07	X			- b c	
Kaneb Services	8.750-08		X		a b c	28
Kaneb Services	8.000-95	-			- - -	28
Kaufman & Broad Home	0.000-04		X		a b c	
Kaufman & Broad Home	7.500-15			-	- - c	
Kellwood	9.000-99		X		- b c	
Kerr-McGee	7.250-12			X	a b c	
Ketema	8.000-03	X			- b c	
Kirby Exploration	7.250-14		X		a b c	
Kirby Exploration	10.500-92		-		- - c	
Koger Properties	9.250-03		X		a b c	
Kollmorgen	8.750-09		X		a b c	
Kulicke & Soffa	8.750-09	X			a b c	
Kurzweil Music Systems	12.000-00	X			- b c	
Lafarge	7.000-13			X	a b c	
Landmark Bancshares	8.750-98		X		- - c	
La Petite Academy	6.500-11		X		a b c	
La Quinta Motor Inns	10.000-02		X		a b c	
Laser Industries	8.000-06	X			a b c	
Leisure + Technology	6.750-96	X			- - c	
Legg Mason	7.000-11		X		a b c	
Leggett & Platt	6.500-06			X	a b c	
LEP Group	7.500-01		X		- b -	29
Liberty Nat'l. Bancorp	8.250-10		X		a b c	
Lionel	8.000-07	X			a b c	
Live Entertainment	7.625-15		X		- - c	
Loews	0.000-04			X	a b c	
Lone Star Technology	8.000-02	X			a b -	
Loral	7.250-10			X	a b c	
Louisiana Land	8.500-00			X	a b c	30

Company	Descript.	Company size, $millions*			Source	FN
		<100	100-500	>500		
LSI Logic	6.250-02		X		a b -	
LTX Corp.	7.250-11	X			a b c	
LTX Corp.	10.500-09	-			- b c	
Lynch Corp.	8.000-06	X			a b c	
M/A-Com	9.259-06		X		a b c	
Magna Group	7.000-99		X		- b c	
Magna Group	7.500-00		-		- b -	
Magna International	7.000-93		X		- b -	
Management Co Entertainment	14.000-09	X			- b c	
Manor Care	6.375-11			X	a b c	
Marcade Group	12.500-99	X			- - -	
Mark IV Industries	7.000-11		X		a b c	
Mark Twain Bancshares	7.000-99		X		- - c	
Masco Corp.	5.250-12			X	a b c	
Masco Industries	6.000-11			X	a b c	
Maxtor	5.750-12		X		a b c	
Maxus Energy	0.000-04			X	a b c	
MCA Inc.	5.500-02			X	a b -	
McCaw Cellular	8.000-08			X	a b c	
McCaw Cellular	0.000-08			-	a b c	
McCormick Capital	12.000-96	X			- b -	
McDonald & Co. Investment	8.000-11	X			a b c	
McDonnell Douglas	4.750-91			X	- b c	
McGraw-Hill	3.875-92			X	- b c	
MCI Communications	0.000-04			X	a b c	
McKesson	9.750-06			X	a b c	
McKesson	6.000-94			-	- b c	
Mead	6.750-12			X	a b c	
Medalist Industries	7.500-01	X			- b c	
Medco Containment	7.500-00			X	a b c	
MEDIQ	7.250-06	X			a b c	
MEI Diversified	8.000-06		X		a b c	
Mellon Bank	7.250-99			X	- b c	
Melville	4.875-96			X	- b c	
Mentor	6.750-02		X		a b -	
Merrill Lynch	0.000-06			X	a b c	
Metro Airlines	8.500-12	X			a b c	
Micropolis	6.000-12	X			a b c	
Microsemi	5.875-12	X			a b c	
Midlantic	8.250-10			X	a b c	31

Company	Descript.	Company size, $millions*			Source	FN
		<100	100-500	>500		
Midway Airlines	8.500-02		X		a b c	
Minn. Mining & Mfg.	7.750-98			X	a b -	32
Moog	9.875-06		X		a b c	
Morgan (J.P.)	4.750-98			X	a b c	
Mortgage & Realty Trust	6.750-91		X		- b c	
Motorola	0.000-09			X	a b -	
Munsingwear	8.000-06	X			a b c	
NAC Re	6.250-11		X		a b c	
Nasta International	12.000-02	X			- b c	
Nat'l. Bancshares Texas	10.000-06	X			a b c	
Nat'l. Convenience Stores	9.000-08		X		a b c	
National Education	6.500-11		X		a b c	
National Enterprises	4.750-96	X			- b c	
National Intergroup	4.625-94		X		- - -	33
Nat'l. Medical Enterprise	0.000-04			X	a b c	
Nat'l. Vision Services	9.500-97	X			- - c	
NBD Bancorp	8.250-10			X	a b c	
NBI Inc.	8.250-07	X			a b c	
NEECO	7.750-12	X			- b c	
Neolens	7.000-98	X			- b -	
NeoRx	9.750-14	X			a b c	
Network Equipment	7.250-15		X		a b c	
New England Critical	7.750-14		X		a b c	
Newport Pharmaceuticals	10.000-02	X			- b c	
New Visions Entertainment	9.500-01	X			a b c	
NIPSCO Industries	4.125-92			X	- - c	34
NMR of America	8.000-01	X			- b -	
Noble Affiliates	7.250-12			X	a b c	
Nortek	7.500-06	X			a b c	
Northwest Natural Gas	7.250-12		X		a b c	
Norton	7.750-12			X	a b c	
Norwest Corp.	6.750-03			X	a b c	
Novell	7.250-13			X	a b c	
NVR L.P.	10.000-02		X		a b c	
Oak Industries	9.625-91	X			- b c	
Oak Industries	10.500-02	-			- b c	
Oakwood Homes	7.500-01	X			a b c	
Oakwood Homes	6.500-12	-			a b c	
O'Brien Energy Systems	7.750-02	X			a b c	
Ogden	5.000-93			X	- b c	

Company	Descript.	Company size, $millions*			Source	FN
		<100	100-500	>500		
Ogden	6.000-02			-	a b -	
Ogden	5.750-02			-	a b -	
Ohio Bancorp	7.750-12	X			a b -	
OHM Corp.	8.000-06		X		a b c	
Old Kent Financial	8.000-10			X	a b c	
Old National Bancorp	8.000-12		X		a b c	
Old Republic Int'l.	8.000-15		X		a b c	
Olsten	7.000-12		X		a b c	
OMI Corp.	7.500-11		X		- - c	
Omnicom	7.000-13			X	a b c	
Omnicom	6.500-04			-	a b -	
On-Line Software	6.250-02	X			a b c	
One Bancorp	7.500-11	X			a b c	
Oryx Energy	7.500-14			X	a b c	
Pacific Int'l. Services	10.000-07	X			- b c	
Pacific Scientific	7.750-03	X			a b c	
Pan Am Corp.	9.000-10		X		a b c	35
Park Communications	6.875-11		X		a b c	
Park Electrochemical	7.250-06	X			a b c	
Parker-Hannifin	4.000-92			X	- b c	
Patten	8.250-12	X			a b c	
Pay'n Save	7.125-06	X			- b c	
Penn REIT	9.750-03		X		- b -	
Peoples Bancorp	8.750-05		X		- b c	
Pep Boys	6.000-11			X	a b c	
Perpetual Financial	7.250-11		X		a b c	
Perry Drug Stores	8.500-10	X			a b c	
Petrie Stores	8.000-10			X	a b c	
Pfizer	4.000-97			X	- b c	
Pfizer	8.750-06			-	a b c	
Pharmacontrol	8.000-02	X			- - c	
Piedmont BankGroup	7.000-11	X			- - c	
Piedmont Natural Gas	12.000-00		X		- b c	
Pinnacle West	10.000-02			X	a b -	
Pioneer-Standard Electric	9.000-98	X			a b c	
Pittston Co	9.200-04			X	a b c	
Plenum Publishing	6.500-07	X			a b c	
Ply-Gem	0.000-08		X		a b c	
PNC Financial	8.250-08			X	- b c	
Pogo Producing	8.000-05		X		a b c	

Company	Descript.	Company size, $millions*			Source	FN
		<100	100-500	>500		
Policy Management Systems	5.500-12			X	a b c	
Pope & Talbot	6.000-12		X		a b c	
Porta Systems	9.250-00	X			a b c	
Potlatch	5.750-12			X	a b c	
Potomac Electric	7.000-18			X	a b c	
Preston	7.000-11	X			a b c	
Price Co	5.500-12			X	a b c	
Price Communications	10.000-04	X			a b -	
Prime Motor Inns	7.000-13			X	a b c	
Prime Motor Inns	6.625-11			-	a b c	
Primerica	5.750-94			X	a b -	
Primerica	5.500-02			-	a b -	
Primerica	4.500-02			-	a b -	36
Primerica	7.250-06			-	a b c	36
Production Operators	9.250-00	X			a b c	
Pulte Home	8.500-08		X		a b c	37
Punta Gorda Isles	6.000-92	X			- b c	
Punta Gorda Isles	6.500-91	-			- b -	
Quantum Chemical	4.500-92			X	- b c	
Quixote	8.000-11	X			a b c	
Ralston Purina	5.750-00			X	- b c	
Ranger Oil	6.500-02		X		- b -	
Raymond James Financial	7.500-06	X			- b c	
Recognition Equipment	7.250-11	X			a b c	
Recoton	8.000-06	X			a b c	
Richardson Electronics	7.250-06		X		a b c	
Riser Foods	6.500-94	X			- b c	38
RJR Holdings	14.700-09			X	- - c	
RMS International	9.750-95	X			- b c	
Robert Half Int'l.	7.250-12		X		a b c	
Rochester Telephone	4.750-94			X	- b c	
Rockwell International	4.250-91			X	- - c	
Rohr Industries	7.000-12		X		a b c	
Rorer Group	7.750-13			X	a b c	
Rorer Group	6.000-01			-	a b -	
Rouse Company	5.750-02			X	a b -	
Rouse Company	5.875-96			-	a b -	
RPM Inc.	5.750-01		X		a b -	
Ruddick	8.000-11		X		a b c	
Salick Health Care	7.250-01	X			a b c	

Company	Descript.	Company size, $millions*			Source	FN
		<100	100-500	>500		
SCI Systems	5.625-12		X		a b c	
SCI Systems	3.000-01	-			a b -	
Seagate Technology	6.750-12			X	a b c	
Seagram Co.	0.000-06			X	a b c	
Secor Bank	7.500-11	X			- b c	39
Selective Insurance	8.750-08		X		a b c	
Semicon	13.000-01	X			- b c	
Service Corp. Int'l.	6.500-11			X	a b c	
Service Corp. Int'l.	8.000-06			-	- b c	40
Service Corp. Int'l.	7.500-98			-	- - -	41
Sherwin-Williams	6.250-95			X	- b c	
SHL Systemhouse	9.000-07		X		- b c	42
Shoneys	0.000-04		X		a b c	
Sikes	7.000-11		X		a b c	
Silicon Graphics	5.750-12		X		a b c	
Silicon Graphics	8.000-04		-		a b -	
Siliconix	8.000-10	X			a b c	
South Carolina Nat'l.	6.500-01			X	a b -	
Southeast Banking	6.500-99			X	a b c	
Southeast Banking	4.750-97			-	a b c	
Southern NE Telecom.	9.750-10			X	a b c	43
Southwest Airlines	6.750-98			X	a b -	
Southwestern Energy	8.500-10		X		a b c	
Spartech	9.000-99	X			a b c	
SPX Corp.	9.000-10		X		- - c	
State Street Boston	7.750-08			X	- b c	
Sterling Bancorp	6.500-90	X			a b c	
Sterling Electronics	10.750-09	X			- b c	
Sterling Software	8.000-01	X			a b c	
St. Paul Companies	7.500-00			X	- - -	
Suave Shoe	5.000-97	X			- b c	
Sudbury Inc.	7.500-11	X			a b c	44
Sun Co.	6.750-12			X	- b c	
Sun Co.	7.500-95			-	- - -	45
Sun Electric	8.000-06		X		a b c	
Sun Microsystems	5.250-12			X	a b c	
Sun Microsystems	6.375-99			-	a b c	
Sunrise Medical	7.250-96	X			- b -	
Sunshine Mining	8.875-08		X		a b c	
Sysco Corp.	0.000-04			X	a b c	

Company	Descript.	Company size, $millions*			Source	FN
		<100	100-500	>500		
Talley Industries	9.000-05	X			- b -	
Team Inc.	13.000-04	X			- b c	
Tele-Communications	7.000-12			X	a b c	
Telesphere International	7.000-97	X			- b c	
Telxon	7.500-12		X		a b c	
Teradyne	9.250-12		X		- b c	46
Terminal Data	11.250-01	X			- b -	
Texas American Energy	12.875-14	X			a b -	
Texas Industries	9.000-08		X		a b c	
Texas Instruments	2.750-02			X	a b -	
Texfi Industries	11.250-91	X			- - c	
Texfi Industries	4.750-96	-			- - c	
Thermo Electron	5.750-12			X	a b c	
Thermo Environmental	6.000-96	X			- b -	
Thermo Instrument	6.750-03		X		- b -	
Thermo Process Systems	6.500-07		X		a b -	
Thortec International	6.500-12	X			- b c	
Tidewater	7.000-10		X		a b c	
Tidewater	7.750-05		-		- b c	
TJX	7.250-10				a b c	47
Traditional Industries	9.500-07	X			- b c	
Trans-Lux	9.000-05	X			- b c	
Transamerica Corp.	7.000-01			X	- - -	48
Transcisco	9.000-96	X			a b c	49
Trans Financial Bancorp	8.500-99	X			- - c	
Traveler's	8.320-15			X	a b c	
Triad Systems	7.000-12	X			a b c	
Tridex Corp.	10.250-96	X			- b c	
Trinity Industries	0.000-01			X	a b c	
Trinity Industries	6.750-12			-	a b c	50
TRINOVA	6.000-02			X	a b -	
Triton Energy	0.000-05		X		a b c	
TS Industries	8.500-01	X			- b c	
Turner Broadcasting	0.000-04			X	a b c	
Tyco Toys	6.875-06		X		a - -	51
Tyco Toys	8.750-14		-		a b c	
TW Services	10.000-14			X	- b -	
UNC Inc.	7.500-06	X			a b c	
Union Carbide	7.500-12			X	a b c	
Union Pacific	4.750-99			X	- - c	

Company	Descript.	Company size, $millions*			Source	FN
		<100	100-500	>500		
United Artists Enter.	6.375-02			X	a b c	
United Brands	5.500-94			X	a b c	
United Dominion REIT	9.000-10		X		- b c	
United Healthcare	7.500-11		X		- b -	
United Insurance	6.750-06	X			a b c	
United Telecommunications	5.000-93			X	- - c	52
Unitrode Corp.	8.000-09	X			a b c	53
Universal Health Services	7.500-08		X		a b c	
USAir Group	6.000-93			X	- b c	
U.S. Home	5.500-96	X			- b c	
U.S. Home (A)	10.000-95	-			- - c	
U.S. Home (B)	10.000-95	-			- - c	
USLICO	8.000-11		X		a b c	
USLICO	8.500-14		-		a b c	
USX Corp.	5.750-01			X	a b c	
USX Corp.	7.000-17			-	a b c	
UtiliCorp United	6.625-11		X		a b c	
UTL Corp.	6.500-11	X			a b c	
Varco Int'l. Financial	8.500-96		X		- b -	
Vestron	9.000-11	X			a b c	
VICORP Restaurants	13.500-09		X		a b c	
Victoria Bankshares	10.500-97	X			- b c	
Vishay Intertechnology	4.750-03		X		a b -	
VLSI Technology	7.000-12	X			a b c	
Volunteer Capital	8.250-03	X			a b c	54
Wainoco Oil	7.750-14		X		a b c	
Walker Telecommunications	11.000-99	X			- b c	
Walshire Assurance	10.000-03	X			- b c	
Wang Labs	7.750-08		X		a b c	
Wang Labs	9.000-09	-			a b c	
Warner Communications	6.000-01			X	a b -	55
Washington Corp.	6.500-91	X			- b c	
Waste Management	0.000-01			X	a b c	
Watsco	10.000-96	X			- - c	
Watts Industries	7.750-14		X		a b c	
Waxman Industries	6.250-07	X			a b c	
Wean Inc.	5.500-93	X			- b c	
Webb (Del E.)	10.375-09	X			a b c	
Weingarten Realty	7.750-03		X		a b -	
Weingarten Realty	8.000-09		-		a b c	

Company	Descript.	Company size, $millions*			Source	FN
		<100	100-500	>500		
Wendy's International	7.250-10			X	a b c	
Western Digital	9.000-14			X	a b c	
Weston (Roy F.)	7.000-02		X		a b c	
Western Inv't. RE Trust	8.000-06		X		a b c	
Western Union	5.250-97	X			a b c	
Westinghouse Electric	9.000-09			X	a b c	
Westwood One	6.750-11		X		a b c	
Willcox & Gibbs	7.000-14		X		a b c	
Wilshire Oil	6.000-95	X			- b -	
Witco	4.500-93			X	- - c	
Witco	5.500-12			-	a b c	
WMS Industries	12.750-96	X			a b c	
Wyle Labs	6.250-02		X		a b -	
Wyse Technology	6.000-02		X		a b -	
Wyse Technology	6.000-02		-		a b -	
Xerox	6.000-95			X	a b c	
XOMA Corp.	9.000-14		X		a b c	
Xyvision	6.000-02	X			- b -	
Zenith Electronics	6.250-11		X		a b c	
Zurn Industries	5.750-94		X		- b c	
Number of companies		217	177	176		
Number of convertible bonds		239	203	213		

Source:
a. Value Line Convertibles
b. The R.H.M. Convertible Survey
c. Standard & Poor's bond guides
*Company size was determined by multiplying the number of common shares outstanding by the stock's price.

Footnotes:

1 Trades as Alleghany Corp.
2 Trades as Amoco Canada Petroleum
3 Trades as Burlington Resources
4 Trades as Hughes Tool
5 Trades as International Paper
6 Trades as Quantum Chemical
7 Trades as Waste Management
8 Trades as Bergen Brunswig
9 Trades as CooperVision
10 Trades as Hazelton Labs
11 Trades as Covington Technology

12   Trades as Custom Energy Services
13   Trades as T-Bar Inc.
14   Trades as Digital Switch
15   Trades as Newmont Mining
16   Trades as Skil Corp.
17   Trades as Liebert
18   Trades as Equitable Gas
19   Trades as Rotorex
20   Trades as General Dynamics
21   Trades as Ford Motor Credit
22   Trades as Patient Technology
23   Trades as Median Mortgage Investors
24   Trades as Ultrasystems
25   Trades as Scan-tron
26   Trades as International Minerals & Chemical
27   Trades as Anitec Image Technology
28   Trades as Moran Energy
29   Trades as National Guardian
30   Trades as Inexco Oil
31   Trades as Midlantic Banks
32   Trades as Dart & Kraft
33   Trades as Granite City Steel
34   Trades as Norther Indiana Public Service
35   Trades as Pan Am World Airways
36   Trades as Williams (A.L.)
37   Trades as Pulte Home Credit
38   Trades as Fisher Foods
39   Trades as Alabama Federal Savings & Loan
40   Trades as Morlan International
41   Trades as Amedco International Financial
42   Trades as Kinburn
43   Trades as United Telecommunications
44   Trades as Sudbury Holdings
45   Trades as Helmerich & Payne
46   Trades as Zehntel
47   Trades as Zayre
48   Trades as Fairmont Financial
49   Trades as PLM Companies
50   Trades as Trinity Industries Leasing
51   Trades as View-Master
52   Trades as United Utiities
53   Trades as Signal
54   Trades as Winners Corp.
55   Trades as Lorimar Telepictures

AN EVALUATION OF INTEREST RATE RISK FOR CONVERTIBLE BONDS

The assumption that long-term interest rates would not change in the near term made it possible to evaluate various convertible strategies with relatively simple graphs and simple arithmetic. However, interest rates do fluctuate. It is thus important to understand the potential impact of interest rate changes on convertibles as well as on traditional strategies employing fixed-income securities.

Exhibit B-1 repeats the convertible price curve for XYZ Corp. 10s of 2010 (Exhibit 3-1, page 28) trading at par, with long-term interest rates at

Exhibit B-1. The Convertible Price Curve

XYZ Corp. 10 percent, 20-year bond trading at 100

- conversion ratio = 40 shares
- straight bond equivalent yield = 12, 16 or 20 percent

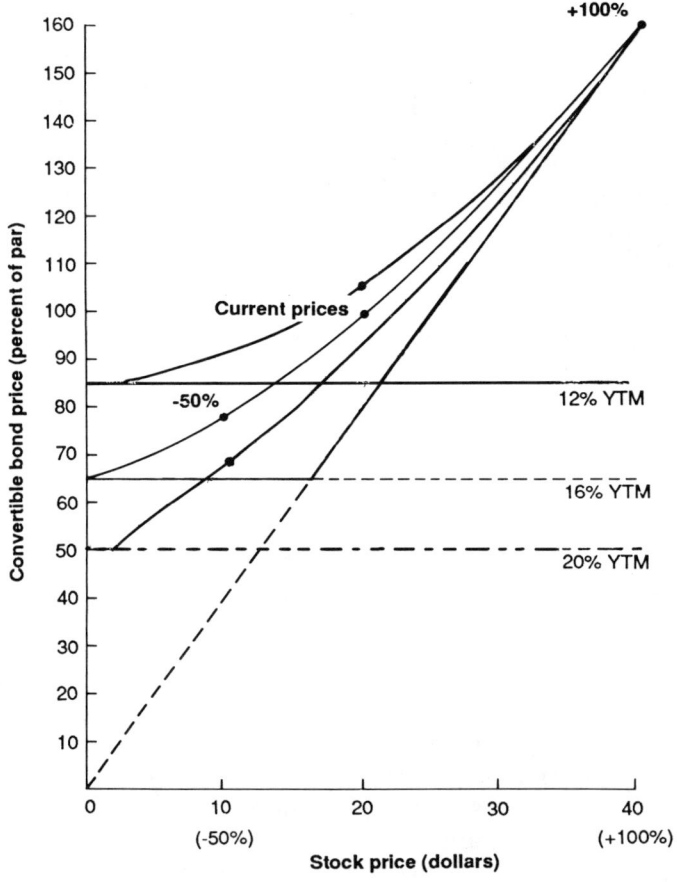

16 percent and adds expected new price curves should interest rates rise to 20 percent or drop to 12 percent. For stock price changes of –50, 0 and +100 percent, the estimated bond prices are as follows:

	Estimated Convertible Bond Price for Stock Price Changes of:		
Long-Term Interest Rates	*–50 Percent*	*0 Percent*	*+100 Percent*
12 percent	90	106	160
16 percent	78	100	160
20 percent	69	95	160

As shown by the price curves, interest rate fluctuations would have little influence on the convertible's price if its stock advanced; upside prices are controlled by the conversion value line, which cannot change. If the stock declined, a higher investment value would moderate the bond's price drop, or a lower investment value would cause a greater decline.

Performance Evaluation

Table B-1 repeats the risk-reward analysis for the XYZ Corp. bond compared to the traditional balanced approach (Table 3-2, page 30).

Tables B-2 and B-3 present new risk-reward calculations for interest rates of 20 percent and 12 percent. Study these calculations and the accompanying conclusions carefully. Pay particular attention to how performance comparisons between the convertible bond and the balanced approach can sharply diverge. They help to explain why the Noddings Large-Cap convertible bond index (Chapter 5) did so much better than the balanced approach during its early years when interest rates were steadily rising and why it substantially underperformed when interest rates plummeted in 1982. Both divergences were quite understandable, given the actual events that unfolded in the stock and straight bond markets.

There are nine possible scenarios for stock/bond combination portfolios based on the specific price action of each security type:

Table B-1. Risk-Reward Analysis: XYZ Corp. 10s of 2010 at 100 versus Common Stock at $20 and Straight Bonds at 16 Percent

	Stock Price Change in 12 Months		
	−50 Percent	*0 Percent*	*+100 Percent*
Balanced approach			
Common stock	−50%	0%	+100%
Straight bonds	+16	+16	+16
50% stock/50% bonds	−17%	+ 8%	+58%
Convertible bond			
Capital gain or loss	−22%	0%	+60%
Interest received	+10	+10	+10
Total return	−12%	+10%	+70%
Convertible advantage	+ 5%	+ 2%	+12%

Stocks	*Bonds*	*Better Performer*
sideways	sideways	Convertibles
sideways	rising	Balanced approach
sideways	falling	Convertibles
rising	sideways	Convertibles
rising	rising	Balanced approach
rising	falling	Convertibles, by far
falling	sideways	Convertibles
falling	rising	Convertibles
falling	falling	Convertibles

As shown by Tables B-1, B-2, and B-3 (summarized above), under-valued convertibles should modestly outperform the balanced approach most of the time. During these six different market scenarios, a convertible portfolio's performance can reasonably be compared to traditional balanced-approach investing. The other three scenarios will cause even most professionals to "throw up their hands in despair" when it comes to evaluating short-term performance results.

Table B-2. Risk-Reward Analysis: XYZ Corp. 10s of 2010 at 100 versus Common Stock at $20 and Straight Bonds at 16 Percent, Assuming Interest Rates Rise to 20 Percent in One Year

	Stock Price Change in 12 Months		
	–50 Percent	*0 Percent*	*+100 Percent*
Balanced approach			
Common stock	–50%	0%	+100%
Straight bonds			
Capital loss*	–20%	–20%	–20%
Interest received	+16	+16	+16
Total return	– 4%	– 4%	– 4%
50% stock/50% bonds	–27%	– 2%	+48%
Convertible bond			
Capital gain or loss	–31%	– 5%	+60%
Interest received	+10	+10	+10
Total return	–21%	+ 5%	+70%
Convertible advantage	+ 6%	+ 7%	+22%

*A 16 percent bond purchased at 100 will drop to about 80 if interest rates rise to 20 percent.

Conclusions

1. Rising interest rates will result in greater losses for both the convertible bond and the balanced approach if the common stock declines. The convertible, however, will retain its advantage over the balanced approach (–21 percent versus –27 percent).

2. If the common stock remains unchanged, the convertible will move modestly lower but will outperform the balanced approach by an even greater margin (+5 percent versus –2 percent).

3. If the common doubles, the convertible will provide the same total return as in a steady interest rate environment (+70 percent) and will significantly outperform the balanced approach; its advantage increases from +12 percent (Table B-1) to +22 percent.

Table B-3. Risk-Reward Analysis: XYZ Corp. 10s of 2010 at 100 versus Common Stock at $20 and Straight Bonds at 16 Percent, Assuming Interest Rates Decline to 12 Percent in One Year

	Stock Price Change in 12 Months		
	−50 Percent	0 Percent	+100 Percent
Balanced approach			
Common stock	−50%	0%	+100%
Straight bonds			
Capital gain*	+30%	+30%	+30%
Interest received	+16	+16	+16
Total return	+46%	+46%	+46%
50% stock/50% bonds	− 2%	+23%	+73%
Convertible bond			
Capital gain or loss	−10%	+ 6%	+60%
Interest received	+10	+10	+10
Total return	0%	+16%	+70%
Convertible advantage	+ 2%	− 7%	− 3%

*A 16 percent bond purchased at 100 will rise to about 130 if interest rates decline to 12 percent (assuming bonds are not callable).

Conclusions

1. Falling interest rates will cushion losses for both the convertible and the balanced approach if the common stock declines. The convertible will lose some of its advantage (0 percent versus −2 percent) at a 50 percent stock decline.

2. If the common stock remains unchanged, the convertible will move modestly higher but will underperform the balanced approach (+16 percent versus +23 percent).

3. If the common doubles, the convertible will provide the same return as in a steady interest rate environment (+70 percent) but the balanced approach will do much better (+73 percent compared to +58 percent from Table B-1).

CLOSING A CONVERTIBLE POSITION VIA THE CONVERSION PROCESS

The limited liquidity for convertible securities works to the investor's advantage since institutional money managers are forced to use the larger markets in stocks and straight bonds. This helps to create undervalued opportunities like those illustrated throughout this book, but it also means that at times a necessary order execution at a fair price may simply be impossible. There are ways to deal with this problem.

Convertible positions are usually closed out after a significant price advance, at which time the convertible is no longer an attractive low-risk alternative to its common stock. However, if the convertible is not actively traded, the best bid may be below its conversion value. Rather than sell at a discount, the most cost-effective method for closing the position often will be to exchange the convertible for common stock and sell the more actively traded common. In actual practice, the common stock usually is sold first, and the stock received later via the conversion process is used to offset the earlier sale.

When considering close out via the conversion process, here are the major factors to consider:

1. Accrued interest is lost when a bond is converted.

2. The capital to carry the position during the conversion period (usually about four weeks) will not be earning any return (90 percent may be released for other investments, but margin interest will be charged on the resulting debit balance).

3. Dividends must be paid if the stock declares a dividend during the conversion period and the record date falls within that conversion period.

4. Brokerage commissions will differ and should therefore be taken into account.

To illustrate these points, consider the XYZ Corp. 10s of 2010. Assume the common stock has risen to $40 per share on May 1 and a 10 bond position (equal to 400 shares) is to be closed out. At $40, the bond's conversion value is 160 ($40 × 40 shares = $1,600) but the best bid is only 155. Assume the bond pays its semiannual interest on June 1 ($50 for each bond) and the common stock declares a $.10 per share dividend to record holders as of May 10 (ex-dividend date is May 3).

Three possible courses of action should be considered: immediate bond sale at 155, sell 400 shares and convert immediately, or sell 400 shares and convert after the June 1 interest date. The arithmetic for evaluating these alternatives is shown in Table C-1.

From the analysis, the normal choice would be to convert after June 1. The extra $394 earned ($16,210 − $15,816) on the position for less than two additional months equates to an annualized rate of return above 15 percent.

Note that the 400 share sale prior to receiving common stock upon conversion is technically treated as a *short* sale. Some investors will not sell stock short for any reason (some institutions are legally prevented

Table C-1.Alternate Methods for Closing a Convertible Position

Immediate bond sale		
Sell 10 bonds at 155	=	$15,500
Accrued bond interest for five months	=	416
Commissions	=	(100)
Net proceeds on settlement date in one week	=	$15,816
Sell 400 shares and convert immediately		
Sell 400 common stock at $40	=	$16,000
Commissions	=	(250)
Net proceeds upon receipt of shares from conversion in about one month	=	$15,750
Sell 400 shares and convert on June 1		
Sell 400 common stock at $40	=	$16,000
Commissions	=	(250)
Dividends paid at $.10 per share	=	(40)
Bond interest received	=	500
Net proceeds upon receipt of shares from conversion in about two months		$16,210

from doing so). If you fit this prohibited category, rather than accept an abnormally low bid, ask your broker if his firm's arbitrage department would be willing to take the position into its inventory at a more favorable price. This question should be asked before opening an account since it is a close-out strategy that you will wish to employ frequently.

RESPONDING TO A CALL NOTICE

The calculations of Table C-1 assume that the bond had not been called; thus interest would be received on June 1. Most companies will call in their convertible bonds when they trade well above par and the usual 30 day notice is frequently timed to fall just prior to the interest payment date. In the example, if the company issued a call notice on April 30, with a May 30 expiration date, bondholders would be forced to convert to obtain the 160 conversion value, but they would not receive any interest. The usual close out procedure is to short the stock and immediately issue conversion instructions to the brokerage firm holding the bonds.

Since most convertible bondholders do not intend to retain common stock received on the exchange, a call notice increases the supply of stock available for sale in the marketplace. Therefore, expect to see a stock price drop when a call notice is issued—the extent of the decline will depend on the bond's size and how active the stock trades. Expecting downward price pressure during the 30-day conversion period, alert bondholders will often sell stock short within minutes after the call notice is announced. Be aware that the short sale is exempt from the uptick rule, so a market order identified as *short exempt* may be executed, if desired.

LARGE-CAP CONVERTIBLES PURCHASED, 1976-89

Background for the Noddings Large-Cap convertible bond index was first presented in the book, *The Investor's Guide to Convertible Bonds*.[1] The original selection parameters, in 1976, were convertible bonds and preferreds on common stocks rated B+ or higher by Standard & Poor's. Most were large capitalization companies listed on the New York Stock Exchange; but occasionally a higher-risk American Exchange or over-the-counter company would have a B+ rating and be included.

Beginning in 1984, the selection criteria was tightened up by excluding companies not listed on the New York Stock Exchange. This refine-

1. Thomas C. Noddings, *The Investor's Guide to Convertible Bonds*. Homewood, Illinois, Dow Jones-Irwin, 1982.

ment was implemented to realize the goal of an index truly reflective of the high-quality convertible market sector. Simultaneously, the rapidly expanding convertible bond market provided increased opportunities for portfolio diversification, allowing the deletion of higher-risk convertible preferreds from the index. These improved selection parameters and updated performance data were presented in the book, *Low Risk Strategies for the High Performance Investor.*

In 1987, as more and more large companies chose to remain on the NASDAQ trading system, additional improvements were effected by replacing the New York Stock Exchange listing requirement with an equity-capitalization parameter. The quality criteria was also updated from Standard & Poor's common stock ratings to their bond ratings. The index currently includes convertible bonds rated BB– or better by Standard & Poor's (or Value Line and Moodys investment grade equivalents) and issued by companies having above $500 million in equity market capitalization (stock price times number of shares outstanding).

Company	Convertible Description	Purchase Data		Sale Data	
		Q-Yr	Price	Q-Yr	Price
Chase Manhattan	4.875-93	——	61.00	2-76	68.25
Federal Nat'l. Mtg.	4.375-96	——	77.75	1-76	82.00
Gulf & Western	5.500-93	——	82.00	1-76	95.50
Tesoro Petroleum	5.250-89	——	82.75	1-77	102.00
United technologies	4.500-92	——	66.50	2-76	88.25
International Tel. & Tel.	$ 2.25 pfd	——	41.00	1-76	45.00
Greyhound	6.500-90	1-76	82.25	3-76	90.75
Grace	6.500-96	2-76	94.12	4-76	99.50
Federal Nat'l. Mtg.	4.375-96	2-76	72.75	4-76	80.75
International Tel. & Tel.	$ 2.25 pfd	2-76	31.25	3-76	38.62
Woolworth	$ 2.20 pfd	3-76	35.00	4-76	37.50
Ford Motor	4.875-98	3-76	82.50	3-78	85.38
Gulf & Western	5.500-93	4-76	90.75	2-77	78.25
National Distillers	4.500-92	4-76	95.00	4-77	87.25
American Hoist	5.500-93	4-76	89.00	2-77	123.00
Continental Telephone	5.250-86	4-76	82.50	3-77	85.25
Beech Aircraft	4.750-93	4-76	81.00	4-77	96.00
Airco	3.875-87	4-76	96.00	2-77	105.00
U.V. Industries	5.750-93	4-76	81.25	3-78	94.71
North Amer. Philips	4.000-92	4-76	77.44	2-77	77.39
Hilton Hotels	5.500-95	4-76	85.50	2-77	87.00
Parker Hannifan	4.000-92	4-76	74.62	2-77	87.00
Storer Broadcasting	4.500-86	4-76	85.00	2-77	86.12
Federal Nat'l. Mtg.	4.375-96	4-76	85.75	3-78	99.00
GAF Corp.	$ 1.20 pfd	4-76	18.58	1-77	18.69
White Consolidated	5.500-93	1-77	101.50	2-77	106.50
City Investing	7.500-90	1-77	99.50	2-77	104.75
Zapata	4.750-88	1-77	77.91	3-77	70.94
Houston Industries	5.500-85	1-77	94.50	4-80	80.50
Citicorp	5.750-00	1-77	94.50	1-78	75.12
E-Systems	4.500-92	1-77	86.25	4-77	84.00
Melville	4.875-96	1-77	89.00	2-78	94.00
Tesoro Petroleum	5.250-89	1-77	94.00	3-77	80.00
Ogden	5.000-93	1-77	71.00	1-78	69.00
Sola Basic	4.500-92	1-77	90.12	2-77	120.00
Woolworth	$ 2.20 pfd	2-77	34.50	4-77	30.00
Dayco	6.250-96	2-77	93.00	3-79	100.00
Castle & Cooke	5.375-94	2-77	79.00	3-78	110.50
Harrah's	7.500-96	2-77	111.50	2-78	147.00
Lear Siegler	$ 2.25 pfd	2-77	41.00	1-78	37.75

Company	Convertible Description	Purchase Data		Sale Data	
		Q-Yr	Price	Q-Yr	Price
Texasgulf	$ 3.00 pfd	4-77	39.50	2-78	38.50
Hilton Hotels	5.500-95	4-77	86.75	2-78	115.00
Pennwalt	$ 1.60 pfd	4-77	23.50	3-78	24.38
Foremost McKesson	$ 1.80 pfd	4-77	28.83	2-78	34.25
Amerada Hess	$ 3.50 pfd	4-77	62.88	2-78	64.00
Gulf & Western	$ 2.50 pfd	4-77	30.25	2-78	34.00
Beech Aircraft	4.750-93	1-78	91.00	1-78	102.00
Chromalloy American	$ 5.00 pfd	1-78	63.00	2-78	92.79
Carrier	$ 1.86 pfd	1-78	27.75	2-78	34.50
Holiday Inns	$ 1.70 pfd	1-78	24.50	2-78	26.22
Humana	6.000-99	2-78	100.00	3-78	122.72
Textron	$ 1.40 pfd	2-78	23.50	2-78	26.66
GAF Corp.	$ 1.20 pfd	2-78	16.42	3-80	17.50
McDermott	$ 2.20 pfd	2-78	31.88	3-78	33.00
White Consolidated	5.500-92	2-78	90.50	2-78	91.00
Gulf & Western	5.500-93	2-78	84.50	1-80	105.00
City Investing	7.500-90	2-78	101.25	3-79	111.50
Wometco Enterprises	5.500-94	2-78	96.00	3-78	111.00
Household Finance	$ 2.50 pfd	2-78	32.50	2-80*	28.50
Zale	$ 0.80 pfd	2-78	13.38	3-78	14.38
Storer Broadcasting	4.500-86	3-78	90.55	2-79	111.50
Frueharf	5.500-94	3-78	76.50	2-79	83.00
Lone Star Industries	5.125-93	3-78	85.00	2-79	95.00
Carrier	$ 1.86 pfd	3-78	33.75	4-78	50.21
Rockwell International	4.250-91	3-78	78.48	1-79	80.75
Federal Nat'l. Mtg.	4.375-96	3-78	92.00	2-79	81.88
Host International	5.250-94	3-78	76.25	3-78	79.00
Chromalloy American	$ 5.00 pfd	3-78	77.25	1-79	76.33
Holiday Inns	$ 1.70 pfd	3-78	30.38	4-78	29.62
Woolworth	$ 2.20 pfd	3-78	30.00	2-79	42.00
Reserve Oil & Gas	$ 1.75 pfd	3-78	23.88	1-79	24.88
U.S. Gypsum	$ 1.80 pfd	3-78	29.50	3-79	32.00
Amfac	$ 1.00 pfd	3-78	12.75	4-79	14.25
Grace (W.R.)	6.500-92	3-78	96.50	4-78	100.50
Owens-Illinois	4.500-92	3-78	84.62	4-78	69.50
Bally Manufacturing	6.000-98	3-78	100.00	4-78	83.25
Amerada Hess	$ 3.50 pfd	3-78	66.58	4-78	63.00
TRW Corp.	$ 4.50 pfd	3-78	75.00	2-79	72.00
Brunswick	$ 2.40 pfd	4-78	33.88	4-78	28.25
Travelers	$ 2.00 pfd	4-78	35.25	1-79	39.50

Company	Convertible Description	Purchase Data Q-Yr	Price	Sale Data Q-Yr	Price
I.U. International	$ 1.36 pfd	4-78	14.00	2-79	14.88
Carrier	5.125-89	4-78	91.50	3-79	97.73
Textron	$ 2.08 pfd	1-79	28.50	1-80	31.62
INA Corp.	$ 1.90 pfd	1-79	22.75	3-80	31.25
Tandy	6.500-03	1-79	104.00	2-79	98.00
Bally Manufacturing	6.000-98	1-79	106.00	1-79	115.00
Amerada Hess	$ 3.50 pfd	1-79	57.50	1-79	62.00
Crocker National	$ 3.00 pfd	1-79	41.50	4-79	43.00
Brunswick	$ 2.40 pfd	1-79	28.50	2-81	34.75
Amax	$ 3.00 pfd	1-79	46.75	2-79	54.00
Arvin Industries	$ 2.00 pfd	1-79	25.00	2-81	25.78
International Tel. & Tel.	$ 4.00 pfd	2-79	46.00	3-80	48.97
FMC corp.	4.250-92	2-79	73.50	3-79*	76.12
Burlington Northern	5.250-92	2-79	89.00	2-79	105.00
Greyhound	6.500-90	2-79	88.00	4-80	80.00
Washington National	$ 2.50 pfd	2-79	38.50	3-79*	39.38
Armco Steel	$ 2.10 pfd	2-79	27.25	4-79	31.12
Carter Hawley Hale	$ 2.00 pfd	2-79	27.25	4-79	31.00
Pitney-Bowes	$ 2.12 pfd	2-79	29.00	2-80	38.00
Woolworth	$ 2.20 pfd	2-79	37.00	3-79*	40.50
Aluminum Co. America	5.250-91	3-79	95.25	1-80	112.00
Dayco	6.000-94	3-79	79.50	3-80	68.12
Insilco	$ 1.25 pfd	3-79	16.12	2-80*	17.00
Phillips-Van Heusen	5.250-94	3-79	64.00	3-79*	62.00
BanCal Tri-State	6.500-96	3-79*	81.25	2-80	99.12
Ford Motor	4.500-96	3-79*	68.50	4-79	55.38
Lone Star Industries	5.125-93	3-79*	95.00	4-79	96.00
North American Philips	4.000-92	3-79*	70.00	4-80	75.93
McDonnell Douglas	4.750-92	3-79*	91.00	4-79	95.00
Riegel Textile	5.000-93	3-79*	70.50	1-80	72.75
Walter, Jim	5.750-91	3-79*	87.50	1-80	81.75
SCM Corp.	5.500-88	3-79*	80.50	1-80	73.50
Amerace	$ 2.60 pfd	3-79*	43.25	4-79	44.25
Arcata	$ 2.16 pfd	3-79*	28.75	2-80	28.75
GK Technologies	$ 1.94 pfd	3-79*	27.25	4-79	28.38
RCA Corp.	$ 4.00 pfd	3-79*	54.00	1-80	51.00
United Technologies	$ 7.32 pfd	3-79*	111.00	4-79	114.00
Western Union	$ 4.90 pfd	3-79*	54.00	2-80*	59.00
Ford Motor	4.875-98	4-79	58.88	2-80	53.25
Cooper Industries	$ 2.90 pfd	4-79	37.25	2-80	41.25

Company	Convertible Description	Purchase Data Q-Yr	Price	Sale Data Q-Yr	Price
Reynolds Metals	4.500-91	1-80	71.92	2-80	69.00
Georgia Pacific	$ 2.24 pfd	1-80	31.75	3-82	24.50
RCA Corp.	$ 2.12 pfd	1-80	19.25	2-80	21.50
Gulf & Western	5.500-93	2-80	87.50	2-80*	100.00
Federal Nat'l. Mtg.	4.375-96	2-80	73.50	2-80	86.00
Foremost McKesson	6.000-94	2-80	75.00	2-80	88.00
McDonnell Douglas	4.750-92	2-80	93.25	4-80	110.00
Bally Manufacturing	6.000-98	2-80	95.00	3-80	107.00
Natomas	$ 4.00 pfd	2-80	58.50	2-80	64.75
United Technologies	$ 3.88 pfd	2-80	51.00	3-80	63.25
Crocker National	5.750-96	2-80	70.00	4-80	85.00
Owens-Illinois	4.500-92	2-80	82.00	1-81	96.00
FMC Corp.	4.250-92	2-80*	66.50	4-80	75.25
Tyco Laboratories	5.875-91	2-80*	89.25	3-80	113.77
Walter, Jim	5.750-91	2-80*	85.00	3-80	89.50
Phillips-Van Heusen	5.250-94	2-80*	55.75	3-80	64.00
RCA Corp.	$ 4.00 pfd	2-80*	50.00	3-80	57.25
Washington National	$ 2.50 pfd	2-80*	37.00	3-80	42.97
Bendix	$ 4.04 pfd	2-80*	41.00	3-80	44.75
Western Union	$ 4.60 pfd	2-80*	51.75	3-80	59.88
I.C. Industries	$ 3.50 pfd	3-80	40.94	3-80	46.12
Citicorp	5.750-00	3-80	66.90	2-81	69.00
Gulf United	9.250-05	3-80	100.25	2-81	98.75
RCA Corp.	$ 2.12 pfd	3-80	22.88	4-80	24.00
Reynolds Metals	4.500-91	4-80	71.25	3-81	66.00
Bally Manufacturing	6.000-98	4-80	85.62	2-81	101.50
Wang Labs	9.000-05	4-80	121.50	2-81	133.00
Household Finance	$ 2.50 pfd	4-80	25.75	1-81	27.38
Signal Companies	5.500-94	4-80	84.50	3-82	64.50
RCA Corp.	$ 2.12 pfd	1-81	22.50	4-80	16.25
Walter, Jim	5.750-91	1-81	74.00	3-81	73.50
Edwards, A.G.	10.500-06	1-81	103.42	2-82*	94.38
Moog	9.875-06	2-81	116.00	4-82	84.00
Dean Witter Reynolds	10.000-05	2-81	113.00	4-81	183.15
Storage Technology	10.250-00	2-81	119.00	4-81	149.50
Trinity Industries	10.000-06	2-81	100.50	2-82	71.00
Hutton, E.F.	9.500-05	2-81	109.00	2-83	159.89
U.S. Air	8.250-05	3-81	104.00	4-81*	80.00
Tiger International	8.625-05	3-81	0.00	1-82	49.00
Hospital Corp. of America	8.750-06	3-81	102.00	3-82	114.50

Company	Convertible Description	Purchase Data		Sale Data	
		Q-Yr	Price	Q-Yr	Price
Nat'l. Medical Enterprises	9.000-06	3-81	74.00	4-81	86.20
Holiday Inns	9.625-05	3-81	116.50	4-81*	138.00
Oak Industries	11.000-00	3-81	110.00	4-81	135.00
Ralston Purina	5.750-00	4-81	74.00	1-82	83.50
Merrill Lynch	9.250-00	4-81	103.60	4-82	150.50
Allied Chemical	7.750-00	4-81	84.00	3-82	74.00
RCA Corp.	$ 4.00 pfd	4-81	40.44	1-82	44.00
Nat'l. Medical Enterprises	9.000-06	4-81	80.00	2-82	74.50
Reading & Bates	$ 2.12 pfd	4-81	33.00	1-82	21.82
Ashland Oil	$ 3.96 pfd	4-81	38.25	3-82	33.00
Motorola	9.125-01	4-81*	87.00	2-82	105.00
Hercules	6.500-99	4-81*	73.00	1-82	73.16
MGIC Corp.	5.000-93	4-81*	80.00	1-82	83.36
Inexco Oil	8.500-00	4-81*	103.25	1-83	70.00
Budd Company	9.000-05	1-82	112.50	1-82	123.40
Bally Manufacturing	6.000-98	1-82	93.00	3-82	111.00
Research-Cottrell	10.500-06	1-82	99.50	2-82*	86.00
General Dynamics	$ 4.25 pfd	1-82	55.31	2-82	67.00
Storage Technology	9.000-01	1-82	100.12	1-83	95.00
Alexander & Alexander	11.000-07	1-82	86.00	2-82	90.25
Heublein	4.500-97	1-82	58.25	4-82	81.50
Mapco	10.000-05	1-82	85.15	3-82	86.08
Oak Industries	10.500-02	1-82	102.00	4=82	75.00
Pogo Producing	8.000-05	2-82	86.50	1-83	82.50
American Medical Int'l.	9.500-01	2-82	89.25	4-83	113.50
RCA Corp.	$ 4.00 pfd	2-82	50.00	4-82	61.00
McDermott	$ 2.20 pfd	2-82	25.00	4-82	23.50
Viacom International	$ 2.10 pfd	2-82	31.67	2-82*	28.50
Toys R Us	9.250-07	2-82	120.00	4-82	143.07
Lifemark	9.000-05	2-82	114.50	2-82*	112.50
Mapco	10.000-05	3-82	84.00	4-82	88.25
Lifemark	9.000-05	3-82	104.50	3-82	115.50
Georgia Pacific	5.250-96	3-82	64.00	4-82	83.00
Bendix	$ 4.04 pfd	3-82	43.81	3-82	47.23
General American Oil	8.500-05	3-82	94.00	1-83	107.00
Bally Manufacturing	10.000-06	3-82	97.75	1-83	99.25
Becton Dickinson	4.125-88	4-82	88.00	4-82	95.00
Storer Broadcasting	8.500-05	4-82	87.00	4-82	96.00
Rowan Companies	$ 2.44 pfd	4-82	30.00	1-83	36.12
Merrill Lynch	8.875-07	4-82	115.00	1-83	128.00

Company	Convertible Description	Purchase Data		Sale Data	
		Q-Yr	Price	Q-Yr	Price
Viacom International	9.250-07	4-82	112.00	1-83	116.00
Wang Labs	9.500-05	4-82	116.00	1-83	139.75
Greyhound	6.500-90	4-82	97.00	1-83	116.86
Paine Webber	8.000-07	4-82	99.00	4-86*	107.00
Nat'l. Medical Enterprises	9.000-06	4-82	107.50	1-83	118.74
Comcast	12.000-96	1-83	108.50	3-83	130.91
Community Psychiatric	11.000-91	1-83	120.00	2-83	158.00
Becton Dickinson	4.125-88	1-83	92.00	2-83	100.50
Mapco	9.000-03	1-83	99.00	2-83	107.13
Lifemark	11.000-02	1-83	116.00	2-83	143.59
Storage Technology	9.000-01	1-83	92.50	2-83	94.50
Bally Manufacturing	6.000-98	1-83	90.00	3-83*	91.00
Walter, Jim	9.000-07	1-83	111.00	2-83	124.57
Goodrich, B.F.	$ 3.12 pfd	1-83	33.75	2-83	34.88
Rowan Companies	$ 2.44 pfd	1-83	36.00	2-83	40.75
Nat'l. Medical Enterprises	12.625-01	1-83	117.50	3-84	108.25
Searle, G.D.	5.250-89	2-83	90.00	3-83	117.00
Quaker State Oil	8.875-08	2-83	106.00	3-86	127.70
MacMillan	8.750-08	2-83	108.50	2-83	124.00
Data Design Labs	12.250-00	2-83	130.50	4-83	125.00
Research-Cottrell	10.500-06	2-83	115.00	1-84	106.20
CPT Corp.	10.000-01	2-83	118.00	4-83	88.50
Comdisco	8.000-03	2-83	102.00	1-84	62.75
Pogo Producing	8.000-05	2-83	80.25	1-85	69.00
Zenith Radio	8.375-05	3-83	128.50	3-83	147.85
Newell Companies	8.750-03	3-83	92.00	2-86	158.33
Leggett & Platt	8.125-01	3-83	111.50	4-85	134.00
Allied Corp.	7.750-05	3-83*	103.12	1-85	107.75
Allied Stores	9.500-07	3-83*	132.00	4-84	137.00
American Maize Products	11.750-00	3-83*	113.00	4-83	111.88
American General	11.000-07	3-83*	126.00	4-84	144.00
Barnett Banks of Florida	12.250-06	3-83*	137.50	4-84	128.88
Celanese	9.750-06	3-83*	113.50	1-85	127.50
Chase Manhattan	6.500-96	3-83*	84.00	3-85	109.00
Conserv	11.000-07	3-83*	80.00	4-83	62.00
Equitable Gas	9.500-06	3-83*	125.25	1-84	139.00
GTE Corp.	10.500-07	3-83*	114.00	2-86	110.87
Lifemark	13.000-01	3-83*	123.00	3-84	164.08
Seagram Company	8.250-08	3-83*	106.25	4-85	115.23
United Telecommunications	5.000-93	3-83*	82.12	2-85	80.35

Company	Convertible Description	Purchase Data		Sale Data	
		Q-Yr	Price	Q-Yr	Price
Walter, Jim	5.750-91	3-83*	88.00	1-86	151.43
Transtechnology	9.000-03	3-83*	99.50	4-83	98.00
McKesson	9.750-06	4-83	103.00	3-86	147.38
Reynolds, R.J.	10.000-08	4-83	112.25	1-85	137.50
Merrill Lynch	8.875-07	4-83	128.50	2-86	129.06
Moran Energy	8.750-08	4-83	95.25	1-86	73.00
Nat'l. Convenience Stores	9.000-08	1-84	103.00	2-86*	97.00
Viacom International	9.250-07	1-84	114.62	1-85	127.00
Southwest Airlines	10.000-07	2-84	124.00	2-85	150.50
SCOA Industries	10.000-07	2-84	102.55	3-85	134.38
Inexco Oil	8.500-00	2-84	83.45	1-85	65.50
Burlington Industries	5.000-91	2-84	80.38	4-84	76.00
Nat'l. Medical Enterprises	9.000-06	3-84	109.25	2-87	114.29
Westinghouse	9.000-09	3-84	100.75	2-86	182.46
Nortek	10.500-04	3-84	104.00	4-86	106.68
Allied Stores	8.750-09	4-84	109.50	3-86	183.98
Grumman	9.250-09	1-85	96.50	2-86*	109.00
Tracor	9.000-07	1-85	111.75	4-86*	107.00
ARX Inc.	9.375-05	1-85	100.00	2-86*	114.00
USAir Group	8.750-09	1-85	119.00	3-87	140.22
Freeport-McMoran	10.500-14	1-85	96.78	3-86	101.05
Lomas & Nettleton	9.000-10	2-85	100.00	3-87*	113.50
Sealed Power	9.000-00	2-85	100.00	4-86*	108.88
Torchmark	7.750-10	2-85	100.00	2-87	106.35
Great Northern Nekoosa	9.500-13	2-85	111.00	2-86	136.14
BASIX Corp.	8.750-05	3-85	105.50	2-86*	111.25
Perry Drug Stores	8.500-10	3-85	100.00	2-86*	126.00
Alaska Air Group	9.000-03	3-85	118.12	4-86*	115.75
Computer Sciences	6.000-04	4-85	103.00	1-86	129.37
American Medical Int'l.	9.500-01	4-85	103.00	2-86	104.00
Limited Inc.	7.500-10	4-85	99.25	2-86	152.19
RCA Corp.	4.500-92	4-85	95.50	2-86	115.29
Toys R Us	8.000-10	4-85	110.50	2-88	138.00
Comdisco	8.000-03	1-86	100.25	1-87	114.57
Sperry Corp.	7.625-11	1-86	107.00	2-86	121.50
Wendy's Int'l.	7.250-11	1-86	108.50	4-87	71.00
Grow Group	8.500-06	1-86	101.00	2-86*	106.00
Bearings	8.500-09	2-86	110.92	4-86*	106.25
Carson Pirie Scott	7.500-11	2-86	110.50	4-86*	110.00
Heinz (H.J.)	7.250-15	2-86	127.00	3-87*	140.63

Company	Convertible Description	Purchase Data Q-Yr	Price	Sale Data Q-Yr	Price
Macmillan	7.500-10	2-86	129.50	2-87	141.63
Merrill Lynch	8.875-06	2-86	94.21	4-86*	99.46
National Education	6.500-11	2-86	100.00	4-86*	97.00
Burroughs	7.250-10	3-86	109.25	4-86*	110.00
Hercules	8.000-10	3-86	135.00	2-89	109.00
Alco Standard	8.500-10	4-86	114.00	3-87	126.43
Corroon & Black	7.500-05	4-86	129.81	2-89	120.00
Flowers Industries	8.250-05	4-86	117.29	2-89	119.50
Int'l. Business Machines	7.875-04	4-86	113.38	2-87	120.77
Mobile Corp.	10.500-08	4-86	120.11	2-88	112.19
Standard Brands Paint	8.375-05	4-86	109.25	4-86*	109.00
Bank of New York	8.250-10	4-86*	125.00	2-89	123.17
Beverly Enterprises	0.000-03	4-86*	27.75	4-87	27.50
Bowater	9.000-09	4-86*	118.50	1-87	140.25
Harcourt, Brace	6.375-11	4-86*	111.50	2-87	164.00
Hechinger Co.	8.500-09	4-86*	125.25	3-87	167.85
Loral Corp.	7.250-10	4-86*	113.75		
Merrill Lynch	0.000-06	4-86*	23.75	1-88	24.00
NWA Inc.	7.500-10	4-86*	118.25	3-87	125.00
Paine Weber	8.250-05	4-86*	103.00	2-87	109.04
Service Corp.	6.500-11	4-86*	113.50	2-89	98.50
Staley Continental	0.000-88	4-86*	34.25	3-87	36.50
Unisys	7.250-10	4-86*	117.25	2-87	149.38
Heileman Brewing	0.000-03	1-87	32.36	3-87*	46.00
Masco	5.250-12	1-87	100.00	3-87*	97.00
Corning Glass	6.500-05	2-87	132.00	3-87*	148.75
Cray Research	6.125-11	2-87	127.33	3-87*	123.00
Federal Co. (Holly Farms)	6.000-17	2-87	100.00	1-89	103.00
Witco Corp.	5.500-12	2-87	101.00		
Zenith Electronics	6.250-11	2-87	112.00		
Browning Ferris	6.250-12	3-87	101.75	2-89	100.50
Stevens (J.P.)	6.000-12	3-87	105.00	1-88	120.00
Dana Corp.	5.875-06	3-87*	109.00	1-88	93.00
General Instrument	7.250-12	3-87*	133.00	2-88	102.50
Hechinger Co.	5.500-12	3-87*	104.00		
Insilco	9.000-10	3-87*	136.00	2-88	117.00
Lomas & Nettleton	7.000-11	3-87*	90.00	4-88	72.00
Norton Co.	7.750-12	3-87*	124.50		
Potlatch	5.750-12	3-87*	98.50	2-88	88.50
Circle K	8.250-05	4-87	93.75	2-88	121.00

Company	Convertible Description	Purchase Data		Sale Data	
		Q-Yr	Price	Q-Yr	Price
Emhart	6.750-10	4-87	92.50	1-89	85.50
First Wachovia	8.750-12	4-87	108.00	2-88	106.50
Johnson Controls	8.500-15	4-87	116.00	4-88	135.11
Kerr McGee	7.250-12	4-87	98.00		
CBS	5.000-02	1-88	89.00		
International Paper	5.875-12	1-88	91.50		
Prime Computer	5.750-12	1-88	75.50	3-89	70.00
Rorer Group	7.750-13	1-88	107.50	4-88	118.89
American Brands	7.750-02	2-88	101.25		
Comcast Corp.	5.500-11	2-88	115.00	4-88	115.50
Freeport-McMoran	8.750-13	2-88	100.25		
Ogden Corp.	6.000-93	2-88	88.50		
Potlach	5.750-12	2-88	82.00	3-89	93.00
Texaco	11.750-10	2-88	111.25	2-89	107.75
Zayre Corp.	7.250-10	2-88	82.00	2-89	92.81
Dana Corp.	5.875-06	3-88	88.50		
General Instrument	7.250-12	3-88	98.50		
Home Federal S&L	6.500-11	3-88	82.50		
Mead Corp.	6.750-12	3-88	101.50		
Prime Motor Inns	6.625-11	3-88	101.75		
American Brands	5.375-03	4-88	118.50	4-88	119.00
Goodyear Tire & Rubber	6.875-03	4-88	90.50	1-89	85.50
Masco Corp.	5.250-12	4-88	79.00	2-89	88.75
Rohr Industries	7.000-12	4-88	91.00	2-89	97.25
Anadarko Petroleum	5.750-12	1-89	96.50	3-89	112.50
CBI Industries	7.000-11	1-89	95.62		
Grace, W.R.	7.000-01	1-89	114.50		
Int'l. Lease Finance	5.750-01	1-89	107.25		
National Education	6.500-11	1-89	98.00		
Texas Eastern	12.000-05	1-89	115.75	1-89	125.00
Comsat International	7.750-98	2-89	101.00		
Fleming Cos.	6.500-96	2-89	102.00		
Humana	8.500-09	2-89	102.25		
Lafarge	7.000-13	2-89	96.13		
Newmont Mining (Galactic)	7.000-95	2-89	85.00		
Omnicom Group	7.000-13	2-89	103.25		
Oryx Energy	7.500-14	2-89	104.50		
Bruno's	6.500-09	3-89	100.12		
Federal Express	5.750-11	3-89	95.00		
Masco Corp.	5.250-12	3-89	83.50		

Company	Convertible Description	Purchase Data Q-Yr	Price	Sale Data Q-Yr	Price
Southeast Banking	4.750-97	3-89	103.25		
Union Carbide	7.500-12	3-89	98.50		
Anadarko Petroleum	7.000-04	4-89	114.25		
Avnet	6.000-12	4-89	82.00		
Berkshire Hathaway	0.000-04	4-89	44.25		
Boise Cascade	7.000-12	4-89	105.50		
International Paper	5.875-12	4-89	95.00		
USX Corp.	5.750-01	4-89	77.00		

*This table presents convertibles purchased for the author's most diversified managed accounts beginning late 1975. Where an account was replaced by a new, more diversified account, end of the quarter prices were used to close out an older convertible not held by the new account or to establish starting prices for convertibles held by the new account not held by the former.

MEDIUM-CAP CONVERTIBLES PURCHASED, 1976-89

The background for the Noddings Medium-Cap convertible bond index was first presented in the book, *The Investor's Guide to Convertible Bonds*. The original selection parameters, in 1976, were convertible bonds and preferreds on common stocks rated below B+ by Standard & Poor's. Most were small- to medium-sized companies listed on the New York or American Stock Exchange.

Beginning in 1984, the selection criteria was changed to include B+ rated companies not listed on the New York Stock Exchange. At the same time, the rapidly expanding convertible bond market provided increased opportunities for portfolio diversification, allowing the deletion of higher-risk convertible preferreds from the index. These improvements and updated performance data were presented in the book, *Low Risk Strategies for the High Performance Investor.*

In 1987, a major change was effected by adding an equity-capitalization parameter. The Medium-Cap index currently includes convertible bonds rated CCC or better by Standard & Poor's (or Value Line and Moodys investment grade equivalents) and issued by companies from $100 to $500 million in equity market capitalization (stock price times number of shares outstanding). Convertibles under $100 million capitalization were switched into a new Small-Cap index.

Company	Convertible Description	Purchase Data Q-Yr	Price	Sale Data Q-Yr	Price
Pan American	7.500-98	——	78.00	2-76	92.75
Occidental Petroleum	$ 3.60 pfd	——	46.88	2-76	57.25
El Paso	6.000-93	1-76	83.00	1-77	93.00
Avco	9.625-01	3-76	103.50	4-76	160.50
Pan American	7.500-98	3-76	76.25	1-77	76.88
Riegel Textile	5.000-93	4-76	77.50	2-78	80.00
Budd Company	5.875-94	4-76	91.88	1-78	142.00
Wallace Murray	6.500-91	4-76	100.00	1-77	118.00
Grumman	4.250-92	1-77	61.50	2-77	69.75
Oak Industries	4.375-87	2-77	70.00	2-77	72.00
Avco	9.625-01	2-77	114.50	3-78	160.50
Pan American	7.500-98	2-77	88.50	3-78	120.00
Arvin Industries	$ 2.00 pfd	2-77	28.00	2-78	33.40
Curtiss Wright	$ 2.00 pfd	2-77	27.25	4-77	26.00
Grumman	8.000-99	3-77	111.00	2-78	109.25
National City Lines	5.500-88	4-77	70.00	3-78	60.00
Republic N.Y.	5.375-97	4-77	74.50	3-78	91.00
Cooper Laboratories	4.500-92	4-77	66.50	3-79*	63.50
Kaiser Cement	$ 2.50 pfd	1-78	34.62	3-78	50.00
Western Airlines	5.250-93	2-78	80.00	2-78	104.00
Allegheny Airlines	9.250-99	2-78	131.00	2-78	182.00
Phoenix Steel	6.000-87	2-78	84.00	1-79	70.00
TRE Corp.	9.750-02	2-78	124.88	3-78	126.00
General Instrument	10.250-96	2-78	124.50	3-78	132.75
Eastern Airlines	10.000-02	2-78	123.50	3-78	137.00
Mohawk Data Sciences	12.000-89	3-78	126.00	3-78	124.00
Litton Industries	3.500-87	3-78	70.00	2-80*	115.00
Ramada Inns	10.000-00	3-78	126.00	3-78	159.00
Kaiser Cement	$ 1.38 pfd	3-78	19.50	3-79	22.50
McDonnell Douglas	4.750-91	3-78	118.00	1-79	114.00
Pan American	9.875-96	4-78	117.00	4-78	122.50
Western Airlines	5.250-93	4-78	84.00	3-79	95.00
Ramada Inns	10.000-00	4-78	117.00	2-79	173.50
Di Giorgio	5.750-93	4-78	74.50	1-79	82.00
El Paso	6.000-93	4-78	90.25	1-79	102.00
LTV Corp.	$ 2.60 pfd	1-79	24.38	2-80	29.50
Punta Gorda Isles	$ 1.10 pfd	2-79	11.75	3-79*	12.88
Texasgulf	$ 3.00 pfd	2-79	41.50	4-79	50.25
Conn. General Mortgage	6.000-96	3-79	81.00	4-80	93.00
Grumman	8.000-99	3-79	102.00	1-80	142.00

Company	Convertible Description	Purchase Data Q-Yr	Price	Sale Data Q-Yr	Price
NFC Corp.	8.000-92	3-79*	93.50	4-80	122.75
Trans World	5.000-94	3-79*	58.00	2-80	44.00
UAL Corp.	4.250-92	4-79	55.00	4-81	40.00
Western Airlines	5.250-93	4-79	75.00	4-79	93.00
Sherwin Williams	6.250-95	4-79	71.00	2-80	73.00
Fairmont Foods	9.000-96	4-79	94.62	2-80	106.00
Phoenix Steel	6.000-97	1-80	65.00	2-80	65.00
National Kinney	5.250-97	1-80	44.00	3-80	39.38
Sanders Associates	7.000-92	1-80	76.50	2-80	82.50
Mattel	$ 2.50 pfd	1-80	20.00	2-80	23.25
Ramada Inns	10.000-00	2-80	109.50	2-81	141.90
Ozark Air Lines	5.250-86	2-80	64.75	2-81	130.64
LTV Corp.	12.000-05	2-80	101.50	1-81	198.35
Cooper Laboratories	4.500-92	2-80*	64.75	4-80	84.60
Warnaco	$ 1.50 pfd	2-80*	29.25	1-81	36.55
Grumman	11.000-00	3-80	117.00	2-82*	123.75
Allegheny Ludlum	4.000-81	3-80	95.80	3-80	100.00
American Airlines	5.250-98	4-80	48.94	1-81	55.50
Zenith Radio	8.375-05	4-80	102.00	3-83	160.09
Energy Resources	9.000-95	4-80	103.80	2-83	92.24
U.S. Realty Investment	5.750-89	4-80	75.82	2-81	88.48
Ampex	5.500-94	4-80	77.50	4-80	84.50
Western Union	$ 4.60 pfd	4-80	56.25	4-81	58.04
Inexco Oil	8.500-00	4-80	119.50	4-81*	103.25
Crystal Oil	11.375-00	1-81	112.58	1-81	150.00
Computer Sciences	6.000-94	1-81	83.00	2-82	66.00
Prime Computer	10.000-00	1-81	130.00	1-81	112.50
Macrodyne	12.500-95	1-81	108.00	4-81*	82.00
Newbery Energy	12.000-95	1-81	87.00	3-82	55.00
Columbia Pictures	8.250-00	1-81	104.00	4-81*	113.12
Vishay Intertechnology	11.000-00	1-81	88.00	3-83	134.14
Instrument Systems	12.000-99	1-81	94.25	3-81	79.50
Eastern Airlines	11.750-05	2-81	96.62	1-82	70.00
Recognition Equipment	11.000-06	2-81	115.00	3-82	58.00
Transtechnology	12.500-01	2-81	98.00	2-83	186.09
GAF Corp.	$ 1.20 pfd	2-81	15.75	2-81	18.94
MGM Grand Hotels	9.500-00	2-81	79.23	3-82	62.31
Energy Management	12.000-96	2-81	104.00	2-82*	72.00
Sanders Associates	7.000-92	2-81	107.00	4-82	104.60
Health Chem	10.375-99	2-81	102.75	3-82	67.67

Company	Convertible Description	Purchase Data Q-Yr	Price	Sale Data Q-Yr	Price
TIE Communications	11.500-01	2-81	114.00	4-82	142.65
Punta Gorda Isles	6.000-92	2-81	73.50	2-82	54.00
Fuqua Industries	5.750-88	2-81	75.00	1-82	99.00
Trans World	12.000-05	2-81	113.00	4-81	96.00
Prime Computer	10.000-05	2-81	124.00	4-81	103.00
PSA Inc.	11.125-04	3-81	108.50	3-82	105.00
Ramada Inns	10.000-00	3-81	108.50	2-83	138.25
National Education	9.875-00	3-81	103.62	4-82	131.62
Tacoma Boatbuilding	10.750-01	3-81	95.50	1-82	103.22
Fairfield Communities	9.750-03	3-81	107.08	4-82	123.53
Crystal Oil	11.375-00	3-81	104.50	1-85	64.00
Galaxy Oil	9.000-94	4-81	100.00	4-81*	96.50
Brunswick	10.000-06	4-81	99.00	3-82	114.86
Pogo Producing	8.000-05	4-81	82.00	4-81*	85.00
Four-Phase Systems	9.125-01	4-81	91.12	4-81*	87.00
Lynch Communications	8.500-99	4-81*	70.00	2-82*	64.00
Zayre	5.750-94	4-81*	72.00	2-82	78.00
U.S. Air	8.250-06	4-81*	80.00	3-82	100.00
Williams Companies	11.000-96	4-81*	97.25	2-83	98.50
Dorchester Gas	8.500-05	2-82	70.68	2-82*	64.00
Trans World	12.000-05	2-82	107.00	2-82*	105.00
Brunswick	10.000-06	2-82	94.00	2-83	186.28
Mattel	$ 2.50 pfd	2-82	35.75	4-82	45.00
Tiger International	8.625-05	2-82	49.00	4-82	52.00
Galaxy Oil	9.000-94	2-82*	62.50	4-82	52.62
Anacomp	9.500-00	3-82	94.25	4-82	117.50
Lynch Communications	8.500-99	3-82	61.50	4-82	72.00
Trans World	5.000-94	3-82	46.00	4-82	50.50
Dorchester Gas	8.500-00	3-82	63.50	4-82*	66.00
Comdisco	13.000-01	4-82	125.50	4-82	136.54
Lifestyle Rest. (Beefsteak)	13.000-97	4-82	103.00	2-86	82.00
U.S. Air	9.250-07	4-82	106.00	1-85	127.27
Financial Corp. of Amer.	11.500-02	4-82	110.25	2-83	189.19
Rohr Industries	$ 3.12 pfd	4-82	31.75	4-82*	31.00
Integrated Resources	$ 3.07 pfd	4-82	31.25	4-82	38.50
Western Union	5.250-97	4-82	78.75	4-82	78.10
Horn & Hardart	11.250-00	4-82	112.50	4-82	117.50
NBI Communications	8.250-07	4-82	101.75	4-82	104.33
Delmed	10.500-02	4-82	101.75	4-82*	103.75
Anacomp	13.875-02	4-82*	117.50	1-83	146.96

Company	Convertible Description	Purchase Data Q-Yr	Price	Sale Data Q-Yr	Price
Mobile Communications	12.000-02	4-82*	148.00	1-85	144.90
Tacoma Boatbuilding	10.750-01	4-82*	136.00	1-83	145.43
Trans World	12.000-05	4-82*	126.00	2-83	151.54
Athlone Industries	11.375-01	1-83	100.00	2-83	140.54
Western Airlines	5.250-93	1-83	69.00	2-83	73.15
Volt Info Sciences	12.125-01	1-83	124.00	2-83	134.97
Saveway Industries	9.750-00	1-83	122.00	2-83	146.41
Mor-Flo Industries	14.000-01	1-83	130.30	2-83	160.79
Delmed	10.500-02	1-83	109.60	2-83	112.66
Southwest Forest Industries	10.000-03	1-83	98.00	1-84	137.50
PSA Inc.	11.125-04	2-83	118.75	2-84	99.36
Andersen Group	10.500-02	2-83	120.00	1-86	98.00
Gulfstream Land	14.375-01	2-83	128.25	3-83	143.61
MGM Grand	9.500-00	2-83	86.00	1-86	102.50
Inter-Regional Financial	11.500-02	2-83	120.00	3-84	67.00
Recognition Equipment	11.000-06	2-83	115.00	2-85	100.00
Delmed	10.500-02	2-83	115.36	4-84	51.00
Crime Control	10.000-97	2-83	112.00	2-86	67.00
Computer Consoles	7.750-98	2-83	118.00	1-86	65.00
Punta Gorda Isles	6.000-92	3-83	75.94	1-84	67.23
Eastern Air Lines	11.750-05	3-83	101.43	3-83	88.78
Dorchester Gas	8.500-05	3-83	78.75	1-84	78.00
Anacomp	13.875-02	3-83	112.92	3-84	55.00
Bowmar Instruments	13.500-95	3-83	116.72	1-84	94.58
Global Marine	18.000-03	3-83	94.50	1-84	89.89
Singer Company	9.000-02	3-83	99.00	4-83	96.00
Graphic Scanning	10.000-01	3-83	100.00	3-86	101.50
American Century	6.750-91	3-83	83.00	1-86	61.75
Prairie Producing	9.250-03	3-83	117.65	4-84	163.00
Brunswick	8.500-98	4-83	125.00	4-83	140.11
Pan American	15.000-98	4-83	133.81	1-84	163.64
Pulte Home	8.500-08	4-83	111.40	1-86	102.00
Lear Petroleum	9.000-03	4-83	83.50	1-84	93.45
American Maize Products	11.750-00	4-83	111.88	3-85	107.00
CPT Corp.	10.000-01	4-83	88.50	4-84	72.38
Data-Design Labs	12.250-00	4-83	125.00	3-84	120.00
Comserv	11.000-02	4-83	62.00	4-85	60.00
Western Airlines	14.000-98	1-84	105.00	4-84	89.00
Pan American	15.000-98	1-84	134.09	3-85	152.53
Koger Properties	9.250-03	1-84	91.00	3-84	87.00

Company	Convertible Description	Purchase Data Q-Yr	Price	Sale Data Q-Yr	Price
American Adventure	10.000-98	1-84	98.00	2-86	20.00
Carl Karcher Enterprises	9.500-07	1-84	111.00	2-85	100.00
Telepictures	10.000-02	2-84	107.50	2-85	155.83
Lear Petroleum	9.000-03	2-84	91.00	3-84	75.00
Southwest Forest Industries	10.000-03	2-84	108.00	1-86	104.00
Walker Telecommunications	11.000-99	2-84	99.50	4-86#	90.00
Rykoff-Sexton	12.000-01	3-84	129.00	3-84	151.26
Inter-Regional Financial	11.500-02	3-84	77.00	3-85	95.00
Anacomp	10.000-95	3-84	69.00	2-86	150.00
Jerrico	8.500-08	4-84	88.25	2-85	98.00
Delmed	10.500-97	4-84	55.00	1-85	55.60
Western Airlines	5.250-93	4-84	63.00	3-85	114.52
Delmed	10.500-97	1-85	60.00	2-86	87.52
Mobile Communications	11.000-04	1-85	122.65	2-86	153.62
Brown & Sharpe Mfg.	9.250-05	1-85	93.38	4-85	92.62
Bowater	9.000-09	1-85	108.00	1-86	122.00
Healthcare USA	8.250-03	1-85	99.00	2-86	76.00
Dixico	8.500-93	1-85	103.00	3-85	131.25
Inexco Oil	8.500-00	1-85	65.50	4-85	63.55
Bally Manufacturing	6.000-98	1-85	68.50	3-86	84.25
Great Western Financial	8.875-07	2-85	102.00	1-86	125.00
Cannon Group	9.000-09	2-85	111.00	1-86	143.74
Eastern Air Lines	11.500-99	2-85	76.65	2-85	82.50
Foothill Group	9.500-03	3-85	107.00	4-86#	94.00
Wedtech Corp.	13.000-04	3-85	113.50	3-86	103.50
Anthony Industries	11.250-00	3-85	102.05	4-86#	103.00
Compaq Computer	9.250-05	3-85	115.00	4-86	166.00
Coeur d'Alene Mines	9.500-05	3-85	108.00	4-85	107.75
Centronics Data	10.000-90	3-85	133.00	2-86	188.46
Astrex	9.500-00	3-85	103.50	4-86#	82.00
Comcast	9.500-09	3-85	136.50	1-86	158.02
Knoll International	8.125-03	4-85	97.75	1-86	115.00
Ozark Holdings	8.750-10	4-85	112.00	3-86	136.25
International Hydron	10.000-10	4-85	97.44	4-86#	99.00
Micron Technology	14.000-10	4-85	116.00	1-88	173.18
Triangle Industries	8.625-11	1-86	106.00	3-86	143.92
Lieberman Enterprises	7.625-05	1-86	120.50	4-86#	106.00
Vestron	9.000-11	1-86	108.00	4-86#	68.50
Ply-Gem Industries	10.000-99	1-86	130.00	3-86	111.76
Gibraltar Financial	9.250-08	2-86	109.75	4-87	70.50

Company	Convertible Description	Purchase Data Q-Yr	Price	Sale Data Q-Yr	Price
Apollo Computer	7.250-11	2-86	115.50	3-86	100.00
Comcast	8.250-10	2-86	131.50	4-86#	130.00
Datapoint	8.875-06	2-86	62.00	4-86	72.82
Cardinal Distribution	8.250-10	2-86	127.50	4-86#	110.00
Mobile Communications	9.000-01	2-86	136.00	3-86	167.00
Ampad	8.000-10	2-86	114.50	4-86#	103.00
Businessland	8.000-06	2-86	108.50	1-89	128.73
Conseco	7.500-06	2-86	127.50	4-86#	108.50
BSN Corp.	7.750-01	2-86	108.00	4-86#	109.50
Patten Corp.	7.250-01	3-86	112.45	1-87	198.25
Hazleton Labs	6.500-06	3-86	100.00	4-86#	104.00
NCA Corp.	10.250-01	3-86	102.00	4-86#	107.00
Durr-Fillauer Medical	8.500-10	3-86	108.00	4-86#	106.25
Energy Factors	8.250-05	3-86	104.00	4-86#	91.00
Network Security	8.000-11	3-86	94.50	4-86#	92.50
Chambers Development	8.000-96	3-86	110.00	2-87	192.30
Countrywide Credit	7.000-11	3-86	114.00	3-88	76.50
TS Industries	8.500-01	3-86	125.50	4-86#	136.00
CooperVision	8.625-05	3-86	95.25	4-88	63.11
Mayflower Group	7.875-06	4-86	95.50	4-86	97.50
Data Switch (T-Bar)	9.000-96	4-86	104.00	4-86#	137.50
PLM Cos.	8.500-96	4-86	109.00	4-86#	121.00
Salick Health Care	7.250-01	4-86	114.00	4-86#	116.00
Environmental Treatment	8.000-06	4-86	126.25	4-86#	129.00
Talley Industries	9.000-05	4-86	109.00		
Airborne Freight	7.500-11	4-86	105.50	3-88	84.38
Adobe Resources	8.750-11	4-86	110.25	2-87	145.09
Bally Manufacturing	6.000-98	4-86	90.00	4-86#	90.25
Medalist Industries	7.500-01	4-86	103.75	4-86#	112.00
Atlantic Research	8.000-08	4-86#	109.00	1-88	104.80
Carson Pirie Scott	7.500-11	4-86#	110.00	2-87	125.00
CCB Financial	8.750-10	4-86#	111.00	3-89*	111.50
Clayton Homes	7.750-01	4-86#	103.00	1-88	100.00
Coleco Industries	11.000-89	4-86#	100.00	4-87	56.50
Comprehensive Care	7.500-10	4-86#	85.50	1-87	82.75
Crane Co.	8.750-05	4-86#	127.00	1-87	141.48
Greenery Rehab Group	6.500-11	4-86#	100.50	2-88	63.00
Grow Group	8.500-06	4-86#	109.50		
Hudson Foods	8.000-06	4-86#	100.00	3-88	72.80
Jamesway	8.000-05	4-86#	106.50		

Company	Convertible Description	Purchase Data Q-Yr	Price	Sale Data Q-Yr	Price
Keystone International	8.500-05	4-86#	111.00	1-87	112.63
Knoll International	8.125-03	4-86#	74.00	1-87	77.50
Leggett & Platt	6.500-06	4-86#	100.25	4-89	100.00
Legg Mason	7.000-11	4-86#	102.00	1-88	70.00
Park Communications	6.875-11	4-86#	115.00	3-89	117.30
Pentair	9.000-10	4-86#	111.75	3-88	148.85
Ruddick	8.000-11	4-86#	107.00	1-88	102.31
Selective Insurance	8.750-08	4-86#	110.00	3-87	124.75
Southmark	8.500-98	4-86#	97.25	3-88	39.50
Standard Brands Paint	8.375-05	4-86#	109.00	4-87	106.70
Timeplex	7.750-08	4-86#	116.00	1-87	113.50
Williams (A.L.)	7.250-06	4-86#	89.50	1-89	82.50
American Fructose	7.500-01	1-87	125.00	3-89	168.29
Enzo Biochem	9.000-01	1-87	107.00	4-87	65.00
Genmar Industries	7.000-06	1-87	102.50	1-88	92.00
Bolt, Beranek/Newman	6.000-12	2-87	100.00	3-89*	51.75
NVRyan	10.000-02	2-87	101.12	1-89	81.00
Ohio Mattress	6.000-12	2-87	104.25	4-88	109.00
Pier 1	6.125-11	2-87	113.50	2-89	122.72
Pope & Talbot	6.000-12	2-87	99.50	2-89	100.00
Quixote	8.000-11	2-87	120.50	4-87	62.00
Richardson Electronics	7.250-06	2-87	112.00	3-88	102.00
SCI Systems	5.625-12	2-87	102.00	3-87	117.50
Thermo Electron	5.750-12	2-87	100.00	3-88	83.15
Trinity Industries	6.750-12	2-87	101.15	3-87	112.00
Essex Corp.	6.000-12	3-87	79.69	3-88	112.50
Guilford Mills	6.000-12	3-87	102.50	2-89	88.00
Hills Department Stores	8.750-02	3-87	104.00	2-88	96.50
Atari	5.250-02	4-87	57.00		
Apache Corp.	7.500-12	1-88	75.75	1-89	82.04
Horn & Hardart	7.500-07	1-88	87.75		
Ranger Oil	6.500-02	1-88	94.50		
SCI Systems	5.625-12	1-88	77.00	1-89	84.50
Texas Industries	9.000-08	1-88	101.25	2-88	113.50
Burnup & Sims	12.000-00	2-88	98.50		
EDO Corp.	7.000-11	2-88	85.00	3-89	55.50
Fieldcrest Cannon	6.000-12	2-88	65.75	3-88	73.00
Hadson Corp.	7.750-06	2-88	89.00		
Kaman Corp.	6.000-12	2-88	92.25		
Lone Star Technologies	8.000-02	2-88	95.50	2-88	92.75

Company	Convertible Description	Purchase Data Q-Yr	Price	Sale Data Q-Yr	Price
UNC Corp.	7.500-06	2-88	82.00	3-89	75.25
Air Wisconsin Service	7.750-10	3-88	86.00	4-89	85.37
Church & Dwight	6.500-11	3-88	83.00	2-89	92.50
CML Group	7.500-12	3-88	93.00		
Environmental Systems	6.750-11	3-88	62.40		
Hudson Foods	14.000-08	3-88	112.00		
RPM Inc.	5.750-01	3-88	92.50		
Sunshine Mining	8.875-08	3-88	99.56		
Thermedics	5.500-96	3-88	108.50	3-89	158.63
Chambers Development	7.000-97	4-88	104.50	2-89	125.58
Clayton Homes	6.000-07	4-88	79.00	3-89*	85.00
Mark IV Industries	7.000-11	4-88	70.00	3-89*	95.50
Olsten	7.000-12	4-88	93.00		
Robert Half Int'l.	7.250-12	4-88	95.00	4-89	93.00
Conner Peripherals	9.000-14	1-89	100.00		
Columbia First Federal	7.500-11	1-89	93.00	3-89*	91.00
Dixie Yarns	7.000-12	1-89	83.00	4-89	75.38
Hexcel Corp.	7.000-11	1-89	104.00	3-89*	88.75
Lionel	8.000-07	1-89	81.70	4-89	64.00
Mentor Corp.	6.750-02	1-89	84.50		
Plenum Publishing	6.500-07	1-89	87.00	2-89	90.50
Recognition Equipment	7.250-11	1-89	71.38	4-89	58.00
SCI Systems	3.000-01	1-89	111.50	4-89	109.75
Barris Industries	6.750-12	2-89	69.00	4-89	77.39
Copperweld	9.920-08	2-89	98.00		
Ingles Markets	9.000-08	2-89	103.75		
Perry Drug Stores	8.500-10	2-89	83.00	3-89	87.00
Watts Industries	7.750-14	2-89	108.00		
Webb, Del E.	10.375-09	2-89	92.00		
Alaska Air Group	7.750-10	3-89	104.00	3-89*	104.00
Diasonics	6.500-01	3-89	106.50		
Graphic Scanning	10.000-01	3-89	113.50		
Guilford Mills	6.000-12	3-89	83.75		
Immunex	7.500-01	3-89	87.25		
J.P. Industries	7.250-13	3-89	87.00		
Midway Airlines	8.500-02	3-89	124.56		
Pulte Home	8.500-08	3-89	92.38	3-89*	92.50
Universal Health	7.500-08	3-89	67.50		
USLICO Corp.	8.000-11	3-89	95.00	3-89*	95.00
PHM Corp.	8.500-08	3-89	92.38		

Company	Convertible Description	Purchase Data Q-Yr	Price	Sale Data Q-Yr	Price
Carolina Freight	6.250-11	3-89*	74.50	4-89	71.75
Clayton Homes	6.000-07	3-89*	85.00		
Vishay Intertechnology	4.750-03	3-89*	96.50		
Alaska Air	6.875-14	4-89	94.00		
Bally Manufacturing	6.000-98	4-89	77.00		
Inspiration Resources	8.500-12	4-89	99.50		
Kirby Exploration	7.750-14	4-89	100.00		
Mark IV Industries	7.000-11	4-89	98.50		
America West Air	11.500-09	4-89	109.75		

*This table presents convertibles purchased for the author's most diversified managed accounts beginning late 1975. Where an account was replaced by a new, more diversified account, end of the quarter prices were used to close out an older convertible not held by the new account or to establish starting prices for convertibles held by the new account not held by the former.

#Convertibles were deleted from the composite if they did not meet revised parameters on 12/31/86. Others were added as additional accounts were included in the composite.

Appendix F

SMALL-CAP CONVERTIBLES PURCHASED, 1987-89

A few small-company convertible bonds were included in the Medium-Cap index (Appendix E) from its inception in 1976; most were listed on the New York or American Stock Exchanges. As over-the-counter companies began issuing convertible bonds more frequently during the mid-1980s, these small issues began to dominate the Medium-Cap index's makeup. Beginning in 1987, companies under $100 million capitalization were assigned to a new index, the Noddings Small-Cap convertible bond index.

Company	Convertible Description	Purchase Data Q-Yr	Price	Sale Data Q-Yr	Price
Advanced Telecommunications	8.000-06	——	125.00	1-87	180.79
America West Airlines	7.750-10	——	95.25	1-89	73.50
Ampad	8.000-05	——	103.00	1-87	105.26
Anthony Industries	11.250-00	——	103.00	2-88	115.48
ARX Corp.	9.375-05	——	114.00	3-87	107.50
Astrex	9.500-00	——	82.00	3-87	55.00
BASIC Corp.	8.750-05	——	90.00	4-87	37.00
Bindley & Western	8.625-10	——	110.50	3-88	76.50
BSN Corp.	7.750-01	——	109.50	4-89	59.12
Builders Transport	8.000-05	——	100.00	3-87	99.25
Cardinal Distribution	8.250-10	——	110.00	1-89	120.88
Central Sprinkler	8.000-10	——	99.00	3-88	130.44
Conseco	7.500-06	——	108.50	1-89	106.00
Continental Info	9.000-06	——	111.50	4-88	34.50
Durr-Fillauer Medical	8.500-10	——	106.25	4-88	121.50
Energy Factors	8.250-05	——	91.00	3-87	73.50
Entertainment Marketing	8.500-06	——	98.00	1-87	139.00
Foothill Group	9.500-03	——	94.00		
Gruntal Financial	7.500-11	——	91.00	3-87	100.00
Hazelton Labs	6.500-06	——	104.00	1-87	132.00
International Hydron	10.000-10	——	99.00	4-87	110.30
Laser Industries	8.000-06	——	100.00	4-88	32.00
Lieberman Entertainment	7.625-05	——	106.00	4-88	115.28
Medalist Industries	7.500-01	——	103.50		
Nafco Financial Group	9.000-03	——	97.00	3-87	88.58
NCA Corp.	10.250-01	——	107.00	3-87	166.67
Network Security	8.000-11	——	92.50	4-87	125.00
New Century Entertainment	9.500-01	——	94.00	4-87	55.00
Owens & Minor	8.500-10	——	119.00	3-87	128.13
PLM Cos.	8.500-96	——	104.00		
Pueblo International	8.500-01	——	119.00	1-88	123.88
Salick Health Care	7.250-01	——	103.00		
TS Industries	8.500-01	——	136.00	2-87	138.13
View Master Ideal	6.875-06	——	98.50	3-88	39.00
Walker Telecommunications	11.000-99	——	90.00	4-87	65.00
Wessex	8.500-06	——	95.00	4-87	50.00
Atalanta Sosnoff	7.125-01	1-87	103.75	4-87	63.00
Bio Response	8.500-01	1-87	106.00	4-87	40.00
Biotechnica International	8.750-96	1-87	107.50	3-89	94.50
Graphic Industries	7.000-06	1-87	103.08		

Company	Convertible Description	Purchase Data Q-Yr	Price	Sale Data Q-Yr	Price
O'Brien Energy Systems	7.750-02	1-87	100.00	3-89	160.53
Park Electrochemical	7.250-06	1-87	112.38	2-89	88.96
Patrick Petroleum	8.000-97	1-87	95.00	2-89	131.25
Ramtek	10.250-02	1-87	100.00	2-88	24.00
Tridex Corp.	9.000-96	1-87	95.50	4-87	62.00
Varco International	10.000-07	1-87	100.00	3-87	219.00
AudioTronics	10.250-02	2-87	95.50	4-88	35.00
Biotechnology General	7.500-97	2-87	91.00	4-87	67.50
Chock Full O'Nuts	7.000-12	2-87	90.00		
Datarex Systems	8.500-02	2-87	100.50	3-88	121.55
Data Switch	8.250-02	2-87	104.00	4-88	95.00
Oakwood Homes	6.500-12	2-87	88.00	2-88	60.00
Spartech	9.000-99	2-87	100.00		
Tyco Toys	8.000-11	2-87	120.00	3-87	137.18
Zehntel	9.250-12	2-87	107.00	4-87	95.00
Bombay Palace	8.000-97	3-87	100.00	3-88	30.00
Carmike Cinemas	8.000-07	3-87	101.20		
Entertainment Marketing	8.500-06	3-87	107.50	4-88	39.50
Intermark	7.375-07	3-87	101.50		
On-Line Software	6.250-02	3-87	104.50	3-88	53.00
Porta Systems	9.250-00	3-87	95.00		
TPA America	10.000-06	3-87	104.00	2-88	47.00
Diagnostic/Retrieval	8.500-98	4-87	100.84	1-88	82.00
Helen of Troy	7.250-07	4-87	102.25	1-89	150.27
Hughes Supply	7.000-11	4-87	86.00	2-88	101.00
Marcade Group	12.500-99	4-87	100.00	3-88	90.00
Medical Imaging Centers	12.000-99	4-87	100.00	2-89	228.00
Nasta International	12.000-02	4-87	101.13		
Silicon Systems	8.500-10	4-87	111.00	2-89	138.00
Sikes Corp.	7.000-11	1-88	85.00	1-89	95.00
Sun Electric	8.000-06	1-88	99.50	1-89	126.90
AmVestors Financial	8.500-12	2-88	94.00	1-89	135.31
DEP Corp.	7.375-01	2-88	104.25	2-89	86.50
Trans-Lux	9.000-05	2-88	81.00		
Tridex Corp.	10.250-96	2-88	65.50		
Waxman Industries	6.250-07	2-88	101.00	2-89	94.00
GIANT Group	7.000-06	3-88	78.62		
Hughes Supply	7.000-11	3-88	95.00	3-89	105.25
Kurzweil Music Systems	12.000-00	3-88	100.00	4-89	50.00
Metro Airlines	8.500-12	3-88	100.00		

Company	Convertible Description	Purchase Data Q-Yr	Purchase Data Price	Sale Data Q-Yr	Sale Data Price
Stanley Interiors	7.000-12	3-88	71.00	4-88	70.00
Sudbury Inc.	7.500-11	3-88	71.00		
Thermo Environmental	6.000-96	3-88	101.38		
Traditional Industries	9.500-07	3-88	117.00		
Ben & Jerry's Homemade	9.500-07	4-88	105.62		
Data Switch (T-Bar)	9.000-96	4-88	98.00		
America West Airlines	11.500-09	1-89	110.00	4-89	109.75
Health Images	6.500-98	1-89	103.00		
AST Research	8.500-13	2-89	73.35		
Daisy Systems	9.000-14	2-89	73.00	4-89	26.50
Data-Design Labs	8.500-08	2-89	82.00		
Ducommun	7.750-11	2-89	53.38		
Jackpot Enterprises	8.750-14	2-89	108.50		
Marcade Group	12.500-99	2-89	96.50		
NEECO	7.750-12	2-89	75.75	4-89	84.67
Sterling Electronics	10.750-09	2-89	100.00		
Wyle Labs	6.250-02	2-89	71.62		
AMDURA	5.500-93	3-89	89.44	4-89	68.00
Conquest Exploration	9.500-14	3-89	100.00		
Howtek	9.000-01	3-89	83.00		
Lynch Corp.	8.000-06	3-89	99.00		
LTX Corp.	10.500-99	3-89	96.00		
Mgt. Co. Entertainment	14.000-09	3-89	130.30		
Renaissance GRX	9.000-96	4-89	100.00		

BASIC EQUITY OPTION STRATEGIES

There are seven basic investment strategies involving equity put and call options: three are bullish, three are bearish, and the neutral seventh is a direct alternative to money market instruments. Each of the seven strategies (listed below) involves the purchase or short sale of common stock (1, 2, . . .) while its alternative (1a, 2a, . . .) excludes the use of stock. Thus, each basic strategy offers two choices. In some cases the choice between the stock strategy and its alternative will be a toss-up; in other cases the risk-reward calculations, brokerage commissions, and income tax consequences will favor one over the other.

For the purpose of this discussion, it is assumed that the most bullish market strategy is the ownership of common stock (Strategy 1); the most bearish is the short sale of stock (Strategy 7). Options may be employed when constructing alternatives to these extremes, or for any risk-reward posture in between. Listed in order of the most bullish to the most bearish, the seven basic strategies are as follows:

Bullish Strategies

1.   Buy 100 shares of stock.
1a. Buy one call and sell one put.
2.   Buy 100 shares of stock and buy one put.
2a. Buy one call.
3.   Buy 100 shares of stock and sell one call.
3a. Sell one put.

Neutral Strategies

4.   Buy 100 shares of stock, buy one put, and sell one call.
4a. Buy Treasury bills.

Bearish Strategies

5.   Short 100 shares of stock and sell one put.
5a. Sell one call.
6.   Short 100 shares of stock and buy one call.
6a. Buy one put.
7.   Short 100 shares of stock.
7a. Buy one put and sell one call.

All other option tactics, such as straddles and spreads, may be analyzed by combining two or more of the basic strategies. The popular straddle sales and purchases are presented later as strategies 8a and 9a.

Before selecting a particular strategy, investors should construct a risk-reward analysis table and profit profile graph similar to the examples in the following pages. These basic tools, unused by most nonprofessional investors, identify a strategy's risk and profit potential.

Unfortunately, most investors who have lost money in "conservative" option strategies and wondered why were simply unaware of the risks they unknowingly assumed. Successful investing demands a thorough understanding of the risks involved.

The risk-reward calculations in the examples are based on certain assumptions that simplify the arithmetic.

- The common stock is trading at $30.
- The common stock pays a $0.15 quarterly dividend (2 percent annual yield).
- A six-month call option, having an exercise (strike) price of $30, is trading at $3.00 ($300 for each at-the-money call on 100 shares of stock), a 10 percent premium.
- A six-month put option, also having a $30 strike price, is trading at $2.12 ($212 for each at-the-money put on 100 shares of stock), a 7 percent premium.
- Each position, an investment of $3,000 based on 100 shares, is held until the options expire in six months.
- Options are assumed to be trading at their intrinsic values at expiration.
- Unused funds, or premiums received from option sales, are placed in Treasury bills (or other risk-free money market instruments) yielding 8 percent.
- Premiums for put and call purchases are assumed to be borrowed at 8 percent.
- Commissions are excluded.

Each strategy is evaluated by a risk-reward analysis for stock prices of $10, $20, $30, and $40 six months later at the option's expiration. A profit profile, which graphically shows gains and losses for any future stock price over the $10 to $40 range, follows each risk-reward calculation table. The $10 and $40 extremes were chosen for analysis purposes simply because they encompass a broad price range; and, while most stocks will not move this far in six months, a stock's halving or doubling are roughly equal probabilities.

The following exhibits evaluate the risk-reward characteristics for each of the strategies. Study the examples carefully; they are not complex if you take a few minutes to become comfortable with them. To check your comprehension after you have finished, go back and look only at the profit profiles. You should be able to identify the strategies without reference to the risk-reward calculation tables.

Exhibit G-1. Bullish Strategies 1 and 1a

	Price	*Prices at Expiration (6 months)*			
Stock	$30.00	15	30	45	60
Call	3.00	0	0	15	30
Put	2.12	15	0	0	0

Strategy 1: Buy 100 shares of stock

Profit or loss on stock	−1500	0	1500	3000
Dividends received	30	30	30	30
Total profit or loss	−1470	30	1530	3030

Strategy 1a: Buy one call and sell one put

Profit or loss on call	−300	−300	1200	2700
Profit or loss on put	−1288	212	212	212
Interest received on $2,912	116	116	116	116
Total profit or loss	−1472	28	1528	3028

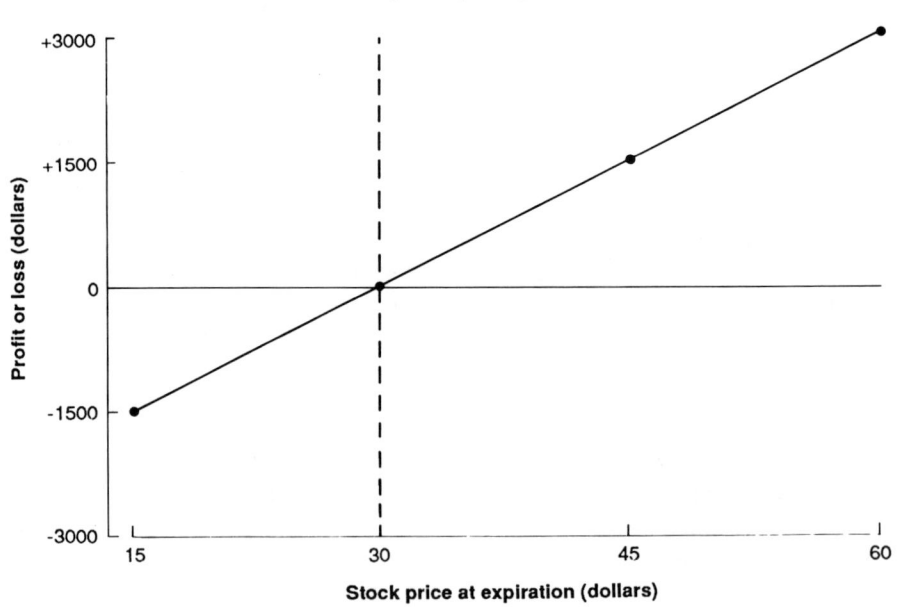

Profit profile (strategies 1 and 1a)

Exhibit G-2. Bullish Strategies 2 and 2a

	Price	Prices at Expiration (6 months)			
Stock	$30.00	15	30	45	60
Call	3.00	0	0	15	30
Put	2.12	15	0	0	0

Strategy 2: Buy 100 shares of stock and buy one put

Profit or loss on stock	−1500	0	1500	3000
Profit or loss on put	1288	−212	−212	−212
Interest paid on $212	−8	−8	−8	−8
Dividends received	30	30	30	30
Total profit or loss	−190	−190	1310	2810

Strategy 2a: Buy one call

Profit or loss on call	−300	−300	1200	2700
Interest received on $2,700	108	108	108	108
Total profit or loss	−192	−192	1308	2808

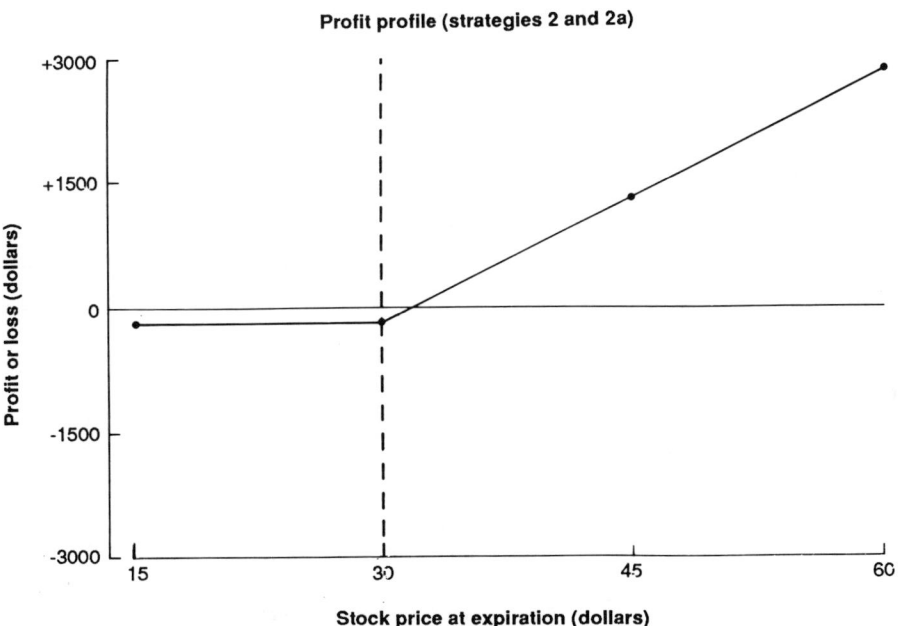

Profit profile (strategies 2 and 2a)

Profit or loss (dollars) vs. Stock price at expiration (dollars)

Exhibit G-3. Bullish Strategies 3 and 3a

	Price	*Prices at Expiration (6 months)*			
Stock	$30.00	15	30	45	60
Call	3.00	0	0	15	30
Put	2.12	15	0	0	0

Strategy 3: Buy 100 shares of stock and sell one call

Profit or loss on stock	−1500	0	1500	3000
Profit or loss on call	300	300	−1200	−2700
Interest received on $300	12	12	12	12
Dividends received	30	30	30	30
Total profit or loss	−1158	342	342	342

Strategy 3a: Sell one put

Profit or loss on put	−1288	212	212	212
Interest received on $3,212	128	128	128	128
Total profit or loss	−1160	340	340	340

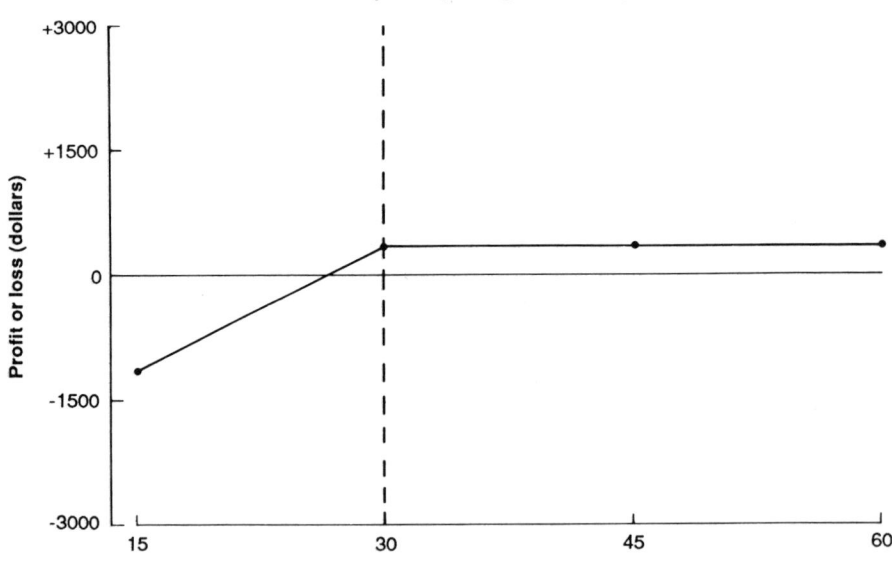

Profit profile (strategies 3 and 3a)

Profit or loss (dollars)

Stock price at expiration (dollars)

Exhibit G-4. Neutral Strategies 4 and 4a

	Price	Prices at Expiration (6 months)			
Stock	$30.00	15	30	45	60
Call	3.00	0	0	15	30
Put	2.12	15	0	0	0

Strategy 4: Buy 100 shares of stock, buy one put, and sell one call

Profit or loss on stocks	−1500	0	1500	3000
Profit or loss on put	1288	−212	−212	−212
Profit or loss on call	300	300	−1200	−2700
Interest received on $88	4	4	4	4
Dividends received	30	30	30	30
Total profit or loss	122	122	122	122

Strategy 4a: Buy Treasury bills

Interest received on $3,000	120	120	120	120

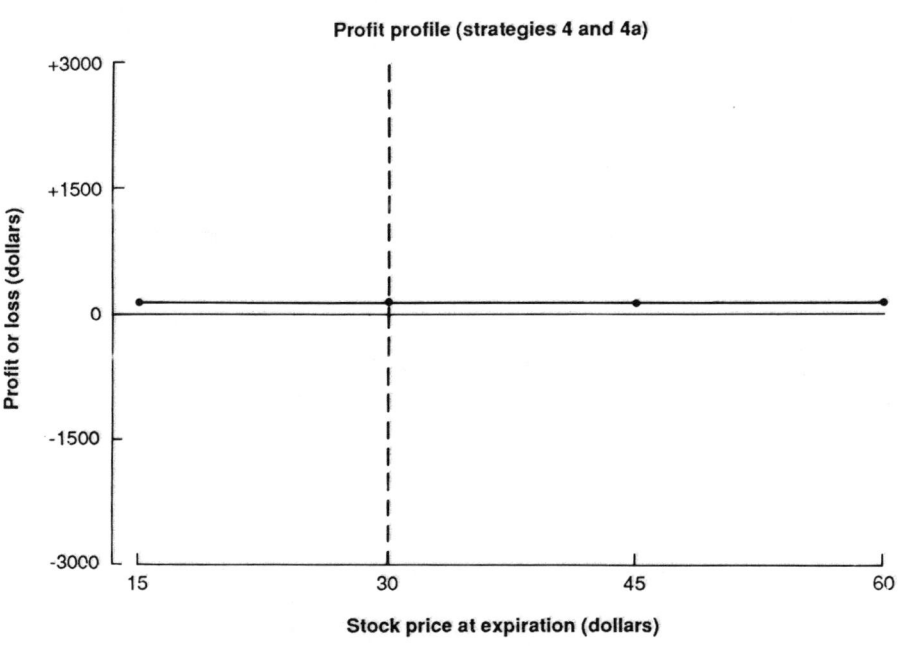

Profit profile (strategies 4 and 4a)

Exhibit G-5. Bearish Strategies 5 and 5a

	Price	Prices at Expiration (6 months)			
Stock	$30.00	15	30	45	60
Call	3.00	0	0	15	30
Put	2.12	15	0	0	0

Strategy 5: Short 100 shares of stock and sell one put

Profit or loss on stock	1500	0	−1500	−3000
Profit or loss on put	−1288	212	212	212
Interest received on $3,212	128	128	128	128
Dividends paid	−30	−30	−30	−30
Total profit or loss	310	310	−1190	−2690

Strategy 5a: Sell one call

Profit or loss on call	300	300	−1200	−2700
Interest received on $3,300	132	132	132	132
Total profit or loss	432	432	−1068	−2568

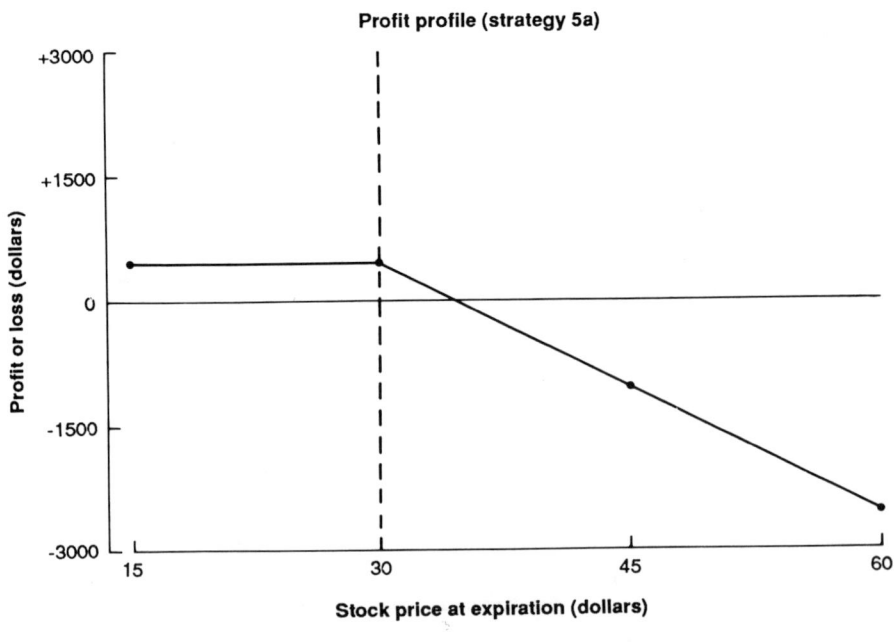

Profit profile (strategy 5a)

Exhibit G-6. Bearish Strategies 6 and 6a

	Price	*Prices at Expiration (6 months)*			
Stock	$30.00	15	30	45	60
Call	3.00	0	0	15	30
Put	2.12	15	0	0	0

Strategy 6: Short 100 shares of stock and buy one call

Profit or loss on stock	1500	0	−1500	−3000
Profit or loss on call	−300	−300	1200	2700
Interest received on $2,700	108	108	108	108
Dividends paid	−30	−30	−30	−30
Total profit or loss	1278	−222	−222	−222

Strategy 6a: Buy one put

Profit or loss on put	1288	−212	−212	−212
Interest received on $2,788	112	112	112	112
Total profit or loss	1400	−100	−100	−100

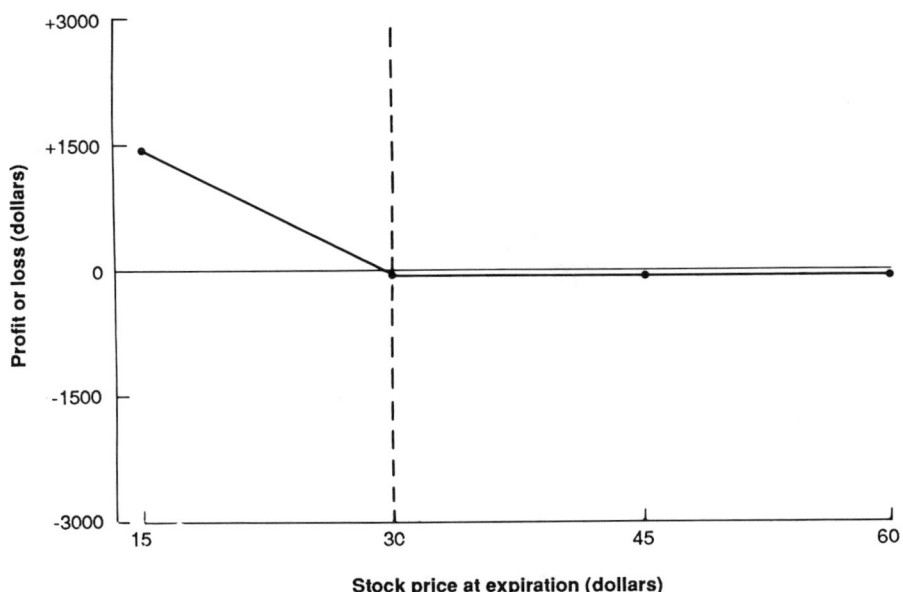

Profit profile (strategy 6a)

Profit or loss (dollars)

Stock price at expiration (dollars)

Exhibit G-7. Bearish Strategies 7 and 7a

	Price	*Prices at Expiration (6 months)*			
Stock	$30.00	15	30	45	60
Call	3.00	0	0	15	30
Put	2.12	15	0	0	0

Strategy 7: Short 100 shares of stock

Profit or loss on stock	1500	0	−1500	−3000
Interest received on $3,000	120	120	120	120
Dividends paid	−30	−30	−30	−30
Total profit or loss	1590	90	−1410	−2910

Strategy 7a: Buy one put and sell one call

Profit or loss on put	1288	−212	−212	−212
Profit or loss on call	300	300	−1200	−2700
Interest received on $3,088	124	124	124	124
Total profit or loss	1712	212	−1288	−2788

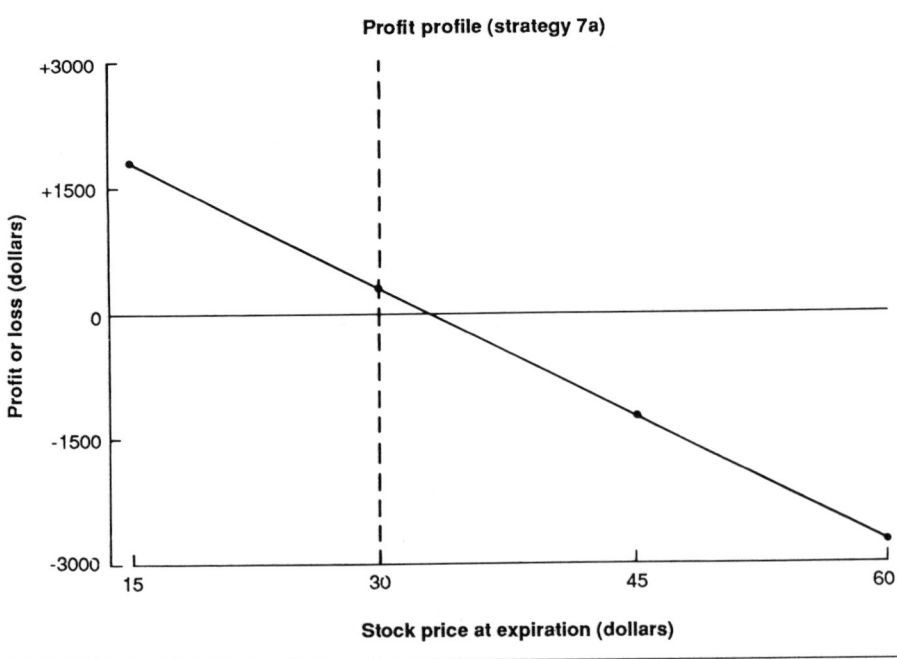

Profit profile (strategy 7a)

Profit or loss (dollars) / Stock price at expiration (dollars)

Exhibit G-8. Option Strategies 8 and 8a

	Price	*Prices at Expiration (6 months)*			
Stock	$30.00	15	30	45	60
Call	3.00	0	0	15	30
Put	2.12	15	0	0	0

Strategy 8: Buy 100 shares of stock and sell two calls

Profit or loss on stock	−1500	0	1500	3000
Profit or loss on calls	600	600	−2400	−5400
Interest received on $600	24	24	24	24
Dividends received	30	30	30	30
Total profit or loss	−846	654	−846	−2346

Strategy 8a: Sell one put and sell one call

Profit or loss on put	−1288	212	212	212
Profit or loss on call	300	300	−1200	−2700
Interest received on $3,512	140	140	140	140
Total profit or loss	−848	652	−848	−2348

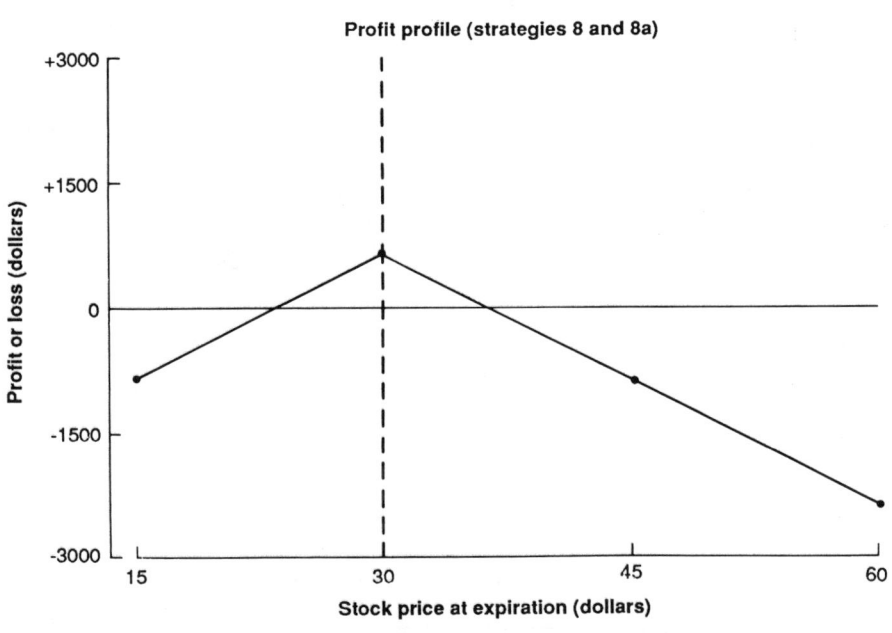

Profit profile (strategies 8 and 8a)

Exhibit G-9. Option Strategies 9 and 9a

	Price	*Prices at Expiration (6 months)*			
Stock	$30.00	15	30	45	60
Call	3.00	0	0	15	30
Put	2.12	15	0	0	0

Strategy 9: Buy 100 shares of stock and buy two puts

Profit or loss on stocks	−1500	0	1500	3000
Profit or loss on puts	2576	−424	−424	−424
Interest paid on $424	−17	−17	−17	−17
Dividends received	30	30	30	30
Total profit or loss	1089	−411	1089	2589

Strategy 9a: Buy one put and buy one call

Profit or loss on put	1288	−212	−212	−212
Profit or loss on call	−300	−300	1200	2700
Interest received on $2,488	100	100	100	100
Total profit or loss	1088	−412	1088	2588

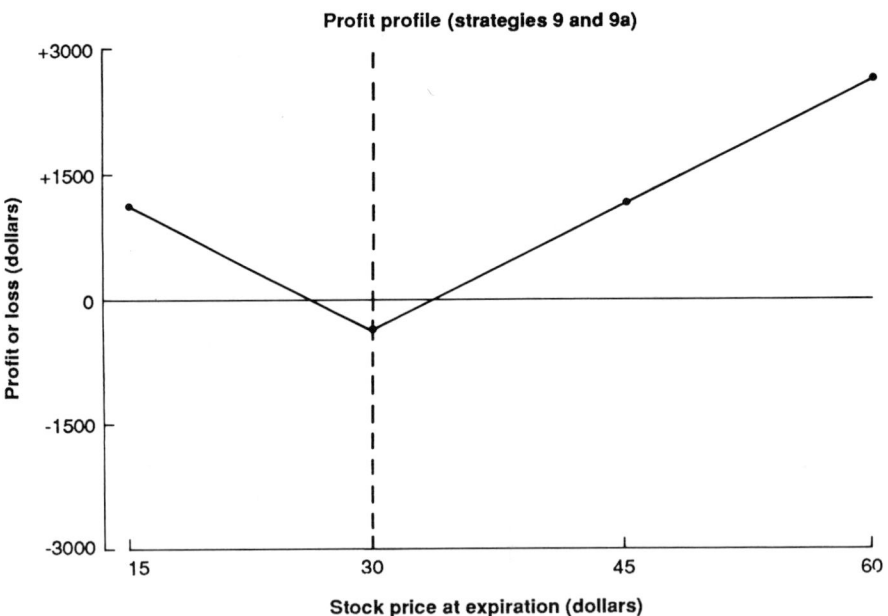

Profit profile (strategies 9 and 9a)

Profit or loss (dollars)

Stock price at expiration (dollars)

SPREADING OPTIONS

Highly touted by some advisory services and stockbrokers as a "low-risk" way to play the market, there is one option strategy that should always be avoided by nonprofessional investors. It is termed *spreading*, the simultaneous purchase and sale of puts or calls having different exercise prices or expiration dates. Variations of this term have alluring names, such as *calendar spreads, bull spreads, bear spreads,* and *butterfly spreads*, among others; however all are virtually guaranteed to destroy one's wealth.

Suffice it to say that professional marketmakers are the only ones who can execute these strategies profitably. Constant access to pricing inefficiencies and minimal clearing costs are their exclusive advantages. Marketmakers are quick to react to under- or overpriced opportunities by taking the other side of the trade. They then protect their positions with another option having a different strike price or expiration month. As prices return to normal, often within minutes, they plan to unwind the spread to capture a small profit. In no way can public investors compete against these highly-skilled, on-the-spot professionals.

This is my advice to those who cannot resist the temptation to trade options. Purchase a seat on an options exchange, roll up your sleeves, and go to work. You will quickly learn that making money by trading options is a full-time, demanding business. Even many professional marketmakers find it hard to survive in this competitive environment.

Appendix H
STRATEGIES USING INDEX PUTS AND CALLS

Tables H-1 and H-2 present back-tested, quarterly calculations to determine theoretical fair-market premiums for put and call options on the S&P 500 and Value Line 1,700 stock indexes. Three hedging strategies are shown in the tables: long puts, short calls, and a combination of the two. The put-call combination is the same as shorting the market on half the value of the index. The fourteen-year time frame (1976-89) was chosen to permit analysis of the Noddings Large- and Medium-Cap convertible bond indexes (since their inception in 1976) if hedged by these index options.

Assuming constant treasury bill rates at 8.0 percent and S&P 500 dividends at 4.0 percent, the fair-value price-spread between S&P 500 3-month at-the-money index puts and calls was calculated as follows:

Treasury bill yield for 3 months = 8.0% × 3/12 =	2.0%
Minus S&P 500 yield for 3 months = 4.0% × 3/12 =	- 1.0%
Price spread = call premium minus put premium =	1.0%

A similar calculation for Value Line options, based on dividends at 3.2 percent, produces a fair-value price-spread of 1.2 percent.

Through trial and error, fair-value premiums for put and call options are calculated by Tables H-1 and H-2. To simplify the calculations, the studies assumed constant option premiums over the fourteen-year period and exclude brokerage commissions. Premiums, of course, will vary as interest rates and index yields change and, as an index's volatility changes.

Tables H-3 and H-4 back test the Noddings Large-Cap convertible bond index if hedged by the S&P 500 and Value Line index options. Tables H-5 and H-6 present similar calculations for the Noddings Medium-Cap convertible bond index.

Table H-1.   Quarterly Returns for the S&P 500 Index if Hedged by 3-Month At-the-Money, Normally Valued Index Puts and Calls—1976-89

Assumptions:
T-bill rate = 8.00 percent
Index yield = 4.00 percent
Put premium = 2.75 percent
Call premium = 3.75 percent
Hedge ratio = 1.00

				Hedging Strategy		
Year-Quarter		*S&P 500 Index**	*S&P 500 Index*	*Long Puts*	*Short Calls*	*Puts & Calls*
1976	1	14.0	15.0	12.3	4.8	8.5
	2	1.4	2.4	-0.3	4.8	2.2
	3	0.9	1.9	-0.9	4.8	2.0
	4	2.1	3.1	0.3	4.8	2.6
		23.7	11.3	20.4	15.9	
1977	1	-8.5	-7.5	-1.8	-3.8	-2.8
	2	2.2	3.2	0.5	4.8	2.6
	3	-3.8	-2.8	-1.8	1.0	-0.4
	4	-1.3	-0.3	-1.8	3.5	0.9
		-7.5	-4.7	5.3	0.2	
1978	1	-5.9	-4.9	-1.8	-1.2	-1.5
	2	7.5	8.5	5.8	4.8	5.3
	3	7.7	8.7	6.0	4.8	5.4
	4	-6.0	-5.0	-1.8	-1.3	-1.5
		6.6	8.2	7.1	7.6	
1979	1	6.1	7.1	4.4	4.8	4.6
	2	1.7	2.7	-0.0	4.8	2.4
	3	6.6	7.6	4.9	4.8	4.8
	4	-0.9	0.1	-1.8	3.9	1.1
		18.5	7.4	19.4	13.3	
1980	1	-5.1	-4.1	-1.8	-0.3	-1.1
	2	12.5	13.5	10.8	4.8	7.8
	3	10.2	11.2	8.5	4.8	6.6
	4	8.5	9.5	6.8	4.8	5.8
		32.5	26.0	14.5	20.2	
1981	1	0.4	1.4	-1.4	4.8	1.7
	2	-3.3	-2.3	-1.8	1.5	-0.1
	3	-11.3	-10.3	-1.8	-6.6	-4.2
	4	5.9	6.9	4.2	4.8	4.5
		-5.0	-0.8	4.0	1.7	
1982	1	-8.3	-7.3	-1.8	-3.6	-2.7
	2	-1.6	-0.6	-1.8	3.2	0.7
	3	10.5	11.5	8.8	4.8	6.8
	4	17.2	18.2	15.5	4.8	10.1
		21.4	21.2	9.2	15.2	

Year-Quarter		S&P 500 Index*	S&P 500 Index	Hedging Strategy		
				Long Puts	*Short Calls*	*Puts & Calls*
1983	1	9.0	10.0	7.3	4.8	6.0
	2	10.1	11.1	8.4	4.8	6.6
	3	-1.2	-0.2	-1.8	3.6	0.9
	4	-0.6	0.4	-1.8	4.2	1.2
			22.5	12.2	18.3	15.3
1984	1	-3.4	-2.4	-1.8	1.3	-0.2
	2	-3.6	-2.6	-1.8	1.2	-0.3
	3	8.7	9.7	7.0	4.8	5.9
	4	0.8	1.8	-1.0	4.8	1.9
			6.2	2.3	12.5	7.3
1985	1	8.2	9.2	6.5	4.8	5.6
	2	6.3	7.3	4.6	4.8	4.7
	3	-5.1	-4.1	-1.8	-0.3	-1.1
	4	16.2	17.2	14.5	4.8	9.6
			31.7	25.1	14.5	19.8
1986	1	13.1	14.1	11.4	4.8	8.1
	2	4.9	5.9	3.2	4.8	4.0
	3	-8.0	-7.0	-1.8	-3.3	-2.5
	4	4.6	5.6	2.9	4.8	3.8
			18.7	16.1	11.2	13.7
1987	1	20.3	21.3	18.6	4.8	11.7
	2	4.0	5.0	2.3	4.8	3.5
	3	5.6	6.6	3.9	4.8	4.3
	4	-23.5	-22.5	-1.8	-18.8	-10.3
			5.2	23.7	-6.6	8.2
1988	1	4.7	5.7	2.9	4.8	3.9
	2	5.6	6.6	3.9	4.8	4.3
	3	-0.7	0.3	-1.8	4.1	1.2
	4	2.1	3.1	0.3	4.8	2.6
			16.5	5.4	19.6	12.4
1989	1	6.1	7.1	4.4	4.8	4.6
	2	7.8	8.8	6.1	4.8	5.4
	3	9.7	10.7	8.0	4.8	6.4
	4	1.1	2.1	-0.7	4.8	2.1
			31.7	18.7	20.4	19.6
Cumulative return			624.6	381.0	380.5	389.0
Annualized return			15.2	11.9	11.9	12.0

*Excluding dividends.

Table H-2.   Quarterly Returns for the Value Line Index if Hedged by 3-Month At-the-Money, Normally Valued Index Puts and Calls—1976-89

Assumptions:
T-bill rate = 8.00 percent
Index yield = 3.20 percent
Put premium = 3.30 percent
Call premium = 4.50 percent
Hedge ratio = 1.00

Year-Quarter		VLE Index*	VLE Index**	Long Puts	Short Calls	Puts & Calls
					Hedging Strategy	
1976	1	25.0	25.8	22.5	5.3	13.9
	2	-0.6	0.2	-2.5	4.7	1.1
	3	-1.2	-0.4	-2.5	4.1	0.8
	4	7.7	8.5	5.2	5.3	5.3
		36.2	22.5		20.9	22.2
1977	1	-3.3	-2.5	-2.5	2.0	-0.3
	2	5.0	5.8	2.5	5.3	3.9
	3	-3.9	-3.1	-2.5	1.4	-0.5
	4	3.0	3.8	0.5	5.3	2.9
			3.8	-2.1	14.7	6.1
1978	1	1.1	1.9	-1.4	5.3	2.0
	2	9.7	10.5	7.2	5.3	6.3
	3	9.9	10.7	7.4	5.3	6.4
	4	-14.4	-13.6	-2.5	-9.1	-5.8
			7.7	10.7	6.1	8.5
1979	1	11.7	12.5	9.2	5.3	7.3
	2	4.2	5.0	1.7	5.3	3.5
	3	8.0	8.8	5.5	5.3	5.4
	4	-1.0	-0.2	-2.5	4.3	0.9
			28.3	14.2	21.8	18.1
1980	1	-12.9	-12.1	-2.5	-7.6	-5.1
	2	16.5	17.3	14.0	5.3	9.7
	3	14.2	15.0	11.7	5.3	8.5
	4	2.1	2.9	-0.4	5.3	2.5
			22.0	23.7	7.9	15.7
1981	1	5.7	6.5	3.2	5.3	4.3
	2	1.7	2.5	-0.8	5.3	2.3
	3	-16.3	-15.5	-2.5	-11.0	-6.8
	4	6.2	7.0	3.7	5.3	4.5
			-1.3	3.5	3.9	3.9
1982	1	-9.1	-8.3	-2.5	-3.8	-3.2
	2	-3.8	-3.0	-2.5	1.5	-0.5
	3	9.4	10.2	6.9	5.3	6.1
	4	20.5	21.3	18.0	5.3	11.7
			18.9	19.9	8.3	14.2

				Hedging Strategy		
Year-Quarter		*VLE Index**	*VLE Index***	*Long Puts*	*Short Calls*	*Puts & Calls*
1983	1	15.5	16.3	13.0	5.3	9.2
	2	16.0	16.8	13.5	5.3	9.4
	3	-1.4	-0.6	-2.5	3.9	0.7
	4	-1.0	-0.2	-2.5	4.3	0.9
		34.8	21.9	20.2		21.4
1984	1	-4.9	-4.1	-2.5	0.4	-1.1
	2	-3.8	-3.0	-2.5	1.5	-0.5
	3	7.4	8.2	4.9	5.3	5.1
	4	-1.0	-0.2	-2.5	4.3	0.9
		0.4	-2.8	11.9		4.4
1985	1	10.9	11.7	8.4	5.3	6.9
	2	4.4	5.2	1.9	5.3	3.6
	3	-4.3	-3.5	-2.5	1.0	-0.7
	4	15.8	16.6	13.3	5.3	9.3
		32.2	21.9	18.0		20.1
1986	1	14.8	15.6	12.3	5.3	8.8
	2	2.9	3.7	0.4	5.3	2.9
	3	-7.8	-7.0	-2.5	-2.5	-2.5
	4	3.4	4.2	0.9	5.3	3.1
		16.2	11.0	13.9		12.5
1987	1	20.7	21.5	18.2	5.3	11.7
	2	1.9	2.7	-0.6	5.3	2.3
	3	5.6	6.4	3.1	5.3	4.2
	4	-24.1	-23.3	-2.5	-18.8	-10.7
		1.8	18.0	-5.2		6.5
1988	1	15.4	16.2	12.9	5.3	9.1
	2	6.6	7.4	4.1	5.3	4.7
	3	-1.1	-0.3	-2.5	4.2	0.8
	4	0.4	1.2	-2.1	5.3	1.6
		25.8	12.1	21.6		17.0
1989	1	7.1	7.9	4.6	5.3	5.0
	2	6.4	7.2	3.9	5.3	4.6
	3	7.3	8.1	4.8	5.3	5.0
	4	-4.2	-3.4	-2.5	1.1	-0.7
		20.7	11.0	18.0		14.5
Cumulative return		798.3	448.6	434.3		455.7
Annualized return		17.0	12.9	12.7		13.0

*Excludes dividends at an assumption of 0.8 percent per quarter.
**Value Line's geometric index (1976-82), arithmetic index (1983-89).

Table H-3.   Quarterly Returns for the Noddings Large-Cap Convertible Bond
Index if Hedged by 3-Month At-the-Money, Normally Valued
S&P 500 Index Puts and Calls—1976-89

Assumptions:
T-bill rate = 8.00 percent
Index yield = 4.00 percent
Put premium = 2.75 percent
Call premium = 3.75 percent
Hedge ratio = 1.00

| | | | | | Hedging Strategy | |
Year-Quarter		S&P 500 Index*	Convert. Index	Long Puts	Short Calls	Puts & Calls
1976	1	14.0	19.2	16.5	9.0	12.7
	2	1.4	6.6	3.9	9.0	6.4
	3	0.9	6.7	4.0	9.5	6.7
	4	2.1	7.6	4.9	9.3	7.1
		45.9	31.8	42.1	37.0	
1977	1	-8.5	-0.5	5.3	3.3	4.3
	2	2.2	7.3	4.6	8.9	6.7
	3	-3.8	-1.0	0.0	2.8	1.4
	4	-1.3	2.3	0.8	6.1	3.5
		8.1	11.0	22.5	16.7	
1978	1	-5.9	3.1	6.3	6.9	6.6
	2	7.5	13.2	10.5	9.5	10.0
	3	7.7	10.3	7.6	6.4	7.0
	4	-6.0	-9.3	-6.1	-5.6	-5.8
		16.8	18.6	17.5	18.0	
1979	1	6.1	10.3	7.6	8.0	7.8
	2	1.7	8.1	5.4	10.2	7.8
	3	6.6	6.8	4.1	4.0	4.0
	4	-0.9	-2.5	-4.4	1.3	-1.6
		24.2	12.8	25.1	18.9	
1980	1	-5.1	-5.8	-3.5	-2.1	-2.8
	2	12.5	22.2	19.5	13.5	16.5
	3	10.2	15.7	13.0	9.3	11.1
	4	8.5	1.6	-1.2	-3.2	-2.2
		35.3	28.8	17.6	23.1	
1981	1	0.4	8.4	5.6	11.8	8.7
	2	-3.3	6.3	6.9	10.1	8.5
	3	-11.3	-9.1	-0.6	-5.4	-3.0
	4	5.9	12.2	9.5	10.0	9.8
		17.5	22.9	28.1	25.6	

Year-Quarter		S&P 500 Index*	Convert. Index	Hedging Strategy		
				Long Puts	Short Calls	Puts & Calls
1982	1	-8.3	-4.7	0.9	-0.9	-0.0
	2	-1.6	-2.5	-3.7	1.3	-1.2
	3	10.5	13.8	11.1	7.1	9.1
	4	17.2	14.9	12.2	1.4	6.8
		21.5	21.0	8.9	15.0	
1983	1	9.0	15.4	12.7	10.2	11.4
	2	10.1	14.5	11.8	8.2	10.0
	3	-1.2	-0.8	-2.4	3.0	0.3
	4	-0.6	-1.9	-4.1	1.9	-1.1
		28.6	17.9	24.9	21.5	
1984	1	-3.4	-1.1	-0.4	2.7	1.1
	2	-3.6	-1.3	-0.5	2.5	1.0
	3	8.7	6.9	4.2	2.0	3.1
	4	0.8	2.4	-0.3	5.4	2.5
		6.9	2.9	13.0	7.9	
1985	1	8.2	9.6	6.9	5.2	6.0
	2	6.3	6.8	4.1	4.3	4.2
	3	-5.1	-1.8	0.5	2.0	1.3
	4	16.2	11.6	8.9	-0.9	4.0
		28.3	21.7	10.8	16.3	
1986	1	13.1	11.6	8.9	2.3	5.6
	2	4.9	3.7	1.0	2.6	1.8
	3	-8.0	-1.9	3.4	1.9	2.6
	4	4.6	1.9	-0.9	1.1	0.1
		15.7	12.6	7.9	10.3	
1987	1	20.3	10.8	8.1	-5.7	1.2
	2	4.0	0.7	-2.1	0.5	-0.8
	3	5.6	2.4	-0.3	0.6	0.1
	4	-23.5	-13.3	7.5	-9.6	-1.1
		-0.9	13.3	-13.9	-0.6	
1988	1	4.7	10.0	7.3	9.1	8.2
	2	5.6	4.3	1.6	2.5	2.0
	3	-0.7	-0.7	-2.8	3.1	0.1
	4	2.1	1.6	-1.2	3.3	1.1
		15.7	4.7	18.9	11.6	
1989	1	6.1	5.6	2.9	3.3	3.1
	2	7.8	4.9	2.2	0.8	1.5
	3	9.7	5.2	2.4	-0.8	0.8
	4	1.1	-1.9	-4.7	0.8	-2.0
		14.3	2.6	4.1	3.4	
Cumulative return			1080.9	658.4	654.4	669.1
Annualized return			19.3	15.6	15.5	15.7

*Excluding dividends.

Table H-4.   Quarterly Returns for the Noddings Large-Cap Convertible Bond
             Index if Hedged by 3-Month At-the-Money, Normally Valued Value
             Line Index Puts and Calls—1976-89

Assumptions:
T-bill rate = 8.00 percent
Index yield = 3.20 percent
Put premium = 3.30 percent
Call premium = 4.50 percent
Hedge ratio = 1.00

| | | | | Hedging Strategy | | |
Year-Quarter		VLE Index*	Convert. Index	Long Puts	Short Calls	Puts & Calls
1976	1	25.0	19.2	15.9	-1.3	7.3
	2	-0.6	6.6	3.9	11.1	7.5
	3	-1.2	6.7	4.6	11.2	7.9
	4	7.7	7.6	4.3	4.4	4.4
		45.9	31.4	27.3	29.9
1977	1	-3.3	-0.5	-0.5	4.0	1.8
	2	5.0	7.3	4.0	6.8	5.4
	3	-3.9	-1.0	-0.4	3.5	1.6
	4	3.0	2.3	-1.0	3.8	1.4
		8.1	2.0	19.3	10.4
1978	1	1.1	3.1	-0.2	6.5	3.2
	2	9.7	13.2	9.9	8.0	9.0
	3	9.9	10.3	7.0	4.9	6.0
	4	-14.4	-9.3	1.8	-4.8	-1.5
		16.8	19.5	14.9	17.3
1979	1	11.7	10.3	7.0	3.1	5.1
	2	4.2	8.1	4.8	8.4	6.6
	3	8.0	6.8	3.5	3.3	3.4
	4	-1.0	-2.5	-4.8	2.0	-1.4
		24.2	10.5	17.8	14.2
1980	1	-12.9	-5.8	3.8	-1.3	1.2
	2	16.5	22.2	18.9	10.2	14.6
	3	14.2	15.7	12.4	6.0	9.2
	4	2.1	1.6	-1.7	4.0	1.2
		35.3	36.4	19.9	28.1
1981	1	5.7	8.4	5.1	7.2	6.1
	2	1.7	6.3	3.0	9.1	6.1
	3	-16.3	-9.1	3.9	-4.6	-0.4
	4	6.2	12.2	8.9	10.5	9.7
		17.5	22.5	23.3	23.1

Year-Quarter	VLE Index*	Convert. Index	Hedging Strategy		
			Long Puts	Short Calls	Puts & Calls
1982 1	-9.1	-4.7	1.1	-0.2	0.5
2	-3.8	-2.5	-2.0	2.0	0.0
3	9.4	13.8	10.5	8.9	9.7
4	20.5	14.9	11.6	-1.1	5.2
		21.5	22.2	9.6	16.0
1983 1	15.5	15.4	12.1	4.4	8.3
2	16.0	14.5	11.2	3.0	7.1
3	-1.4	-0.8	-2.7	3.7	0.5
4	-1.0	-1.9	-4.2	2.6	-0.8
		28.6	16.2	14.4	15.6
1984 1	-4.9	-1.1	0.5	3.4	2.0
2	-3.8	-1.3	-0.8	3.2	1.2
3	7.4	6.9	3.6	4.0	3.8
4	-1.0	2.4	0.1	6.9	3.5
		6.9	3.4	18.6	10.8
1985 1	10.9	9.6	6.3	3.2	4.8
2	4.4	6.8	3.5	6.9	5.2
3	-4.3	-1.8	-0.8	2.7	1.0
4	15.8	11.6	8.3	0.3	4.3
		28.3	18.2	13.6	16.0
1986 1	14.8	11.6	8.3	1.3	4.8
2	2.9	3.7	0.4	5.3	2.9
3	-7.8	-1.9	2.6	2.6	2.6
4	3.4	1.9	-1.4	3.0	0.8
		15.7	10.0	12.7	11.5
1987 1	20.7	10.8	7.5	-5.4	1.0
2	1.9	0.7	-2.6	3.3	0.4
3	5.6	2.4	-0.9	1.3	0.2
4	-24.1	-13.3	7.5	-8.8	-0.6
		-0.9	11.5	-9.7	0.9
1988 1	15.4	10.0	6.7	-0.9	2.9
2	6.6	4.3	1.0	2.2	1.6
3	-1.1	-0.7	-2.9	3.8	0.5
4	0.4	1.6	-1.7	5.7	2.0
		15.7	2.9	11.1	7.1
1989 1	7.1	5.6	2.3	3.0	2.7
2	6.4	4.9	1.6	3.0	2.3
3	7.3	5.2	1.9	2.4	2.1
4	-4.2	-1.9	-1.0	2.6	0.8
		14.3	4.9	11.5	8.1
Cumulative return		1080.9	578.5	547.5	580.3
Annualized return		19.3	14.7	14.3	14.7

*Excluding dividends.

Table H-5.   Quarterly Returns for the Noddings Medium-Cap Convertible Bond Index if Hedged by 3-Month At-the-Money, Normally Valued S&P 500 Index Puts and Calls—1976-89

Assumptions:
T-bill rate = 8.00 percent
Index yield = 4.00 percent
Put premium = 2.75 percent
Call premium = 3.75 percent
Hedge ratio = 1.00

| | | | | Hedging Strategy | | |
| | | S&P 500 | Convert. | Long | Short | Puts & |
Year-Quarter		Index*	Index	Puts	Calls	Calls
1976	1	14.0	10.3	7.6	0.1	3.8
	2	1.4	10.5	7.8	12.9	10.3
	3	0.9	6.1	3.4	9.0	6.1
	4	2.1	7.9	5.2	9.6	7.4
			39.5	25.9	34.8	30.5
1977	1	-8.5	3.0	8.8	6.8	7.8
	2	2.2	7.2	4.5	8.8	6.6
	3	-3.8	0.7	1.8	4.5	3.1
	4	-1.3	2.7	1.3	6.5	3.9
			14.2	17.0	29.1	23.0
1978	1	-5.9	10.9	14.1	14.7	14.4
	2	7.5	12.1	9.4	8.4	8.9
	3	7.7	17.7	15.0	13.8	14.4
	4	-6.0	-5.6	-2.4	-1.9	-2.1
			38.1	40.0	38.7	39.3
1979	1	6.1	14.9	12.2	12.5	12.3
	2	1.7	9.1	6.4	11.2	8.8
	3	6.6	9.4	6.7	6.6	6.6
	4	-0.9	3.3	1.4	7.1	4.3
			41.7	29.0	42.7	35.8
1980	1	-5.1	-3.5	-1.2	0.3	-0.5
	2	12.5	17.2	14.5	8.5	11.5
	3	10.2	11.9	9.2	5.5	7.3
	4	8.5	8.6	5.9	3.9	4.9
			37.4	30.7	19.1	24.8
1981	1	0.4	13.2	10.5	16.6	13.5
	2	-3.3	2.8	3.4	6.6	5.0
	3	-11.3	-11.7	-3.1	-8.0	-5.5
	4	5.9	5.1	2.4	2.9	2.6
			8.0	13.2	17.7	15.5

Year-Quarter		S&P 500 Index*	Convert. Index	Hedging Strategy		
				Long Puts	Short Calls	Puts & Calls
1982	1	-8.3	-0.1	5.5	3.7	4.6
	2	-1.6	2.6	1.4	6.4	3.9
	3	10.5	9.6	6.9	2.9	4.9
	4	17.2	20.0	17.3	6.5	11.9
		34.8	34.0		20.8	27.4
1983	1	9.0	13.1	10.4	7.9	9.1
	2	10.1	21.7	19.0	15.4	17.2
	3	-1.2	-6.5	-8.1	-2.8	-5.4
	4	-0.6	-1.1	-3.3	2.7	-0.3
		27.3	16.8		24.2	20.5
1984	1	-3.4	1.9	2.6	5.7	4.1
	2	-3.6	-6.9	-6.1	-3.2	-4.6
	3	8.7	4.4	1.7	-0.5	0.6
	4	0.8	1.3	-1.5	4.3	1.4
		0.3	-3.5		6.1	1.3
1985	1	8.2	13.4	10.7	9.0	9.8
	2	6.3	5.8	3.1	3.3	3.2
	3	-5.1	0.8	3.1	4.6	3.9
	4	16.2	3.5	0.8	-9.0	-4.1
		25.2	18.5		7.1	12.8
1986	1	13.1	8.6	5.9	-0.8	2.6
	2	4.9	9.0	6.3	7.9	7.1
	3	-8.0	-2.6	2.7	1.2	1.9
	4	4.6	3.8	1.1	3.0	2.0
		19.7	16.7		11.5	14.1
1987	1	20.3	13.7	11.0	-2.8	4.1
	2	4.0	-1.5	-4.3	-1.8	-3.0
	3	5.6	0.1	-2.7	-1.7	-2.2
	4	-23.5	-19.6	1.1	-15.9	-7.4
		-9.9	4.6		-21.1	-8.5
1988	1	4.7	10.7	8.0	9.8	8.9
	2	5.6	6.4	3.7	4.6	4.1
	3	-0.7	1.0	-1.1	4.8	1.9
	4	2.1	1.5	-1.3	3.2	1.0
		20.7	9.3		24.0	16.5
1989	1	6.1	3.1	0.3	0.8	0.5
	2	7.8	5.9	3.2	1.9	2.5
	3	9.7	6.6	3.9	0.7	2.3
	4	1.1	-6.2	-9.0	-3.5	-6.3
		9.2	-2.1		-0.4	-1.2
Cumulative return			1318.0	820.4	793.0	822.3
Annualized return			20.9	17.2	16.9	17.2

*Excluding dividends.

Table H-6.   Quarterly Returns for the Noddings Medium-Cap Convertible Bond Index if Hedged by 3-Month At-the-Money, Normally Valued Value Line Index Puts and Calls—1976-89

Assumptions:
T-bill rate = 8.00 percent
Index yield = 3.20 percent
Put premium = 3.30 percent
Call premium = 4.50 percent
Hedge ratio = 1.00

				Hedging Strategy		
Year-Quarter		VLE Index*	Convert. Index	Long Puts	Short Calls	Puts & Calls
1976	1	25.0	10.3	7.0	-10.2	-1.6
	2	-0.6	10.5	7.8	15.0	11.4
	3	-1.2	6.1	4.0	10.6	7.3
	4	7.7	7.9	4.6	4.7	4.7
		39.5	25.5	19.6	23.1
1977	1	-3.3	3.0	3.0	7.5	5.3
	2	5.0	7.2	3.9	6.7	5.3
	3	-3.9	0.7	1.3	5.2	3.3
	4	3.0	2.7	-0.6	4.2	1.8
		14.2	7.8	25.7	16.5
1978	1	1.1	10.9	7.6	14.3	11.0
	2	9.7	12.1	8.8	6.9	7.9
	3	9.9	17.7	14.4	12.3	13.4
	4	-14.4	-5.6	5.5	-1.1	2.2
		38.1	41.3	35.7	38.6
1979	1	11.7	14.9	11.6	7.7	9.7
	2	4.2	9.1	5.8	9.4	7.6
	3	8.0	9.4	6.1	5.9	6.0
	4	-1.0	3.3	1.0	7.8	4.4
		41.7	26.5	34.5	30.6
1980	1	-12.9	-3.5	6.1	1.0	3.6
	2	16.5	17.2	13.9	5.2	9.6
	3	14.2	11.9	8.6	2.2	5.4
	4	2.1	8.6	5.3	11.0	8.2
		37.4	38.2	20.5	29.3
1981	1	5.7	13.2	9.9	12.0	11.0
	2	1.7	2.8	-0.5	5.6	2.6
	3	-16.3	-11.7	1.3	-7.2	-2.9
	4	6.2	5.1	1.8	3.4	2.6
		8.0	12.8	13.5	13.3

		VLE	Convert.	Hedging Strategy		
				Long	Short	Puts &
Year-Quarter		Index*	Index	Puts	Calls	Calls
1982	1	-9.1	-0.1	5.7	4.4	5.1
	2	-3.8	2.6	3.1	7.1	5.1
	3	9.4	9.6	6.3	4.7	5.5
	4	20.5	20.0	16.7	4.0	10.4
		34.8	35.2	21.8	28.5
1983	1	15.5	13.1	9.8	2.1	6.0
	2	16.0	21.7	18.4	10.2	14.3
	3	-1.4	-6.5	-8.4	-2.0	-5.2
	4	-1.0	-1.1	-3.4	3.4	0.0
		27.3	15.0	14.0	14.8
1984	1	-4.9	1.9	3.5	6.4	5.0
	2	-3.8	-6.9	-6.4	-2.4	-4.4
	3	7.4	4.4	1.1	1.5	1.3
	4	-1.0	1.3	-1.0	5.8	2.4
		0.3	-3.0	11.5	4.1
1985	1	10.9	13.4	10.1	7.0	8.6
	2	4.4	5.8	2.5	5.9	4.2
	3	-4.3	0.8	1.8	5.3	3.6
	4	15.8	3.5	0.2	-7.8	-3.8
		25.2	15.1	10.0	12.7
1986	1	14.8	8.6	5.3	-1.7	1.8
	2	2.9	9.0	5.7	10.6	8.2
	3	-7.8	-2.6	1.9	1.9	1.9
	4	3.4	3.8	0.5	4.9	2.7
		19.7	14.0	16.2	15.2
1987	1	20.7	13.7	10.4	-2.5	4.0
	2	1.9	-1.5	-4.8	1.1	-1.9
	3	5.6	0.1	-3.2	-1.0	-2.1
	4	-24.1	-19.6	1.2	-15.1	-7.0
		-9.9	3.0	-17.1	-7.1
1988	1	15.4	10.7	7.4	-0.2	3.6
	2	6.6	6.4	3.1	4.3	3.7
	3	-1.1	1.0	-1.2	5.5	2.2
	4	0.4	1.5	-1.8	5.6	1.9
		20.7	7.4	16.0	11.8
1989	1	7.1	3.1	-0.2	0.5	0.2
	2	6.4	5.9	2.6	4.0	3.3
	3	7.3	6.6	3.3	3.8	3.6
	4	-4.2	-6.2	-5.3	-1.7	-3.5
		9.2	0.2	6.6	3.4
Cumulative return			1318.0	725.8	661.4	714.4
Annualized return			20.9	16.3	15.6	16.2

*Excluding dividends

TERMS APPLYING TO CONVERTIBLE BONDS AND HEDGING STRATEGIES

Accrued interest. Interest earned on a bond since its last interest payment date. The buyer of the bond pays the market price plus accrued interest to the seller and is entitled to the next interest payment in full. Exceptions include bonds in default and income bonds, which trade flat (without accrued interest).

Adjustable-rate bond. A bond whose interest rate may be adjusted periodically to keep the rate in line with changing market conditions.

Antidilution clause. Provisions contained in most convertible bond indentures calling for adjustment of the conversion ratio in the event of stock splits, stock dividends or the sale of new stock at a price below the conversion price of existing convertibles. In some cases, adjustment is not made for small stock dividends (e.g., under five percent in any single year or ten percent during the life of the convertible).

Arbitrage. See "Convertible arbitrage."

Beta. A measure of the sensitivity of a stock's price to overall movements in the prices of other stocks, as reflected in Standard & Poor's 500 stock index or a similar benchmark.

Bond indenture. The contract under which bonds are issued. It describes terms of the agreement such as interest rate, interest payment dates, date of maturity, redemption terms, conversion privileges and antidilution clauses.

Bond price quotation. Bonds are quoted as a percentage of par (usually $1,000). Thus, 90 represents 90 percent of a $1,000 bond, or $900. 110 means 110 percent of par, or $1,100.

Bond value. See "Investment value."

Break-even time. The time period over which a convertible bond recaptures any premium paid over conversion value when bond interest exceeds the common stock's dividend.

Call option. An option granting the holder the right to purchase an asset at a specified price for a specified period of time.

Call price. The amount of money a corporation agrees to pay, expressed as a percentage of par, if it chooses to redeem its convertible bonds. It is normally set somewhat above par, commencing a few years after issuance, and is periodically reduced.

Callable. Term applied to a convertible bond with an indenture containing a provision giving the issuer the right to retire the issue prior to its maturity date. See "Call price."

Call protection. Newly issued convertible bonds are usually protected against call for a number of years. If they are not callable under any circumstances, they have absolute protection. Provisional protection allows bonds to be called when the stock's price reaches a certain level.

Capital market line. A graphic representation of long-term risk-reward relationships for traditional financial instruments.

Coefficient of variation. An investment strategy's quarterly standard deviation divided by its average return. The result is then multiplied by 100. When comparing different strategies, the one having the lowest coefficient of variation is usually considered the best.

Conversion parity. Price the convertible sells for is equal to the current market value of the common shares to be received upon conversion. As an example, if the conversion ratio was 40 shares and the common was trading at $30, conversion parity is 120 (40 shares × $30 = $1,200). When the convertible trades above conversion parity, it is better to sell the convertible rather than to convert.

Conversion premium. Difference between a convertible's market price and its conversion value expressed as a percentage above conversion value.

Conversion price. The price at which the underlying common stock must trade in order for the bond to be worth par value if converted. As an example, if the conversion ratio was 40 shares the conversion price is $25 ($1,000 / 40 = $25).

Conversion ratio. The number of common shares to be received upon conversion.

Conversion value. The worth of a convertible bond if it is converted into common stock. It is calculated by multiplying the number of shares to be received upon conversion by the current market price of the common.

Convertible arbitrage. A simultaneous purchase and sale of related securities for an immediate profit upon conversion. This technique generally involves the purchase of a convertible bond that is trading at a price below its conversion value, and the full short sale of its common stock. The stock received from the bond's conversion offsets the short sale.

Convertible bond. A debt instrument exchangeable at the option of the holder into common stock or other securities in accordance with the terms of the bond indenture.

Convertible hedging. An investment strategy which takes advantage of an undervalued convertible bond while further reducing risk via the short sale of common stock or the use of put and/or call options.

Convertible price curve. A graphic representation of the expected convertible bond price for any stock price over the near-term future.

Convertible strategies line. A graphic representation of risk-reward relationships for various investment strategies involving undervalued convertible securities.

Current yield. The interest paid annually divided by the current price of the bond.

Debt floor. See "Investment value."

Debt value. See "Investment value."

Default. Failure of the bond issuer to meet a contractual obligation, such as payment of interest, maintenance of working capital requirements or payment of principal via a sinking fund or at maturity.

Delayed convertible bond. A convertible bond which is exchangeable into common stock commencing on a specified future date.

Discounted bond. A bond selling below par value.

Equity options. Puts and calls on common stocks.

Equity value. See "Conversion value."

Exercise price. The price at which an option is exercisable. Also called the strike price.

Expiration of conversion privileges. Termination date of a convertible bond's conversion privilege.

Fabricated convertible bond. A combination of warrants plus bonds usable for exercise purposes at par value in lieu of cash.

Forced conversion. Holders of convertible bonds are forced to convert in order to capture conversion value if the bonds are called for redemption, if there is an adverse change in their conversion terms, or as an expiration date comes due.

Indenture. See "Bond Indenture."

Index options. Puts and calls on stock indexes.

Investment floor. See "Investment value."

Investment grade bonds. Convertible or straight bonds receiving a BBB or better by Standard & Poor's or Baa or better by Moody's.

Investment value. The estimated value of a convertible bond without consideration of its conversion privilege. Also known as the investment floor or debt value.

Investment value premium. The difference between a convertible's market price and its investment value expressed as a percentage above investment value.

Junk bond. A straight bond having a Standard & Poor's rating below BBB.

Maturity date. A fixed date when the company must redeem a bond by payment of the full par value to the bondholder.

Nonconvertible bond. See "Straight bond."

Parity. See "Conversion Value."

Par value. The value of a bond which the company promises to pay upon maturity. It is usually $1,000 for convertible bonds.

Plus-cash convertible bond. A convertible bond which requires an additional cash payment on conversion.

Premium over conversion value. See "Conversion premium."

Premium over investment value. See "Investment value premium."

Profit profile. A graphic presentation of a risk-reward analysis which permits a visual comparison of investment alternatives.

Provisional call protection. See "Call protection."

Put option. An option granting the holder the right to sell an asset at a specified price for a specified period of time.

Redemption. The act of retiring part or all of a bond issue prior to its maturity date. If a convertible bond issue is selling above the redemption price when it is called by the issuing company, redemption is equivalent to a forced conversion of the issue.

Registered bond. A bond which is issued in the name of the holder. Interest is paid by check to the holder. Most convertible bonds are registered.

Risk-reward analysis. A mathematical evaluation of a convertible bond relative to its common stock, or a combination of common stock and straight bonds, used to identify undervalued investment alternatives.

Sharpe measure. An investment strategy's average quarterly return minus the three-month Treasury bill rate divided by the standard deviation. When comparing different strategies, the one having the highest Sharpe measure is considered the best.

Sinking fund provisions. A requirement calling for the company to begin retiring a convertible issue prior to its maturity date.

Standard deviation. A statistical measurement of the tendency of individual values to differ from the mean (average). Where investment strategies are similar, such as when evaluating different portfolios of large capitalization stocks, the various portfolio standard deviations indicate relative levels of historical volatility, or risk.

Stock value. See "Conversion value."

Straight bond. A bond which is not convertible into common stock.

Straight bond equivalent yield. The yield to maturity for a convertible bond assuming that it did not contain conversion features. Used for determining the convertible bond's investment value.

Subordinated debenture. A bond which is subject to the prior claim of other senior securities and usually not secured by any specific property. Most convertible bonds are subordinated debentures.

Synthetic convertible bond. A combination of call options or warrants with money market instruments.

Undervalued convertible bond. A convertible bond having superior investment characteristics relative to its common stock or a combination of common stock and straight bonds, as determined by a risk-reward analysis.

Unit convertible bond. A bond which is exchangeable for a package of more than one security that may or may not include common stock.

Yield advantage. The difference between the yield of a convertible bond and its underlying common stock.

Yield to maturity. The effective yield of a bond, taking into account its premium or discount from par, if one holds it to maturity when it is expected to be redeemed by the company at par value.

INDEX